We
Belong
Here

We Belong Here

Gentrification,
White Spacemaking,
and a
Black Sense of Place

Shani Adia Evans

The University of Chicago Press
Chicago and London

The University of Chicago Press, Chicago 60637
The University of Chicago Press, Ltd., London
Published 2025
Printed in the United States of America

34 33 32 31 30 29 28 27 26 25   1 2 3 4 5

ISBN-13: 978-0-226-83776-5 (cloth)
ISBN-13: 978-0-226-83775-8 (paper)
ISBN-13: 978-0-226-83777-2 (e-book)
DOI: https://doi.org/10.7208/chicago/9780226837772.001.0001

Library of Congress Cataloging-in-Publication Data

Names: Evans, Shani Adia, author.
Title: We belong here : gentrification, White spacemaking, and a Black sense
  of place / Shani Adia Evans.
Description: Chicago : The University of Chicago Press, 2025. | Includes
  bibliographical references and index.
Identifiers: LCCN 2024031897 | ISBN 9780226837765 (cloth) |
  ISBN 9780226837758 (paperback) | ISBN 9780226837772 (ebook)
Subjects: LCSH: Gentrification—Social aspects—Oregon—Portland. | African
  American neighborhoods—Oregon—Portland. | African Americans—
  Segregation—Oregon—Portland. | Gentrification—Oregon—Portland—
  Public opinion. | Urban African Americans—Oregon—Portland—
  Attitudes. | Albina (Portland, Or.)
Classification: LCC HT177.P6 E93 2025 | DDC 307.1/4160979549—dc23/
  eng/20240912
LC record available at https://lccn.loc.gov/2024031897

⊖ This paper meets the requirements of ANSI/NISO Z39.48-1992 (Permanence
of Paper).

In memory of my mother,
Gloria Page Evans (1949–1998),
who taught me to love being human.

Contents

1 Introduction

As a child in the 1990s, Troy's social life was lived in the courtyard of his apartment complex. After school, Troy would play with his neighbors who, like him, were Black and poor or working class: "You know kids, we figured out a way to play. We played baseball. We played kickball. That was something that was good for us, that we always went outside. We went outside every day and played. Even if it was just rocks, throwing rocks or playing tag or talking, it was a community of color, so people looked like me. They were in the same income bracket. We all were trying to figure it out, but we had a good time. We had a really good time." At forty-five years old, Troy offered a positive account of growing up in "low-rent public housing" in Portland, Oregon: "It was good. First of all, it was good because of community. We had community. We could go to community centers, community church, sports. Everything was here. It was all accessible for us." While he recollects good times, Troy also remembers that the built environment that surrounded his apartment consisted of run-down and empty buildings: "They just let them fall apart for years and years and years. My childhood, all throughout my childhood."

Then, when Troy was in his twenties and thirties, a major transformation occurred. By 2010, most of the run-down homes in his childhood neighborhood had been renovated. Developers tore down old houses and built large contemporary-style homes and condominiums.

The commercial streets were increasingly busy with boutiques, tattoo parlors, coffee shops, yoga studios, and restaurants where a mostly White clientele shopped and socialized. For Troy, the shift was bewildering: "Then boom, it just happened. Now they got thousands of buildings. You walk down the street and eat what you want to eat, watch a movie, all kinds of stuff."

Although there is now a lot more to do and eat, Troy, who maintains rental properties, is not pleased by the changes. His childhood neighborhood has turned into a place where he feels unwelcome.

It sucks. Because you go over there, and they treat you like a visitor. They treat you like you don't belong, or "what are you doing in my neighborhood?" Not realizing that this is my neighborhood. You're not even from here, or if you are from here, you didn't originate in this neighborhood. It sucks because of that and because there's nothing you can do to prove or to explain or you don't have the time to talk to people and tell them, "I'm supposed to be here. I used to be here. I lived here." Nobody cares about that.

The neighborhood where Troy grew up gentrified in the late 1990s and early 2000s and became a majority middle-class area. It has also become a space dominated by Whiteness.[1] Now when Troy goes to his old neighborhood, White residents question his presence and look at him as if he does not belong.

Portland is recognized as a politically progressive city, but Troy suggests that symbols of progressive politics and anti-racism conflict with a reality of racial exclusion and racialized displacement. For example, he said that it's "kind of a slap in the face" to see Black Lives Matter signs in his old neighborhood, saying "Black lives didn't matter enough for you to not push us out of our houses." Still, rather than focusing on individual newcomers, Troy attributed the shift in his childhood neighborhood to real-estate profiteering and systemic racism: "It's not their fault. . . . I think [it's] greed. The whole plan was—We got redlined. We tried to have businesses, and banks wouldn't lend to us in this neighborhood. Nobody will lend to you to upgrade your house. Nobody will lend to you because it's redlined. It's a 'dangerous area.' It's a 'nonprofitable area.' Once they get us out, now it's booming. . . . It's San Francisco. It's booming now. Everybody loves it. It's the greatest, hottest, freshest neighborhood and it's the same neighborhood." In this commentary, Troy identifies racism as fundamental to the story of his neighborhood. Racism prevented Black residents from accessing the economic resources that would have allowed them to maintain and develop their homes and businesses. And racism is what defines White neighborhoods as inherently valuable, "the greatest, hottest, freshest."

Although Portland, Oregon is widely known as "America's Whitest city," Black adults who grew up there have a different perspective.[2] They view a group of neighborhoods in Northeast Portland—including Boise, Eliot, Humboldt, King, and Woodlawn—often collectively called "Albina," "Inner Northeast," or "North/Northeast," as a historically Black place and the hub of Black culture and community (figure 1.1 and figure 1.2). Until recently, White people from other parts of the city saw the area as a slum or a ghetto.[3] But a demographic and economic shift occurred at the beginning of the twenty-first

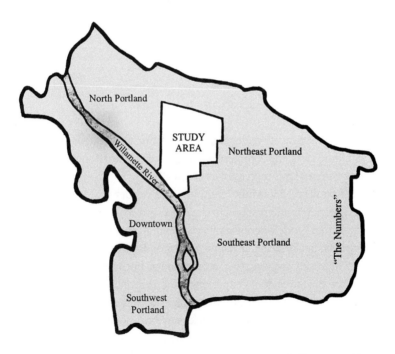

FIGURE 1.1. Map showing location of the study area within Portland, Oregon. This area is often called "Albina," "Inner Northeast," or "North/Northeast."

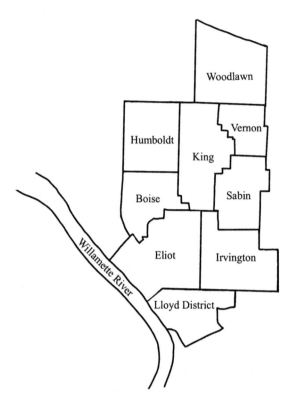

FIGURE 1.2. Map of neighborhoods within the study area.

century. Today, most residents of Northeast neighborhoods are White and middle class, the commercial streets are busy with shops, and the housing prices have increased dramatically.[4]

This book considers how longtime Black residents of Portland, Oregon experience and respond to the racial and economic transition of the neighborhoods where they were raised. Across the United States, many historically Black urban neighborhoods have become majority White in recent decades. However, little has been written about how longtime Black residents experience and respond to the Whitening of historically Black places. This book asks how and why the racial transformation of historically Black neighborhoods matters to long-term residents. And it defies leading assumptions in urban sociology about life in majority Black urban neighborhoods in the late twentieth century. Instead of presuming that disadvantage is the central theme in any account of Black urban life, my analysis emphasizes the varied experiences and sensemaking of Black Portland residents.

I introduce *White spacemaking* as a framework for analyzing the remaking of neighborhoods as White space. Here, I draw on Elijah Anderson's theorization of White space as predominantly White contexts where Whiteness is positioned as the default identity and Black people and other non-Whites are looked upon with suspicion.[5] White space is not simply where White people are in the majority. It describes spaces where "culture is deployed" to make White people feel at ease, while non-Whites are treated as bodies out of place.[6] Whites interpret unknown Black people who enter White space as representative of negative stereotypes.[7] Consequently, Black people may attempt to show Whites that they are not a threat by following White cultural norms, presenting credentials, or staying "in their place" as subordinates.[8]

In scholarly and popular accounts, the transformation of a historically Black place into White space is typically called "gentrification."[9] However, my research reveals that gentrification is an inadequate framework for analyzing the racial transition of a neighborhood. Gentrification is principally understood as a process of social class change. For example, Jackelyn Hwang defines gentrification as "the socioeconomic upgrading of previously low-income, central city neighborhoods."[10] Similarly, Loretta Lees describes gentrification as "the transformation of a working-class or vacant area of the central city into middle-class residential or commercial use."[11] Given their focus on social class change, gentrification scholars tend to attribute the racialized outcomes of neighborhood change to the relationship between race and class—i.e., Black and Latinx people are displaced from gentrifying neighborhoods because they are more likely to be poor. While some scholars assert that gentrification is an inherently racial process because space and urban development are racialized, they nonetheless define gentrification as social class change.[12]

There is no framework for studying racial change in an urban neighborhood without presuming that the significance of that change is dependent on class. Consequently, when Black people describe feeling out of place in gentrified neighborhoods, researchers often attribute that feeling to class-based exclusion rather than racialized exclusion.[13] The prevailing usage of gentrification as class, and therefore racial, change indicates a broader problem in sociology—the frequent conflation of race and class.[14] It also reflects a theoretical trajectory in urban studies that prioritizes class exploitation over other forms of domination.[15] With White spacemaking, I invite urban scholars to consider how raced and classed processes intersect to shape urban experiences and outcomes in potentially unexpected ways.

When I began this project, I had lived in Portland for one year and knew little about its Black history. In 2015, I moved with my family to accept a fellowship at Reed College, a liberal arts institution in Portland. We arrived there after living in West Philadelphia for a decade. As a Black woman coming from a racially mixed, but predominantly Black, Philadelphia neighborhood, I found the racial landscape of Portland jarring. I could go days without seeing another Black person. White people often seemed startled when I turned the corner in my neighborhood grocery store, as if they were not quite sure how to respond to my presence. I became interested in what it was like to be Black and grow up in this context. However, when I talked to long-time Black residents, it became clear that, to them, Portland in 2015 was a very different place from the Portland they knew growing up. Most adults remembered when there was a predominantly Black area in the city. By 2015, such an area did not exist. I set out to learn about residents' experiences with this transition.

A BLACK SENSE OF PLACE

American sociologists have studied Black urban neighborhoods since the early days of the discipline. W. E. B. Du Bois's *The Philadelphia Negro*, published in 1899, was one of the first systematic studies of urban life.[16] In addition to racial discrimination and substandard housing conditions in Philadelphia, Du Bois and his team documented the agentive behavior of residents who joined churches and beneficial societies, opened businesses, and supported each other through mutual aid. Nearly fifty years later, *The Black Metropolis* described place-based disadvantage on Chicago's South Side. However, its authors, St. Clair Drake and Horace Cayton, also assert that residents experienced the South Side as a place where they "can temporarily shake off the incubus of the White world."[17] They did not simply suffer through systematic disadvantage, they "live[d] in the Black belt and to them it is more than the 'ghetto' revealed by statistical analysis."[18]

The Philadelphia Negro and *Black Metropolis* are exemplars of a tradition that understands majority Black urban neighborhoods as both the consequence of racist oppression and a site of meaningful community life.[19] More recent examples include Marcus Anthony Hunter and Zandria Robinson's *Chocolate Cities*, which demonstrates how Black migrants from the South brought cultural customs to segregated cities where they established Black places or "villages" and "deliberately used their ability to densely occupy space to obscure the white gaze and develop an intricately dynamic lifeworld."[20]

Despite a long history of nuanced portrayals of urban life in American sociology, most social science research on Black urban neighborhoods emphasizes place-based disadvantage. In the twentieth century, millions of Black Americans moved north and west, seeking new opportunities.[21] But they settled in cities where White landlords, realtors, property owners, and neighborhood associations worked together to exclude Black residents and maintain all-White neighborhoods.[22] The introduction of the thirty-year mortgage meant that homeownership became an option for more Whites, many of whom moved into Whites-only suburban communities.[23] At the same time, most banks would not lend to Black people, thereby limiting their ability to buy and maintain property.[24] Urban landlords divided apartments into small, crowded units and charged high rents to Black tenants who had few choices about where to live.[25] Whites and urban elites then attributed poor living conditions in Black urban neighborhoods to cultural pathology and labeled them "blighted" slums.[26] Black urban neighborhoods became the site of political unrest in the 1960s, and the federal government and urban planners sought to "revitalize" the urban core by clearing neighborhoods to make room for redevelopment projects.[27]

Social scientists do the important work of revealing how Black people and Black neighborhoods have been disadvantaged by discriminatory policies and exclusionary practices. In the 1970s and 1980s, urban scholars became especially interested in the "underclass," poor Black urban residents who were left unemployed and purportedly isolated from "mainstream" (i.e., White middle-class) culture as employers and the Black middle class abandoned the city.[28] Since the 1980s, urban sociologists have focused much of their attention on poverty, drug addiction, and violence in Black neighborhoods.[29] Researchers study inequities in schools, housing, employment, policing, and health.[30] While research on Black disadvantage and dispossession may be necessary, the drawback is that much of this work equates Blackness and Black place with suffering.[31]

Social scientists who exclusively associate disadvantage with Black neighborhoods overlook the fact that Black people live, create, and make meaningful places within spaces demarcated by racist oppression.[32] The geographer Katherine McKittrick argues that by continually defining Black people as those "without," scholars signal that Black experience only pertains to discussions about loss and exclusion. Equating Black experience with disadvantage is dehumanizing because it assigns the status of perpetual "other" to Black subjects, who are juxtaposed with the fully human (White) social scientist. McKittrick asserts that a "Black sense of place" reveals that "racial violences . . . shape, but do not wholly define, Black worlds." I draw on this framework to examine Black experiences with neighborhood change. A Black sense of place elicits analyses that move beyond "describing and re-describing" racial violence to show how Black people live and contest anti-Black ideologies within racialized spaces.[33]

HOMEPLACE

White racial dominance, or White supremacy, refers to the political, economic, and cultural systems that create and reproduce White advantages and prioritize White interests while disadvantaging non-Whites. White racial dominance is evident in the United States in the representation of Whiteness as the norm, or the standard American identity, while non-White people are othered and racially marked. White culture operates as "mainstream" culture, even while extracting and appropriating cultural practices from non-White groups. Using what the sociologist Joe Feagin calls the White racial frame, many White people perceive Black people through racist stereotypes and presume that racial inequality is neutral and legitimate.[34]

Black neighborhoods have long provided a place where Black people can avoid the risks and stresses of interpersonal White racism, if only temporarily. bell hooks maintained that Black people create homeplace, "however fragile and tenuous (the slave hut, the wooden shack)," where one can rest and recover from the violence of the White world.[35] A homeplace is "about the construction of a safe place where Black people could affirm one another and by so doing heal many of the wounds inflicted by racist domination." Homeplace is a refuge from the dehumanizing forces of White racism: "Despite the brutal reality of racial apartheid, of domination, one's homeplace was the one site where one could freely confront the issue of humanization, where one could resist. . . . African Americans have recognized the subversive value of homeplace, of having access to private space where we do not directly encounter racist aggression."[36] Within a society founded on the dehumanization of Black people, a homeplace provides an opportunity for Black people to interact as fully human subjects. To be clear, the homeplace does not resolve the material consequences of systemic racism. However, homeplace can help neutralize the physical, psychological, and emotional toll of everyday racism.[37]

Many sociological studies of Black urban life rely on assimilation theories that presume that Black experience and outcomes should be judged according to how well Black people assimilate into dominant, White, "mainstream" culture.[38] But White logic is not the only framework for determining social status or value. Black people have alternative understandings of stigma or esteem.[39] The homeplace is where people can develop understandings of self and place that do not rely exclusively on White definitions of worthiness.

In some Black neighborhoods, residents reconsider the meaning of property and the value of place.[40] Earl Lewis contends that Black residents of segregated communities transformed *segregation into congregation*. During most of the twentieth century, Black families were confined in segregated majority Black neighborhoods, as Whites worked to maintain exclusively White communities and banks limited access to mortgages and home improvement loans. Property values in Black neighborhoods were (and are) depressed relative to comparable houses in similar White neighborhoods, while rents were high.[41] Lewis suggests that "Afro-Americans discovered that even though they could not always secure the range of improvements desired, they could begin to frame their own reality."[42] Instead of prioritizing property values, which were out of their control, Black residents focused on the value of interconnected community life. By turning segregation into congregation, Black residents created use value in communities where exchange value was systematically diminished.[43]

In the context of spatial containment, George Lipsitz contends that Black people developed a "Black spatial imaginary." While reaffirming Lewis's "segregation into congregation" concept, Lipsitz asserts that Black residents of segregated communities developed new ways to interpret the value of space.[44] According to Lipsitz, the Black spatial imaginary privileges "sociality over selfishness, and inclusion over exclusion." He contrasts the Black spatial imaginary with the "hostile privatism and defensive localism" of a White spatial imaginary.[45] Rather than trying to create value by controlling space and excluding others, the Black spatial imaginary "turned sites of containment and confinement into spaces of creativity and community making."[46] The Black spatial imaginary does not imply that all Black people think about space in the same liberatory way. Rather, it is an ideology that emerged in the context of spatial and racial subordination and resistance. Referring to the street parades that allowed a young Louis Armstrong to move across segregated New Orleans, Lipsitz associates the Black spatial imaginary with a "collective and communal cultural politics of the street."[47]

While many writers agree that Black neighborhoods provided a place for residents to be "at home" in the first half of the twentieth century, some suggest that these neighborhoods stopped filling this role by the end of the 1960s as a result of urban renewal, political unrest, and economic decline in the central city.[48] However, the interview data I collected for this project steered me to bell hooks's homeplace and Lipsitz's Black spatial imaginary. I found that these theories closely mapped onto the experiences and perspectives that were shared by interviewees. Specifically, longtime Black residents report feeling "at home" and protected from interpersonal White racism in majority Black Northeast Portland neighborhoods during the 1970s, 1980s, and 1990s. Strikingly, this was the same time during which Northeast Portland reportedly hit economic and social "rock bottom."[49] *We Belong Here* indicates that places can simultaneously expose residents to severe structural disadvantage and provide protection from *some* forms of racial violence.

Other scholars dismiss the association of Black neighborhoods with homeplace as fictional recollections of a "golden age" in urban

Black communities.[50] The notion that poor and middle-class Black people worked together in congregation is presumed to be false or misguided nostalgia.[51] For example, writing about gentrification in Northeast Portland, Matt Hern critiques scholars who "fall prey to nostalgic reifications of the past." Nostalgia is often disparaged as false consciousness based on memories of a utopian period that never existed.[52] But nostalgia expresses an emotional longing for something one does not have now. It is erroneous to assume that longing for some aspects of the past implies that the past was without difficulties or conflict. In chapter 3, Black Portland residents describe their formerly segregated neighborhood as a homeplace, a place characterized by congregation and protection from some forms of White racism. However, these findings do not imply that life in Northeast Portland neighborhoods was idyllic or without internal conflict.[53] A homeplace or "place of respite" does not necessarily refute other systems of oppression, including capitalist exploitation and classism, patriarchy, or heterosexism.[54]

The fact that many Black people experienced Northeast Portland neighborhoods as a homeplace does not mean that all Black people always worked together for collective liberation. For example, we know from research in Chicago and Harlem that Black middle-class residents sometimes promote strategies and policies that enrich themselves at the expense of their less advantaged neighbors.[55] Nor does it mean that appeals to Black collectivity are always in the interests of all Black people. Demands for Black unity have been used to advocate agendas that harm those who are less advantaged (e.g., poor and working-class people, women, queer people, etc.). In sum, racial identity politics has been deployed in ways that reinforce inequality and domination. Yet Black group solidarity is frequently called upon to create spaces of refuge, creativity, resistance, and support within a White-dominated society that dehumanizes all Black people.

WHITE SPACEMAKING

To learn about Black experiences with racial change in Northeast Portland, I interviewed longtime Black residents and spent time in Northeast neighborhoods talking with people and attending Black-focused events. Much of what I heard from interviewees aligns with sociological research on Black experiences in White space.[56] Their experiences suggest that *White spacemaking* is taking place in Northeast Portland. White spacemaking describes a process by which places are reconfigured as White space. White spacemaking represents the assertion of White racial dominance in place. It redefines space to make White dominance feel normal and natural, while making non-Whites feel out of place.[57] White spacemaking habitually disrupts homeplace. It appropriates spaces that had provided refuge from *some* forms of racist oppression. White spacemaking also evokes racialized surveillance of Black behavior, which I term *White watching*, in a place that previously served as a haven from interpersonal racism.[58]

White watching is one mechanism by which social settings are designated as White space. Black people routinely experience White watching in neighborhoods, pools, parks, stores, and offices. Moreover, if a Black person fails to appease the watcher, White watching can quickly turn into accusations, threats, violent attacks, and calls to the police (who often do the bidding of the White watcher).[59] The sociologist Eduardo Bonilla-Silva stresses that these are "regular White folks acting as agents of racial control," not "bad apples." He contends that White people are often socialized to reap satisfaction, or even pleasure, from enforcing racial boundaries.[60] White watching also has emotional consequences for Black people, who share the emotional toll of constant surveillance, misrecognition, and violent threat in White space.[61] Constant exposure to negative racialized emotions can harm one's physical and mental health. Thus, White spacemaking exposes Black residents to symbolic and interpersonal violence.

Some sociologists question scholarship that locates White space in predominantly White social settings. For example, Wendy Leo Moore uses "White space" or "White institutional space" to convey that White supremacy is structured in, and reproduced by, organizations and institutions. She contends that racially diverse places can also function as White space because they are shaped by "racial dynamics of advantage and disadvantage, control and exploitation."[62] Moore asserts that by emphasizing the racial demographics of White space, researchers falsely imply that racial diversity is enough to disrupt racialized power structures and racialized culture.

To be sure, an analysis of White space that only considers racial demographics will miss the various ways anti-Black racism and White supremacy are implemented and institutionalized. White space is also defined by who has symbolic ownership, cultural dominance, economic advantage, and political power in place.[63] At the same time, definitions of White space that foreground institutions may neglect the micro processes that shape everyday experience. Anderson's conception of White space focuses specifically on the experiences of Black people who enter spaces where their presence is unexpected and often challenged. The distinct experience of being perceived by Whites as "bodies out of place" in predominantly White spaces is widely shared among Black Americans.[64] A theory of White institutional space, which suggests that racially diverse and predominantly Black spaces may also be White space, does not capture this specific racialized experience of spatial exclusion. According to Moore's definition, Northeast Portland was White space when it was predominantly Black and continues to be White space now. However, longtime Black residents did not experience Northeast Portland in this way. "White space" and "White institutional space" index two aspects of White supremacy that may overlap, but cannot be flattened into a singular concept.

White spacemaking draws on Anderson's theory of White space to describe a process by which historically Black neighborhoods are remade by and for Whites. However, my characterization of race and space departs from his analysis in two important ways. First, while Anderson equates Black urban place with "the iconic ghetto," I understand Black urban neighborhoods to be varied places where people live, find joy, and make meaning, even as they are injured by structural racism and place-based disadvantage.[65] Second, Anderson's work on White space has focused on middle-class Black people who must prove to Whites that they "did not start from the inner-city ghetto" and are therefore deserving of "decent treatment or trusting relations." His analysis concentrates on the ways middle-class Black people are misrecognized as representative of ghetto stereotypes; however, it does little to disrupt the stereotypes themselves.[66] By contrast, my analysis explicitly asserts that poor and working-class people who "start from the inner-city ghetto," including those who are not "law-abiding" and those who reject some norms of "conventional society," are also misrecognized by dehumanizing stereotypes.[67]

Researchers have shown that White space can remake urban neighborhoods.[68] However, existing work tends to conflate race and class and emphasize class culture as the mechanism of exclusion. In other words, the culture of White space is often presented as equivalent to middle-class culture.[69] When the transformation of a historically Black neighborhood entails both social class change (gentrification) and racial change (White spacemaking), multiple forms of displacement are possible.[70] Longtime Black residents may be displaced by the emplacement of middle-class culture, the assertion of Whiteness, or an amalgamation of the two. Moreover, the specific responses to these different types of neighborhood change might be tied to the class status of the Black resident.

Displacement does not refer only to physical relocation; rather, it concerns the relationship between people and place. When that relationship is disrupted, long-term residents may experience "unhoming" or a sense of losing one's home.[71] Cultural displacement occurs when the norms, behaviors, and values of newcomers become dominant, while the tastes and preferences of long-term residents are marginalized.[72] Political displacement occurs when longtime residents lose political power as newcomers take over local decision-making processes.[73]

The fact that Black people are experiencing displacement in US cities is widely discussed in both academia and popular media. However, these accounts do not explain why racialized neighborhood change has such a deep and emotional effect for longtime Black residents. Existing accounts emphasize the economic significance of closing Black-owned businesses, losing Black-owned homes, or being priced out of the rental market. Some commentary prioritizes cultural displacement and mourns the loss of jazz clubs and barbershops. Other commentary points out that, regardless of race, people experience acute loss when their home community is physically, socially, or culturally disrupted.[74] While not inaccurate, these interpretations deemphasize the role of racism in shaping the meaning and experience of place. A White spacemaking framework reveals that racialized displacement can mean the loss of homeplace, a place that provides refuge from interpersonal White racism and facilitates Black communal life.

LIMITS OF GENTRIFICATION

When I began this project, I thought I was studying Black experiences with gentrification in a majority White city. Indeed, gentrification did occur in Portland. And most people refer to the changes in Portland's Black neighborhoods as "gentrification." However, as my research progressed, it became clear that gentrification was an insufficient framework for explaining interviewees' experiences. When the racial makeup of a neighborhood changes, the meaning of that change is not equivalent to the meaning of social class change. In fact, gentrification does not always entail racial transition. White working-class neighborhoods have been gentrified by an influx of White middle-class residents.[75] Similarly, Black middle-class residents have gentrified poor and working-class Black neighborhoods.[76]

The effects of anti-Black racism on Black residents' experiences with racial neighborhood change are muddled when studied only as a form of gentrification (i.e., social class change). Using gentrification to describe both race and class change prevents researchers from observing potential contradictions in how people experience social class change and racial change. For example, Black residents might endorse gentrification, but lament racial change. Black middle-class residents have supported gentrification in Chicago by promoting the interests of homeowners while opposing affordable housing.[77] Similarly, in Harlem, some Black gentrifiers understood their interests to be at odds with those of poor and working-class residents.[78] In her study of gentrification in Washington, DC, Sabiyha Prince finds that poor and working-class Black residents of gentrifying neighborhoods felt excluded by middle-class newcomers, regardless of their race.[79] These studies, like most research on gentrification, are most often conducted in places where the Black population is shrinking but is still quite large (e.g., Washington, DC, Harlem, Brooklyn, Chicago, Philadelphia). It is probable that social class has greater salience for Black people in cities with a large Black population. A large Black population may facilitate the enforcement of intra-racial distinctions, making residents more discriminate about Black people and places. Alternatively, the fact that many public places in gentrifying cities like Washington, DC, remain predominantly Black or racially diverse may mean that Black residents are less exposed to racialized exclusion and are therefore less motivated to seek Black places as a refuge from White space. Less is known about how Black residents respond to a drastic reduction in the Black population of an area, particularly one located in a majority White city. This question can be examined by studying White spacemaking in Portland, as a process distinct from, yet linked to, gentrification.

White spacemaking often facilitates and underpins gentrification, but the two are not interchangeable processes. Scholars like Zawadi Rucks-Ahidiana and Prentiss Dentzler point out that social class transition in urban neighborhoods is dependent on racial processes. Race and racism influence both residential mobility and the ability to profit from gentrification and urban development.[80] While White property ownership has been facilitated and protected by the state and by financial institutions, Black people, who were once defined as property, have been systematically excluded from property ownership.[81] There are also ongoing processes that further racialize gentrification. For example, banks target Black borrowers and majority Black neighborhoods for subprime loans, which increases rates of foreclosure among Black homeowners, reduces opportunities to build equity, and exacerbates the racial wealth gap.[82]

In sum, gentrification cannot be separated from racism. Because space and economic processes are racialized, neighborhood "upgrading" is an inherently racial process.[83] Racial distinctions undergird economic processes, including the commodification of housing and space. Urban spaces are most valued when associated with Whites. Correspondingly, places that are associated with Black people are devalued in the real estate market. In the view of most appraisers and realtors, the presence of Black people downgrades the desirability of a neighborhood.[84] Therefore, the process of "improving" or upscaling neighborhoods is often contingent on changing their racial demographics. Still, when scholars explain its racial (racist) foundations, gentrification is nonetheless defined as social class change. With White spacemaking, one can study racial change in a neighborhood without presuming that the mechanisms and meanings of the transition are always class-dependent.

There are some similarities between White spacemaking and settler colonialism; however, the two processes should not be conflated.

Settler colonialism is the ongoing process by which settlers seek to eliminate indigenous people through land theft and genocide.[85] The state of Oregon and the United States are settler colonial projects. White spacemaking in a previously Black neighborhood is not equivalent to settler colonialism because Black people are not indigenous to the places from which they are displaced. Black people in the United States, most of whom are the descendants of enslaved Africans, were removed from their homelands to provide free labor for the settler state. For Black people, the harm of racialized displacement in the United States is not based in indigenous rights to land. It is founded in dehumanization, subordination, and the experience of being perpetually out of place in White supremacist society.[86] Nonetheless, the way gentrification and White spacemaking are discussed by White newcomers, the press, city officials, investors, and others indicates an understanding of neighborhood change that is based in settler colonial frameworks.[87] Black neighborhoods are often portrayed as empty places that need to be saved and brought back to life by Whites. White newcomers are often called "pioneers," while the boundaries of gentrifying neighborhoods are referred to as "frontiers."[88] While gentrification and White spacemaking are not comparable to settler colonialism, they do emerge from colonial ontologies and "settler logics."[89]

A CRITICAL STUDY OF BLACK LIFE AND NEIGHBORHOOD CHANGE

This book asks how longtime Black residents experience, understand, and respond to the transformation of historically Black neighborhoods into White space. In recent decades social scientists have turned much of our attention to the study of structural racism rather than examinations of individual racist acts or experiences. In the tradition of colorblind racism, scholars try to understand how racial inequality and racist oppression persists when so few people claim to participate in racism.[90] If we want to understand how racial inequality and oppression continues, we have to study structural processes. However, the study of interpersonal racism also remains important if we are to understand how various forms of racist violence affect people in their daily lives. Moreover, the macro and micro are linked, such that studying the interpersonal helps to explain how macro processes unfold.[91]

As Barbara Harris Combs contends, "everyday racism is still racism." Combs's bodies out of place (BOP) framework provides a way for social scientists to make sense of the "social processes [that] produce everyday forms of violence against Black bodies." Although contemporary anti-Black racism is often less overt than it was in the past, it persists in "nuanced, complex, and multi-layered ways." Combs's everyday racism emphasizes that racialized mistreatment is a "normalized part of everyday life." White people call the police, threaten, and otherwise sanction Black people for engaging in such routine activities as eating lunch, opening one's car door, or laughing.[92]

Moreover, BOP draws attention to the role of space and place in everyday racism. Anti-Black racism is enforced when individual actors assert their ability to control Black bodies by "stating dictates about what Black bodies can and cannot do and where they can and cannot be." Importantly, Combs points out that individuals may act on racist beliefs about where Black people belong, while simultaneously professing anti-racist rhetoric. Everyday racism harms the physical, emotional, and psychological well-being of Black people. BOP is an apt framework for examining everyday experiences with White space and White spacemaking.

This book is not just about White spacemaking; it is also about Black placemaking. Black placemaking refers to the ways Black people live, not just survive, even as the burdens of interpersonal and structural anti-Black racism persist. Black placemaking also builds on the notion of linked fate, which suggests that Black people believe that their individual well-being is tied to the fate of the Black race.[93] However, this collective racial identity does not preclude internal conflict or intra-racial marginalization. "Black place making refers to the ability of residents to shift otherwise oppressive geographies of a city to provide sites of place, pleasure, celebration, and politics," write Hunter, Pattillo, Robinson, and Taylor. A Black placemaking analysis assumes that Black residents are capable of influencing the conditions of their own lives, such that Black urban life is not reducible to suffering.

To some, it may seem odd to write a book about Black life in Portland, Oregon, as it is often depicted as the Whitest major city in the

United States.⁹⁴ However, it is precisely for this reason that Portland provides an especially fruitful case for the study of White space, Black placemaking, and urban change. Much of Portland operates as White space where Whiteness is normalized and non-Whites are unexpected. But Northeast Portland has long served as a hub for Black life. In the 1940s, thousands of Black migrants arrived in the city seeking new industrial opportunities. Redlining and other forms of discrimination made Northeast the only place where many Black Portlanders were able to settle for much of the twentieth century. Even for those who did not live there, Northeast was the place where Black Portlanders went to spend time with other Black people, find services like the barbershop or the salon, and partake in Black culture. Studying Black experiences in Portland is pertinent to broader questions about Black communities in predominantly White cities across the United States. By examining gentrification and White spacemaking as separate but interconnected processes, this book also suggests new ways of thinking about neighborhood change in the typical sites of urban sociological research, including Chicago, New York, Los Angeles, and Philadelphia.

A narrative that is often repeated by city officials and local media is that Northeast Portland was a thriving Black community in the 1950s. While Black people were prevented from living in other parts of the city, Northeast residents made the most of their containment and created a "vibrant community."⁹⁵ However, urban renewal projects cleared Black neighborhoods and destroyed Black community life in the 1950s and 1960s. In the 1960s, Black youth rioted in Northeast, damaging storefronts and otherwise bringing chaos to the area. In the 1980s, Northeast residents joined gangs, sold and used drugs, and became increasingly violent. According to this narrative, by the late 1980s Northeast was a barren wasteland that needed to be revitalized. Regrettably, when public and private investment increased, so did housing costs. Black people were inadvertently priced out and the area accidentally became a White space. This widespread narrative also suggests that Portland was once a racist city, but has since become a progressive stronghold that rejects racism of all kinds.

Although this story about change in Northeast Portland is prevalent, I hesitate to call it "dominant" because it has been the focal point of extensive contestation. Black residents and community groups have forced the city to acknowledge the harms of urban renewal and to recognize the city's role in Black displacement. While the city was made to acknowledge past racism, the prevalent narrative nonetheless legitimizes gentrification and White spacemaking by suggesting that Northeast Portland was so empty of value by the late 1980s that the changes that occurred were both necessary and inevitable. It also relegates racism, and racially motivated urban change, to the past.

Black people who grew up in Portland offer a different account of the remaking of Northeast Portland in the late twentieth century.[96] The experiences that were shared with me by current and former Black Portland residents counter both (1) dominant depictions of Black urban life in social science research and (2) local narratives about the trajectory of neighborhood change in Northeast Portland. My priority in this work is to tell the truth as the research participants understand it. My hope is that by taking this approach, this work will help disrupt taken-for-granted narratives about Black urban life and neighborhood change and will open new pathways for future research on race, space, and place.

Between 2017 and 2019 I conducted in-depth interviews, and one focus group, with forty-five Black adults who had spent most of their lives in Portland.[97] Nearly all were born in Portland and spent part or all of their childhood in Northeast Portland neighborhoods. Most interviewees were between the ages of thirty and sixty; however, the full range was nineteen to seventy-eight (see Appendix for more information about the sample and the research process). Some were property owners and landlords, while others lived in apartment complexes or subsidized housing. The social class status of interviewees varied widely, but most interviewees are in the lower middle class. With this sampling strategy, I am able to compare and contrast the experiences of Black residents with different economic and social resources. Some interviewees still live in Northeast Portland while others have moved to other parts of the metro area. While their daily experiences diverge, I did not find major differences in how these two groups perceive neighborhood change. In addition to interviews and the focus group, I observed events and community meetings. To better understand the city and its history, I analyzed contemporary and historical documents, including flyers, newspaper articles, and policy reports.

My analysis considers Black residents' experience with White space. When recruiting interviewees, I included anyone who identified as Black. The racial and ethnic landscape of Portland is not just Black and White; however, this book is not intended to provide a holistic account of race and ethnicity in the city. I use "Black" and "White" to refer to socially constructed classifications, not essential human differences. As Michael Omi and Howard Winant assert, race is made and remade over time through political struggle and social conflict.[98]

Because there is no single Black experience in Portland, I also highlight the many differences that emerged from the interview data. Moreover, this study is less about being Black in a White city, and more about the firsthand experiences of Black people living through racial change. There are many Black people in Portland who moved there in recent years and never knew Northeast as a Black place. Others may have grown up in Portland but spent little time in Northeast. Since they did not live through racial change, their experience is not the focus of this study.

NEITHER DEFICIT NOR ASSET

Early in my fieldwork I attended a leadership development workshop with a group of Black Portland residents, most of whom were in their twenties and thirties. One of their first activities was a brainstorming session. The twenty attendees split into two groups. I remained with Group One while Group Two moved to another room. The facilitator asked Group One to make a list of the root problems facing Portland's Black community and then to identify solutions for those problems. For most of the activity, Group One discussed complex social dilemmas, trying to determine which were root causes and which were symptoms of deeper issues. Eventually, they decided upon a set of problems and a list of potential solutions. But they acknowledged that the solutions were inadequate given the magnitude of the problems, which included White supremacy, poverty, mass incarceration, and "theft of historical knowledge."

At the end of the activity, members of Group One appeared tired and emotionally drained. They seemed overwhelmed by the weight of

TABLE 1. Summary of notes from brainstorming session

GROUP ONE: SOLUTIONS	GROUP TWO: DREAMING
• Fair policies • Equal representation in the justice system, education and political arena • Economic access • Creating an empowering curriculum that depicts our history	• Community center • Black-owned and -run school • A community for us: Black-owned community • Financial education/generational wealth building • Food cart pods • Gathering spaces • Memberships for services, farming, and food production • Communications—podcast • Affordable summer programming for youth

the troubles they had just itemized. By contrast, at the end of the activity, Group Two energetically bounded into the room, ready to join Group One in a discussion. Unbeknownst to them, the two groups had been given different tasks. Group Two was asked to identify the resources that already exist in Portland's Black community and then dream of a future they would like to realize. Group Two listed local Black-serving organizations, youth-support programs, community leaders, and Black community events as resources that already exist. While Group One identified structural problems and systemic solutions, members of Group Two imagined change that could be generated through their own agency. The members of Group One were in awe of the ideas produced by Group Two.

The facilitator explained that Group Two used an Appreciative Inquiry Model, while Group One used a deficit framework. The Appreciative Inquiry Model is based on the idea that people and organizations "move in the direction of what they study."[99] If they study problems, they are likely to find more problems. If they study resources, achievements, and best practices, they will develop more of the same. The facilitator's goal was to show participants that their potential to make positive change was limited by deficit thinking. She explained, "we can't control White supremacy, so when we think about what we want, why should we start with the reality of White supremacy?" The workshop participants seemed impressed, and they vowed to continue using the Appreciative Inquiry Model in the future.

Referencing the film *Get Out*, one participant said, "We should have something to remind us when we start [using a deficit framework] 'Come back—you're going to the sunken place. Come back.'"

This brief story exemplifies a dilemma in research about structurally disadvantaged Black communities. Social scientists tend to study the mechanisms of inequality while paying far less attention to Black urban residents' agency. This practice of "describing and re-describing" marginalization reifies disadvantage by defining Black people as those "without" [subjectivity, efficacy, resources, opportunity, power].[100] It suggests that solutions can only come from the outside, from fully human White policymakers and researchers. For this reason, there has been a call for more research on Black urban life that uses an assets-based approach and considers how people live, experience joy, find respite, and resist racial domination. An assets-based approach focuses on the agency and creativity of Black urban residents.[101] The exercise above suggests that an assets-based approach can produce knowledge that motivates and inspires. By design, an assets-based approach also underemphasizes the constraints of social structures like White supremacy and the legal system. In the current work I use neither an asset- nor a deficit-based approach. Instead, I simultaneously study structure and agency by investigating how Black longtime residents experience and respond to the assertion of White space and make Black place within the context of a White-dominated city, state, and nation. By prioritizing everyday experience, not deficits or assets, this work provides insight into the social processes by which "structure and agency are mutually constituted."[102]

SUMMARY OF CHAPTERS

In chapter 2, I show how race, space, and place have been co-constructed in the state of Oregon and the city of Portland.[103] The chapter draws on historical research to present an account of Northeast, the larger city, and the state. While many people have written about Black disadvantage in Portland, this chapter uses a relational framework to emphasize that Black disadvantage and White advantage are interdependent, and often spatial, processes.[104] I describe the establishment of Oregon as a White settler state that defined Black

Americans as people without rights to property or political power. I examine the processes by which residential opportunities have been limited for Black people in Portland, while Black placemaking has been repeatedly interrupted by urban renewal and serial displacement.[105] I provide this historical account of systemic racism because it continues to shape economic and social life in contemporary Portland.

In chapter 3, I draw on bell hooks's notion of "homeplace" to consider how interviewees remember Northeast in the 1970s, 1980s, and 1990s. Participants share memories of Northeast that denote an experience of being at home. Most describe their childhood neighborhood as a place where they were known by neighbors and felt protected from interpersonal aspects of White racial dominance. I show that these memories of place were shared by people with vastly different backgrounds and family lives. Although some interviewees experienced many of the challenges that are stereotypically associated with life in Black urban neighborhoods, including gang violence and a highly visible drug trade, they were nonetheless thankful for having grown up in a neighborhood that felt like home. I conclude this chapter by describing interviewees' early experiences outside of homeplace. I show that they only perceived Portland to be White space when they left Northeast neighborhoods and experienced anti-Black interactions firsthand elsewhere.

Chapter 4 presents interviewees' perspectives on the changing relationship between race and space in Northeast Portland. Interviewees describe the changes that have occurred in their community and in the built environment. While some interviewees appreciate the aesthetics of new contemporary buildings, others insist that they are built for White tastes and do not fit in the neighborhood. I examine interviewees' perceptions of how and why these changes occurred. While interviewees mention some economic mechanisms, they identify several explicitly racial processes that, in their view, facilitated Black displacement and White emplacement. My goal in this chapter is not to objectively explain how Northeast became a gentrified White space, but to portray the process of racialized neighborhood change through the subjective experience of interviewees.

Chapter 5 demonstrates that interviewees experience contemporary Northeast as "White space" where Whiteness is centered and non-Whites are treated with suspicion. Here I focus on interviewees' experiences with *White watching* in their everyday interactions on sidewalks and in retail establishments. Interviewees describe the look on the faces of Whites they encounter, which conveys an exclusionary message: "what are *you* doing here?" Notably, this experience is shared across social class groups by people who still live in the neighborhood as well as by those who have moved. Being looked at as if one does not belong is a particularly painful experience because it occurs in a place that once felt like home. Additionally, many interviewees believe that the new shops and boutiques that have opened in the neighborhood are "not for us," that store employees are unwelcoming, and that the products they carry are directed toward upper-middle-class White tastes.

In chapter 6, I demonstrate how long-term residents have responded to neighborhood change. I show that some residents work to create Black place, or homeplace, within Portland, despite the absence of Black neighborhoods. I reveal how Black leaders and activists have intervened to redirect public and private resources toward projects that narrate Black history and affirm the belonging of Black people in Portland. I also consider the risks that previous studies have associated with projects that emphasize Black aesthetics or a romanticized history of place. These risks include the potential commodification of local culture as well as the mobilization of nostalgia to achieve the political goals of community elites.

In the concluding chapter I summarize the claims I make in the book. I argue that there is a need to study White spacemaking as a separate process that often facilitates, and intertwines with, gentrification. Throughout the book, interviewees describe a desire to live in the city without being alerted that they are "bodies out of place." Some scholars suggest that attachment to historically Black neighborhoods is just romantic nostalgia about a fictional past. But what interviewees share is a longing for homeplace and a wish to avoid interpersonal racism in everyday life.

A note on terminology: for decades, "Albina" has been used to refer to the areas in Northeast Portland where Black people live. Albina was once an independent city on the eastern side of the Willamette River. It consolidated with Portland in 1891.[106] As I explain in chapter 2, Black people began to move into the Albina area in the early 1900s. In subsequent decades, the majority Black area of Portland

was called "Albina," even as the precise geographic location of predominantly Black areas changed over time. The Albina area contains
multiple city-recognized neighborhoods. However, the boundaries
of Albina are not exact and often vary. In recent decades, "Albina"
has been less frequently used, except to refer to formerly Black areas
as "historic Albina." Interviewees use "Northeast Portland," "Inner
Northeast," "North/Northeast Portland," and "Albina" to describe
the historically Black areas in Portland. For simplicity, I use "Northeast" and "Northeast Portland" and occasionally, "Albina." However,
most of the area that the city demarcates as "Northeast Portland" was
never majority Black.

2

From White Space to Black Place and Back Again

The reputation of Portland, Oregon, as America's Whitest major city was solidified in popular culture when *Portlandia* (2011–2018), a sketch comedy television show, parodied the city's eccentric hipster culture. One *Portlandia* episode portrays Portland as "a dream of the '90s . . . an alternative universe where Gore won . . . cars don't exist, people ride bikes or double decker bikes . . . flannel shirts still look fine." This fantasy alludes to a stereotypically White and progressive worldview. In another skit, the mayor calls for "DNA testing on all the citizens of Portland" to prove "that we are actually very diverse." According to the *New York Times*, Northeast Portland is the best area in which to experience the city's famed White hipster culture. One *Times* article profiles a White Northeast Portland business owner who declared, "We've gone from the worst neighborhood in the city to one of the hottest and coolest."[1]

A story of gentrification and Black displacement in Northeast Portland has been told and retold in dozens of magazine articles, newspaper stories, policy reports, and academic papers.[2] These accounts describe a "vibrant" Black community, mostly symbolized by Black-owned businesses, in the 1940s and 1950s that was destroyed by urban renewal projects in the 1960s and 1970s. Financial disinvestment in the 1980s contributed to further deterioration. Then, the area became a dangerous "slum" where "no one" wanted to live.[3] In the late 1990s, the neighborhood began to "revitalize" and housing became more expensive. According to this recurrent narrative, Northeast is now a beautiful place to live and shop, but many Black people have been priced out. Moreover, the thriving Black community that existed in the 1940s, 1950s, and early 1960s never recovered.

The fact that this widely shared account recognizes a pattern of Black displacement is testament to the efforts of Black residents and activists to influence the terms of the conversation about the past and future of Northeast Portland. Nonetheless, this prevailing account relies heavily on White, middle-class perspectives on Black space. It presumes that predominantly Black sections of Northeast Portland were abysmal places where "no one" would want to live in the 1980s and 1990s, reflecting a commonly held view among Whites that majority Black places are inherently dangerous and undesirable.[4] Terms like "gang-infested," "crime-ridden," and "blighted" are used to depict Black urban neighborhoods of the 1980s and 1990s as dead or dying, dangerous places to avoid.[5] Indeed, the *New York Times* article cited above quips, "You may still fear for your life here, but only if you're Starbucks." This joke about the rejection of corporate establishments (e.g., Starbucks) and the predominance of anti-establishment hipster culture in Northeast Portland relies on the assumption that (White) readers share widespread and taken-for-granted beliefs about the inherently life-threatening danger of Black space.

Additionally, while public discussions about gentrification in Portland increasingly mention Black displacement and loss, they remain silent about White advantage and White spacemaking. The fact that many Black people are "left out" or "pushed out" of new economic opportunities in gentrifying neighborhoods is only part of the story. At the same time, White property owners, newcomers, and investors benefit from the redefinition of Northeast as a "nice" neighborhood, "the hottest and coolest," as *White space*. There is a circular logic at play, whereby White people depict White spaces as desirable, White people acquire resources (e.g., loans and property assessments) based on these depictions,[6] and then White homeowners and investors profit from the presumed desirability of White space.[7]

OREGON'S RACIST HISTORY

In recent years, scholars have written more extensively about Oregon's multilayered history of anti-Black racism.[8] However, this racist history is often portrayed as incompatible with the city's progressive present. In many respects, contemporary Portland does diverge from the Portland of the nineteenth and twentieth centuries, when Whites worked explicitly to create and maintain White racial dominance. Portland's prolonged racial justice protests in 2020 provide evidence of this shift. Still, the process of disinvestment in Northeast Portland in the 1960s, 1970s, and 1980s and reinvestment since the late 1990s reveals the persistence of structural racism. Moreover, the reverence for White hipster culture and the advancement of White spacemaking in Northeast Portland reflect an ongoing commitment to reproducing the profitability of Whiteness.[9]

In this chapter, I examine how Portland, Oregon, has been created and recreated over time through a process of White spacemaking. At the same time, Black Portlanders have made Black places, "both in resistance to, and in spite" of racism and racial segregation.[10] Oregon is the only state in the union whose constitution contained a racial exclusion clause.[11] But Oregon is not a uniquely racist state. In fact, many of the mechanisms by which individuals and institutions worked to create and maintain White dominance in Oregon were widespread throughout the United States. Moreover, the dominant logic that defines White space as the most desirable and profitable social space prevails across the United States, even as some White residents, politicians, and business leaders claim to value racial diversity.[12]

Founding of a White State

Portland was established on the homeland of several indigenous groups, including bands of Chinook-speaking people, Kalapuya, Clackamas, and others.[13] The original inhabitants established villages, fished, hunted, and gathered. Some built canoes and traded with other groups along the Columbia River. In the late eighteenth century, British and Anglo-American traders began to arrive in increasing numbers. Early traders were a multiracial and multicultural group, including people of African ancestry.[14] These traders brought diseases that killed 50 to 90 percent of the indigenous population and decimated community life.[15]

By the 1840s, settler colonialism was well underway in Oregon. In 1843, Peter H. Burnett, a leader in Oregon's provisional legislature, stated, "We came not to establish trade with the Indians, but to take and settle the country exclusively for ourselves."[16] Settlements first formed at the "new town of Portland" in 1845.[17] Encouraged by the US government, more than 53,000 European and Anglo-American migrants moved into the area between 1840 and 1860. In 1849, the territorial (provisional) legislature sent a memo to Congress requesting Indian removal, purportedly to benefit both "the White race" and the conditions of indigenous people. They wrote: "The moral and civil interests of the White race, equally with the claims of humanity, require the removal of [Indians] to some place where . . . their condition may be improved."[18] As White settlers went about establishing the White-dominated state of Oregon, Indian schools and missions attempted to assimilate indigenous children. Tribes were dissolved and surviving members were forcibly moved off their land and onto reservations.

Early White settlers quickly passed laws to ban Black people from the region. The provisional government first outlawed slavery in 1843. Then, an 1844 law banned any "free negro or mulatto" from living in Oregon. Excluding Black migrants preserved economic opportunity for Whites. Moreover, because exploiting the labor of enslaved Africans and African descendants produced great wealth for slaveowners, banning slavery hindered the development of a White elite class. By excluding Black people, enslaved or free, some Whites hoped to create a more egalitarian White society.[19] In addition, the involvement of free Black people in the Oregon economy would undermine the settler colonial project by obfuscating the social system of White racial dominance. White leaders worried that Black and indigenous people might collaborate to unsettle White power.[20]

Although the Black population in Oregon remained very small, leaders of the provisional government were preoccupied with Black exclusion. A revised exclusion law was passed in 1849. In 1857, Black exclusion was ratified in the state constitution. The punishment for Black people who remained in the state was five lashes. While records indicate that the punishment was enforced only once, the exclusion laws, which also prevented Black people from voting, holding public office, making contracts, or testifying against a White person in court, effectively deterred most Black people from entering the state.[21] Despite the risk, 128 Black people were living in Oregon in 1860.

Racial exclusion laws were fundamental to White spacemaking in Oregon. But just as essential was the Donation Land Claim Act (DLCA) of 1850, which allowed single White men to claim 320 acres of land. It also enabled each member of a White married couple to claim 320 acres in his or her own name. Eager to take advantage of new opportunities to acquire land under the DLCA, thousands of White people migrated to Oregon from the Mississippi River Valley, the Midwest, and the South. More than seven thousand grants were recorded for the territory, totaling approximately three million acres. Oregon's White population increased from 11,873 in 1850 to 60,000 by 1860.[22]

The Donation Land Claim Act authorized the removal of indigenous people from their land. This act of racialized land theft was a critical step in establishing Oregon as White space. The DLCA linked Whiteness to land entitlement and property ownership. Simultaneously, DLCA classified indigenous, Black, Chinese, and Pacific Islanders as people who did not have the right to access land or racialized advantage. Property ownership affords political power; thus, the DLCA reified White supremacy in thousands of land claims. Since property owners decide the succession of ownership, and since most Whites refused to transfer property to non-Whites throughout the nineteenth and twentieth centuries, the act underwrote the reproduction of White political and social domination for more than a century.

Critical historians and legal scholars demonstrate that Black exclusion laws and the Donation Land Claim Act helped to establish Oregon as a White-dominated state.[23] However, others treat Black exclusion as a marginal aspect of Oregon's history.[24] These scholars acknowledge that Black exclusion harmed Black residents (and discouraged Black residency), but do not consider how Black exclusion benefited and continues to benefit Whites. Such accounts treat White dominance in Oregon as natural and unremarkable.[25]

MAKING BLACK PLACE/PROTECTING WHITE SPACE

Early Migration, 1870–1941

A localized Black community began to emerge in Portland in the late 1800s after the Fourteenth Amendment rendered the Black exclusion law unenforceable. Fewer than one hundred Black people lived in Portland in 1850.[26] The first Black church was established in 1862; a second followed in 1883.[27] In 1890, a group led by Black church leaders unsuccessfully organized to repeal Oregon's Black exclusion laws, then still on the books, which prohibited Black people from entering the state, owning property, or voting. Although these laws were moot, the exclusionary language in the state constitution maintained their symbolic significance. Voters passed a repeal of the Black exclusion laws in 1926 after similar referenda failed to pass in 1900 and 1916.

The Black population slowly increased as more people came to Portland seeking opportunities in the service industry. By 1910, there were more than a thousand Black Portlanders.[28] Black men came to work in hotels and on the railroad, as cooks, barbers, and Pullman porters. Black women worked largely as domestics and dressmakers. The positions available to Black migrants were those that affirmed their subservient relationship to Whites.[29] There were few opportunities for Black men and women to gain professional employment. For example, Portland hospitals refused to train Black women to be nurses.[30] The school district did not hire Black teachers until the 1940s.[31]

Before World War I, the majority of the city's Black residents lived in Old Town, on the west side of the Willamette River. This area was most convenient to hotel, restaurant, and railroad jobs. In the early twentieth century, most Black Portlanders held stable and relatively (i.e., compared to other Black workers in the US) well-paying jobs. Despite ongoing discrimination, the Black community grew and Black-owned businesses catered to Black clientele. Black-owned newspapers and civic organizations were founded during this time. The Oregon Federation of Colored Women was established in 1912, and a branch of the NAACP was organized in 1914.[32]

As industry began to take over Old Town, the Black community moved to Lower Albina, on the east side of the Willamette River, especially after the Broadway bridge opened in 1913.[33] This area had been settled in the late 1800s as an ethnic neighborhood for Scandinavians, Poles, and German-Russians. As Black home seekers moved into Albina, the children of European immigrants relocated to newer housing in the "streetcar suburbs" that excluded Black people.[34] By 1940, more than half of the city's two thousand Black residents lived in the Williams Avenue district in Albina. Black churches, organizations, and businesses also moved across the river.[35]

Realtors began to treat Lower Albina as Portland's Black district and urged each other to only sell and rent to Black people in that area. As they did across the United States, realtors argued that allowing Black people to live in White neighborhoods threatened Whites' ability to maintain and increase property values.[36] They also claimed that they would lose White business if they provided their services to Black home seekers. In 1919, the Portland Realty Board declared it "unethical for an agent to sell property to either Negro or Chinese people in a White neighborhood."

White developers and neighborhood groups also began to implement restrictive covenants on Portland properties, and these measures were enforced by the state.[37] These covenants in the property deeds prohibited homeowners from selling to non-Whites. Restrictive covenants were one strategy through which homeowners and developers ensured that White neighborhoods remained White. Few Black families attempted to buy in neighborhoods that were reserved for Whites. Those who did faced violent protest. For example, Dr. De-Norval Unthank, a Black physician and civic leader, bought a home in all-White Ladd's Addition in 1931. The Unthank family had already been forced to move from four other homes.[38] Whites presented the family with a petition demanding that they leave, signed by seventy-five neighbors. After receiving threats and having their house vandalized, the Unthanks moved out of the neighborhood.[39]

Wartime Migration and Vanport, 1942–1948

The US entered World War II in December 1941. Beginning in 1942, Portland experienced a rapid increase in population, driven by wartime industry. The largest recruiter was the Kaiser Shipbuilding Company, which sent trains to eastern and southern states to bring workers to Oregon, Washington, and California. Black men and women went to Portland looking for economic opportunity. By the end of 1943, 100,000 White and 23,000 Black workers had arrived in Portland. The city population increased by 50 percent in just one year. The Black population increased 1,000 percent. Before this influx, Black Portlanders knew where they could go and which businesses would serve them. But as the Black population expanded, "White Trade Only" signs proliferated in shop windows.[40] The *People's Observer*, a Black newspaper and "valiant defender against segregation and its related evils," documented escalating racist incidents, police harassment, and conflict in the boilermakers' union.[41]

There was not adequate housing to accommodate the new shipyard workers, but Portland's housing bureau was reluctant to build housing for them in the city. City leaders and residents did not want the shipyard workers, especially those who were Black, to become permanent residents of Portland. Portland Mayor Earl Riley privately said that the increase in the Black population threatened Portland's "regular way of life."[42] Black migrants had few options for housing because Whites protested when they heard rumors that Black people might be moving into their neighborhood.[43]

Even though Albina was the only place where Black people might be able to find housing, Whites living there also spurned Black migrants. On October 7, 1942, a group of White residents attended a Portland City Council meeting to protest a rumored "negro colony" to be built in Albina. Hundreds signed a petition against the purported project. One leader of the group proclaimed: "To deliberately plant a colony of negroes in the midst of a well-established White community is to deny the very foundations of that freedom and equality with which the negro and his friends so misguidedly prate. The truth is the negro needs to learn to make himself worthy of the White companionship he craves." Jesse James Clow, a Black minister and community leader, responded, "I think some of these people have forgotten the history of their country or didn't know it. . . . The negroes have everything they have got tied up in America and we are insisting that the majority of America let us breathe the free air."[44]

In late 1942, Kaiser and the US Maritime Commission responded to the housing shortage and White resistance by building Vanport, the largest public housing development in the United States. Kaiser bypassed the city's authority by using federal funds and building just outside the city limits.[45] Built on the Columbia River floodplain, the planned city contained 10,000 units. At its height, the population in Vanport exceeded 40,000. Vanport's structures were rapidly built, and the quality of their construction was poor. The development housed a racially diverse group of wartime workers in segregated housing. After the war ended, bankers, politicians, and business leaders wanted to dismantle Vanport and use the area for industry. They said they wanted to "turn a troublesome blighted area into a constructive community asset."[46]

In 1945, the City Club, a group of men from the civic and financial elite, invited Edwin C. Berry, of the Pittsburgh Urban League, to come to Portland and address the "race problem."[47] They wanted Berry to encourage Black people who arrived during the war to leave the city. Instead, Berry established Portland's Urban League and successfully organized to get equal protection laws passed in the state. Still, many Black workers *did* leave Portland after the war. They knew that few White employers would hire them. Between 1945 and 1955, Portland's Black population decreased from 18,000 to 11,000.[48]

On May 30, 1948, a dike broke and Vanport flooded, washing away the small city. Although the Vanport population shrank significantly after the war, the 17,000 remaining residents were displaced by the flood, 6,000 of them Black.[49] The flood left Vanport residents without a place to live. While some left Portland, Black residents who remained had little choice but to move into the Albina district. They had few other options, as White residents, landlords, and realtors excluded Black home seekers from housing in other parts of the city.

Albina: Portland's Black Place

Albina was already becoming a hub for Black life before World War II. This status was further established when thousands of displaced Vanport residents moved into the area in 1948. As the Black population increased, many White residents came to see many Northeast neighborhoods as undesirable.[50] There were also realtors who engaged in the common practice of blockbusting.[51] They took advantage of Whites' racist fear and Black residents' constrained housing opportunities to profit off the racial transition of the neighborhood.[52] In the second half of the twentieth century, the great majority of Black Portlanders lived in Northeast.[53] The map in figure 2.1 shows where Portland's Black residents were concentrated between 1910 and 1980.

After many failed attempts, the Oregon state legislature passed a public accommodations bill in 1953. The bill made racial discrimination illegal in restaurants, social clubs, hotels, and amusement places, including swimming pools, theaters, and skating rinks. This state law would have likely failed if it had been put to a popular vote. In fact, a City of Portland civil rights ordinance was defeated in 1950. The state public accommodations bill was momentous, but it did not transform Portland into a welcoming place for Black people. For example, in a 1957 survey of 92 employers, only 28 (of the 48 who replied) said they hired Black people.[54] Housing discrimination persisted and Black Portlanders remained segregated in the Albina area.

Black residents were not welcome in most of the city. In Albina, Black residents were active in churches and fraternal organizations. In 1956, there were more than 135 businesses and churches on North Williams between Clackamas and Killingsworth streets, most owned by and catering to Black people. These included "meeting halls, taverns, cocktail lounges, jazz clubs, and billiard halls."[55]

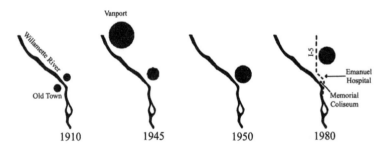

FIGURE 2.1. Map showing the sites of concentrated Black population in and around Portland in 1910, 1945, 1950, and 1980. Adapted from Burke and Jeffries, *The Portland Black Panthers*, and Millner, Abbott, and Galbraith, "Cornerstones of Community."

Urban Renewal

Urban renewal was a federal program intended to "rehabilitate" central cities by clearing "slums" and building new developments, or restoring historic properties, that would attract the middle class to the city.[56] Throughout the United States, urban planners, developers, and city elites disparaged central city neighborhoods, particularly those inhabited by Black people, as "blighted," "ghettos," and "slums." City planners claimed that these areas would be better used for industry, retail, transportation, or luxury housing.[57] Urban renewal empowered public agencies to use eminent domain to demolish buildings and to resell the cleared tracts to developers.[58] Urban renewal occurred in several older Portland neighborhoods in the 1960s, but it displaced Black families in Northeast at disproportionately high rates.[59] Although replacement housing was often promised, renewal resulted in the loss of thousands of housing units.[60]

Beginning in the 1950s, renewal projects displaced Black residents from Lower Albina neighborhoods. Hundreds of Black-owned homes, fraternal lodges, and businesses were torn down to make room for the Veterans Memorial Coliseum, a sports stadium and early urban renewal project that was approved in 1956 and completed in 1960. In 1958, voters approved an amendment to the city charter to establish the Portland Development Commission (PDC), which would oversee urban renewal projects. The PDC published the Central Albina study of 1962, which identified much of Albina as blighted and requiring clearance. It paved the way for future renewal projects. Approximately 1,600 housing units in Albina were lost between 1960 and 1980.[61] The PDC rarely engaged residents in their decision-making about what projects were appropriate for the neighborhood.[62]

In 1966, the PDC hoped to use newly available federal funds to initiate a "Model Cities" program that would continue clearance efforts. Neighborhoods in Northeast Portland (and throughout the city), however, began to organize to challenge urban renewal and make their own neighborhood plans. Moreover, the federal government wanted cities to involve community members in Model Cities programs. Albina's Black community demanded a say in the planning process. One flyer that was distributed in the neighborhood effectively portrayed the Model Cities Program as a White spacemaking project: "The MCP [Model Cities Program] unless halted Now—will follow other Urban Renewal (Negro Removal) programs in this city . . . like the memorial coliseum, where Black people were forced out to build a 'palace' for them (Whites)."[63] The mayor compromised with Albina leaders and residents by creating a Citizens Planning Board (CPB) that could veto decisions made by the mayor or the city council. Eventually, more than 30 percent of Albina's Black population participated in Model Cities meetings or committees.[64] But Ira Keller, the head of the PDC, became angry and dismissive when members of CPB, working with Portland State University's Urban Studies Center, wrote a plan that called out racism and the harmful effects of urban renewal.[65] The PDC did not want to acknowledge or address the ongoing effects of racialized exclusion and White racial dominance in Portland. Nonetheless, the efforts of CPB and the activism of Portland's Black Panthers forced the PDC to forfeit some of its control over the planning process.[66]

The Emanuel Hospital expansion project was the most controversial and impactful urban renewal project in Northeast Portland. A PDC report claimed that the area around the hospital, a hub of Black-owned businesses, had a "greater concentration of urban blight" and needed to be renewed.[67] In 1967, the PDC declared that the Emanuel Hospital Urban Renewal Project would be the first component of the Model Cities Program; however, the first public community meeting about the project was not held until 1970.[68] A 1971 City Club of Portland report chastised the PDC for its failed communication with community residents, writing that the commission "exhibited a pompous, condescending attitude and did not directly state the nature of the proposed project or its effect on residents of the project area."[69] Throughout the Emanuel Hospital urban renewal process, residents complained that they were not getting a say in what would happen in the area.[70]

To circumvent Model Cities rules requiring community participation, the PDC withdrew the Emanuel Hospital expansion from the Model Cities Program.[71] The PDC demolished 188 homes and businesses in the mid-1960s for the Emanuel Hospital Project. Additionally, the hospital acquired and cleared 101 properties between 1963 and 1969.[72] Many residents and business owners complained that the project disrupted their lives and did not provide adequate compensation.[73] Strikingly, the project was largely abandoned in 1973 because of loss of federal funds, leaving a large open lot that remained vacant as of 2024.

The PDC has continued to initiate new urban renewal projects in Northeast Portland, while Black residents and community groups have continued to demand more political power. The construction of the Fremont Bridge and its ramps to Interstate 5 "shredded the southern end of Albina" in the 1970s.[74] More homes were demolished to build the headquarters of the Portland Public Schools, which opened in 1978. Many residents were opposed to the light rail that was proposed in 2000 and built between 2001 and 2004. Harold Williams, the head of the Portland African American Chamber of Commerce, considered suing to stop the light rail. Recounting the city's record of clearing Black neighborhoods, Williams proclaimed, "we had restaurants, clothing stores, pharmacies . . . small business shops, barbershops, nightclubs. . . . And they were all wiped out—like . . . a breeze just came through and we no longer exist!"[75]

Black Power and Political Action

In the 1960s, when urban renewal was clearing housing and businesses, social problems were also pervasive. Employers continued to discriminate against Black prospective employees, and there were few job opportunities. The police were a pervasive presence in Albina. Black people made up less than 5 percent of the population, but they made up 45 percent of arrestees in Portland.[76] The public school system was characterized by vast racial disparities. It was a time of enormous conflict. As Jeffries and Burke write in *The Portland Black Panthers*, "Portland—from the streets, schools, and businesses of Albina to the offices of urban planners and politicians—found itself in the midst of a growing civil war for space and place."[77]

Albina, like Black neighborhoods in other US cities, erupted in revolt during the late 1960s.[78] On July 30, 1967, a nonviolent protest in Irving Park became a political uprising. The event was initially focused on community building and "opposition to racist employment, housing, and urban renewal practices."[79] Participants also opposed police presence and police brutality. One participant asked, "Where else but in Albina do cops hang around the streets and parks all day like plantation overseers?"[80] As the day progressed, some attendees began throwing rocks and bottles at White passersby. The mayor enacted a curfew and sent four hundred police officers and sheriff's deputies to the Irving Park area. Businesses were looted or damaged. A second multi-day clash between police and Albina youth took place in June 1969.[81] With no evidence, Black pastors and other prominent leaders claimed that the unrest was initiated by outside agitators, while Black teenagers complained that the city's older Black leadership "won't listen to what we have to say and have lost all contact with people on the street."[82]

Conversely, racial inequality in the public school system was a source of frustration for Black people of all ages. After the *Brown vs. Board of Education* decision, Portland Public Schools (PPS) initially claimed to have an equitable education system and planned to make no policy changes. After the NAACP put pressure on them, the PPS later acknowledged racial disparities in schools. However, a PPS report maintained that integration would harm Black children. According to the report, "a small group of Negro children of deplorable home background" would be "regarded as strangers, outsiders, subjected to ridicule and paternalism." The PPS approach presumed that Black students were culturally deficient and came from terrible homes. Instead of desegregation, PPS began a program that sent more resources to the schools the majority of Black students attended. The schools began to improve, but with increasing White flight they became more segregated. In 1968, 73 percent of Black students were enrolled in just nine of the ninety-four elementary schools.[83]

After the 1969 uprising, PPS decided to try to address segregation, which some understood to be a root cause of unrest.[84] The plan to desegregate schools transitioned Albina K-8 schools to K-5 schools, but opened no middle school in Albina. Approximately 600 mostly middle school students would be bused out of Albina to attend majority White schools. Although they made up a tiny portion of PPS enrollment, two-thirds of bused students were Black. In 1977, the program was extended to high school students. Initially, many Black parents supported busing, but they became increasingly irritated that their children were being transported across the city while White students largely remained in their neighborhood schools. An additional source of aggravation was an analysis by the *Portland Observer*, a Black newspaper, showing that PPS allowed many White students in Northeast to transfer schools rather than enroll at majority Black Jefferson High School, which only increased segregation.

Education became a focus for racial justice efforts in the 1970s. After years of Black organizing and activism, PPS began to acknowledge that the school curriculum was prejudiced and centered Whiteness. Simultaneously, young Black people in Portland were becoming more involved in the Black Power movement. They advocated more revolutionary, rather than reformist, strategies for pursuing racial justice. A group of recent Reed College graduates that included Ron Herndon, Joyce Harris, and Frank Wilson established a program that taught African American History and Culture. The Black Education Center was founded as an after-school and summer program in 1970, and transitioned to a full-time private school in 1978.[85]

Later, Herndon and Harris drew on their experience at Black Education Center to introduce African American history and culture into the Portland public school curriculum. In the late 1970s and early 1980s, Black political activism continued to intensify.[86] The Portland Black United Front threatened to boycott public schools, thereby persuading PPS to end the busing program in 1979. PPS proposed closing majority Black schools as a strategy to integrate the school system. In 1982, Black parents successfully fought PPS efforts to close Boise, a predominantly Black elementary school in Northeast. Although many parents supported integration efforts, they opposed approaches that would eliminate neighborhood schools in Albina (figure 2.2).

The role of the police in Northeast Portland also continued to be a major concern for many Black residents. The police were highly visible in Albina and would stop and interrogate people without cause. At the same time, police were slow to respond to requests for help.[87] In 1981, Washington and Oregon had the most disproportionate rates of Black imprisonment in the nation.[88] Despite comprising only 4 percent of the population, Black people were 22 percent of those incarcerated in Multnomah County. In 1985, police used a chokehold to kill Lloyd Stevenson, a bystander, who happened to be at the scene of a 7-Eleven robbery. An off-duty security guard, Stevenson was trying to calm 7-Eleven employees after the robbery when the police

FIGURE 2.2. Black United Front School Board protest, April 12, 1982. Those pictured include Bobbi Myrick, Venita Myrick, Alice Wysingle, and Gloria Johnson. Source: City of Portland (OR) Archives, AP/6041.

arrived and attacked him. After Stevenson's murder, hundreds of Black people organized to protest racialized police violence, particularly in Albina.[89]

Disinvestment

The built and social environment in Albina deteriorated significantly in the 1980s and 1990s. In "Bleeding Albina: A History of Disinvestment, 1940–2000," Karen Gibson writes that "Albina hit rock bottom" as a result of "a process of private sector disinvestment and public sector neglect."[90] Properties in Albina were assessed at 58 percent of the city median in 1989. There were also high rates of real estate tax delinquency. Gibson illustrates how these processes of disinvestment ultimately made Albina a profitable location for speculation, and subsequently for gentrification.

The fact that banks approved very few mortgages in Albina was a major economic calamity for Albina residents.[91] A 1990 analysis by *The Oregonian*, a Portland newspaper, found that banks provided loans to

Black neighborhoods at one-sixth the rate of other Portland neighbor-hoods.[92] In the absence of traditional banks, predatory lenders were able to thrive. In the 1990 report, "Blueprint for a Slum," *The Oregonian* reported on the illegal and harmful lending practices of Dominion Capital, a local firm that would buy up houses and sell them to people for more money than they were worth and at high interest rates during the 1980s and early 1990s. With nowhere else to turn for a mortgage, Albina homeowners would accept unfair and unfavorable terms. Moreover, some people thought they owned their homes, only to learn that the property was purchased "on contract" and belonged to Dominion. *The Oregonian* reported that Dominion took possession of more than 140 homes through these schemes. Property owners were also unable to borrow for property maintenance. Properties fell into extreme disrepair and many houses were abandoned by the 1980s and early 1990s. Landlords saw little reason to maintain properties, which they increasingly held as a form of real estate speculation. Dilapidated and abandoned housing spread throughout Northeast as many residents who were able to moved to other neighborhoods.[93]

In the late 1980s, public drug sales and gangs became a prevalent concern in Northeast Portland. Reportedly, members of the Bloods and Crips came from Los Angeles looking for opportunities to tap into a new drug market.[94] Even before gang-related violence was documented in Portland, the local press became focused on the problem of Los Angeles gangs.[95] In 1988, *The Oregonian* published 150 articles about the *impending* gang problem. At the time there were active White skinheads and Asian gangs in Portland; however, the coverage focused primarily on the threat of LA Crips and Bloods. According to the political scientist Sarah Cate, "what emerges is a chain of equivalence between Black, Los Angeles, crack, gangs, and youth."[96] The discourse around Portland's "problem of crime" was "monolithic and exaggerated."[97] It was also racialized and spatialized to equate crime with "Black" and "Albina."

In the 1980s, many White Portlanders saw Northeast Portland as a "dilapidated, crime-ridden" place where "no one" would want to live.[98] Outsiders often presume that poor neighborhood conditions in Black urban neighborhoods were caused by the choices of residents.[99] Research suggests that Black and White people use drugs at similar rates. However, in the mind of many Whites, drug use and drug selling are viewed as specifically Black and urban problems.[100] Some presume that the culture of poor Black people includes practices—such as poor property maintenance, drug use, and gang involvement—that cause neighborhood destruction and property devaluation. These dominant narratives about race and place in newspapers and media overlook the impact of racial disparities in lending, real estate, hiring, education, and public investment on producing severely unequal neighborhoods.

Increasing public drug sales, drug addiction, and gang-related violence were also a source of fear and worry for many Black people who lived in Albina in the late 1980s and 1990s. The consequences of these problems were especially impactful in Albina for a number of reasons. Drug transactions in poorer neighborhoods, like Albina, often occur outside, thereby disrupting life in public places. In addition, with few employment opportunities, some Albina youth were highly motivated to participate in the illegal drug trade. Third, Portland police disproportionately arrested Black drug users, resulting in high rates of incarceration in Albina, further disrupting community life.[101] Finally, because of constraints on property ownership and limited access to financial capital, Black families were less likely to have a safety net that could provide stability during a family member's addiction-related crisis.[102]

The influx of gangs and public drug sales impacted everyday life in Albina neighborhoods. However, the specific experiences of Northeast residents varied greatly, depending on age, where they lived, and their own social networks. For people who grew up in the 1980s and 1990s, certain blocks became associated with particular groups, while residents of other blocks became rivals. Older residents worked with city officials to try to mitigate the presence of gangs and drugs in the streets.[103] Several neighborhood-based institutions, including the Urban League, Albina Head Start, and the Black United Fund, worked to support Albina residents and provide a path to educational, occupational, and social opportunities. Although many people in Albina faced new difficulties in the 1980s and 1990s, they continued to live their lives. They went to Black churches on Sunday, had barbecues and picnics in the park, saw friends in the barbershop, shopped at Talking Drum Bookstore, rode bikes on the streets, and spent time with their neighbors on their front porches.[104]

Reinvestment and Gentrification

In the 1990s, Alberta Street and surrounding blocks began to attract artists from other parts of the city who were looking for housing and studio spaces that were more affordable than the gentrified Pearl District on the west side of the river. After years of disinvestment and neglect, developers began to renovate and construct new residential and commercial properties. The attractive housing stock, low cost, and central location made the area appealing to middle-class Whites. In 1996, *The Oregonian* reported that "White, middle-class professionals [were] *discovering* pockets of Albina as a refuge from Portland's pricier neighborhoods" (italics added).[105]

Since 1997, a monthly art walk and summer street festival called Last Thursday has helped to promote Alberta Street as an arts district and bohemian destination.[106] Through Last Thursday, artist newcomers took symbolic ownership of one section of Northeast Portland, redefining it as the Alberta Arts District.[107] These were prime conditions for developers and landlords to invest in the neighborhood and profit from the ensuing increases in rent and property value. During the 1990s, home prices in Inner Northeast neighborhoods rose rapidly, many tripling or quadrupling.[108] By 2005, the *Seattle Times* described Alberta Street as "a mile-long commercial stretch . . . where local entrepreneurs have turned the 'hood into a hip hub for food, art and new ideas." Donna Guardino, then president of Arts on Alberta, told the paper, "there was nothing here essentially, and there was nowhere to go but up."[109]

There were other factors at play in Northeast's transformation besides economic expedience and cultural entrepreneurship. Longtime residents of Northeast neighborhoods had been working for decades to make the area safer and better resourced. Organizations such as the Albina Ministerial Alliance worked to create job opportunities for Albina residents, who experienced high rates of unemployment. Local nonprofit organizations also endeavored to renovate and build high-quality housing. In addition, community members participated in the city's urban planning process. Produced over several years of meetings, the Albina Community Plan was completed in 1993. The plan calls for infill development and allows for more density with smaller lot sizes. The plan reflects authors' (perhaps contradictory) concerns about keeping housing affordable while growing property values. In addition to the Albina Community Plan, each neighborhood association completed its own plan. The resulting documents reveal that community members were concerned about gentrification and displacement and wanted to ensure that longtime residents could stay in the neighborhood. At the same time, many neighborhood associations opposed building affordable housing, which they feared would attract crime and further depress property values. While it was often White residents who resisted affordable housing, some Black property owners did as well.[110]

Additionally, the neighborhood plans did not consider how racism might influence neighborhood change. For example, unemployment is identified as an important issue in the Albina Community Plan, but there is no reference to decades of racial discrimination in hiring. Similarly, the Boise Neighborhood Plan proposed to "train police to be sensitive to the racial and cultural diversity of the Boise neighborhood." However, it did not explicitly mention discrimination in policing and disproportionate levels of arrest and incarceration.[111] Instead of addressing racism and the racialized risk faced by Black residents, the plans make vague assertions about the desirability of racial diversity.[112] This approach, which defined displacement as undesirable but simultaneously avoided discussion of racialized disadvantage or racial violence, undergirds much of the development that subsequently occurred in Northeast Portland. The Portland Development Commission and city offices (housing, city planning, transportation) endeavored to revitalize the neighborhood through urban renewal and tax benefits for developers (tax exemptions, TIF, an Enterprise Zone), without specifying how they would undo or address decades of public and financial neglect.

Moreover, while residents developed the plans that specifically raised concerns about displacement, the PDC rarely involved residents in final decision-making.[113] Given that the unspoken definition of a "good" neighborhood is one that attracts middle-class Whites, conceptions of "revitalization" in a Black neighborhood often necessitate demographic change.[114] For example, in 1995 Portland's planning director insisted that it was not his goal to turn "poor Black neighborhoods . . . into yuppie attractions"; however, he conceded that "you cannot be successful without some displacement."[115]

As the neighborhoods developed, many lower-income residents could no longer afford to pay the rent in Northeast Portland neighborhoods. Low-income families who rented their homes, many of whom were Black, left the neighborhood as middle-class Whites moved in. However, Black middle-class people and property owners also left Northeast in large numbers in the late 1980s and early 1990s. Gibson reports that "the vast majority of the change in housing occupancy among Blacks in Upper Albina (96 percent) and Lower Albina (63 percent) represented Black owners selling homes."[116] Gibson further suggests that Black homeowners who moved to the neighborhood in the 1940s sold their homes as they approached the end of their lives. Other homeowners moved to better resourced neighborhoods as housing discrimination lessened in other parts of the city. Interviewees suggest that, at the time, they could not imagine that Northeast Portland would ever cease to exist as a Black place.

Redevelopment in Northeast Portland is the result of diverse actors' efforts and actions. Developers, investors, and public officials wanted to create a more profitable neighborhood with higher property values. As Gibson describes, Black and interracial groups of longtime Northeast residents worked for safer and better resourced neighborhoods, as well as property value growth. However, both the city and community groups worked within a far-reaching racial logic that equates "improving" the neighborhood with increasing its White population.[117] This link between White residents and perceived neighborhood quality is often both taken for granted and rendered invisible in discourse about urban development.

BACK TO WHITE SPACE

The demographics of Northeast Portland changed drastically between 1990 and 2010 (figure 2.3). The Black population in Northeast neighborhoods continues to shrink. In 1990, there were seven census tracts where more than 50 percent of the population was Black. By 2018, there were no census tracts that were more than 20 percent Black. In the census tracts that are typically defined as Albina, the

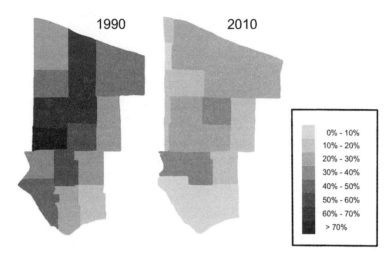

FIGURE 2.3. Map showing change in the Black population in Northeast Portland between 1990 and 2010.

racial breakdown was 65 percent Black and 29 percent White in 1990; in 2018 the same four tracts were 71.8 percent White and 16.3 percent Black. Between 1990 and 2018, the Black population decreased from 6,718 to 2,277, while the White population increased from 3,005 to 10,053. The number of Black people in the wider region of North and Northeast Portland decreased from 13,000 to 5,000 between 1990 and 2018.

Many Black Portland residents moved further east, away from central Portland. The area east of 82nd Avenue is commonly called "the Numbers," referring to the high street numbers near the eastern edge of the city. The boundary of the Numbers is imprecise, with some people including parts of Gresham, the city that abuts Portland on the east, in their conception. People who cannot afford to live in the city often find more affordable housing in and around Gresham. In my interviews, people use "Gresham" and "the Numbers" to symbolize an under-resourced place to which Black people were displaced. Although parts of Gresham are racially and ethnically diverse (including Asian, Latinx, Black, and Native American residents), it is nonetheless a predominantly White city. Black people from Northeast have also moved to other Portland neighborhoods or nearby suburbs, or have left the metro area altogether.

The history of segregation, housing and mortgage discrimination, and urban renewal in Portland shares much in common with other US cities that have been the focus of gentrification research, including New York, Chicago, Washington, DC, and Los Angeles. However, Portland is unlike these racially diverse cities that have multiple Black neighborhoods in that neighborhood change in Portland did not relocate Black neighborhoods from one section of the city to another.[118] Instead, Black people are now spread out over large areas of the city, particularly the eastern outskirts of Portland. The recent demographic shifts in Northeast Portland have resulted in a city where no neighborhood is majority Black, and few neighborhoods are racially diverse.

The lack of majority Black spaces in a city is sometimes perceived positively because it means that Black people are less racially segregated. But racial integration is only beneficial if it provides Black residents with more access to the resources and opportunities that are lacking in the segregated neighborhoods.[119] In addition, material and structural resources in a neighborhood are not the only features that matter. It is also important to consider residents' daily interactions. Much of the city is experienced by Black Portlanders as White space where Whiteness is normalized. In this respect, Portland is similar to predominantly White cities like Seattle, Washington; Denver, Colorado; Austin, Texas; and Asheville, North Carolina. Nonetheless, the experiences of Black Portland residents have relevance beyond other majority White cities. Black places are disappearing in some multiracial cities, including San Francisco and Los Angeles.[120] Moreover, Black people can encounter White space in any city. While my analysis focuses on a city, White spacemaking may also be applicable to studies of racial change in suburbs and small towns.[121] Additionally, the pervasive paradigm that defines White space as the most desirable and profitable is pervasive throughout the United States.[122]

3   Homeplace

Barry Smith (b. 1980) has positive memories of growing up in Kenton,
a predominantly White North Portland neighborhood. But there was a
shift in Barry's neighborhood experience when he moved to a majority
Black section of Woodlawn at age eleven. Now a social service case
manager, Barry reflects on those early days in Woodlawn:

> I just liked that I saw Black folks. I felt like I was safer, and I can't
> even explain why. I just felt like when I would see a Black person, they
> would wave, especially the elders in the neighborhood like, "Hey, baby.
> How you doing?" I just felt safe. I felt like they knew who I was, I knew
> who they were. I don't remember having that feeling when I lived in
> North Portland. I don't remember feeling that from the neighbors
> or feeling that acceptance, like it was *my* neighborhood. I felt that in
> Northeast Portland.

As Barry continues to describe life in Woodlawn, it becomes clear that
it was not just a neighborhood where his family lived. Woodlawn felt
like home.

> It was like being around family. You could feel—I wouldn't have
> noticed that there was anything wrong with it if I would've came to
> Northeast Portland and nobody spoke. I would've just thought it's

normal. But when I came to Northeast Portland and people were acknowledging and they'd wave. If I went to the store, they asked me, "What's your name?" so when I'd walk in, they'd know who I am and know me by name. I didn't get that when I was in North Portland. I got that in Northeast.

Barry's experience in Northeast Portland echoes those of many interviewees. They describe feelings of connection and affirmation in the 1980s and 1990s. It was a place that provided protection and recognition. It felt like home.

To be "at home" is to feel that one belongs. Home is where we relax and rejuvenate; it's where we can freely occupy space and experience a sense of belonging.[1] When neighborhoods experience substantial change, long-term residents can feel that they have lost the familiar home they once knew.[2] While having somewhere to feel at home is important for anyone, it has particular significance for Black people living in the United States, a society characterized by White racial dominance, or White supremacy. The geographers Anne Bonds and Joshua Inwood define White supremacy as "the presumed superiority of White racial identities, however problematically defined, in support of the cultural, political, and economic domination of non-White groups."[3] Here, I also draw on David Gillborn's account of White supremacy as "a comprehensive condition whereby the interests and perceptions of White subjects are continually placed center stage and assumed as 'normal.'"[4]

In Portland, Oregon, the interests of White people have long been placed center stage. The city and state's history of racial exclusion is explicit and pronounced. As interviewees often reminded me, it was by no accident that the Black population in Oregon remained quite small. Today, interviewees experience much of the city as White space, and several called Portland "White folks' mecca." At work, interviewees describe feeling like the "fly in the ointment" or the "chocolate in the milk."[5] In chapter 5, I show that interviewees feel perpetually surveilled by Whites in Northeast Portland since it became majority White.

Looking back, interviewees put particular value on having grown up around other Black people. Not only did the neighborhood feel familiar; it also provided respite from interpersonal forms of White racial dominance in the larger city. Referring to the homemaking work of Black women, bell hooks wrote that homeplaces are "where we could restore to ourselves the dignity denied us on the outside in the public world." Black neighborhoods, like homeplaces, have long served as a haven from interpersonal racism in American cities.[6] Some scholars suggest that by the late twentieth century, neighborhoods no longer served this purpose, that post-1960s Black neighborhoods are characterized only by conflict, exploitation, and poverty. For example, the sociologist Loïc Wacquant associates the emergence of the stigmatized "Black American ghetto" with "the loss of a humanized, culturally familiar and socially filtered locale with which marginalized urban populations identify and in which they feel 'at home' and in relative security."[7] But my respondents reported that Northeast Portland continued to provide protection from interpersonal racism, even while simultaneously subjecting residents to structural racism and socioeconomic disadvantage.

Interviewees remember Northeast Portland during the 1980s and 1990s as a refuge from Whiteness, a place where their humanity as Black people was affirmed and they were shielded from interpersonal racism. White people were present, but Whiteness, as a category of racial dominance, was not centered in place. Structural racism excluded Black residents from residential and business loans, jobs, quality education, public amenities, city permits, and other opportunities.[8] But the area was nonetheless a place where Black people could recover and live without the incessant stress of anti-Blackness in White space.

The development of an interconnected community in Northeast was a response to the exclusion of Black people in most other regions of the city. It also closely resembles a cultural emphasis on civility in the segregated South. Describing her childhood in Kentucky, bell hooks writes that she was raised to believe that civility is an act of affirming one's humanity: "The etiquette of civility then is far more than the performance of manners: it includes an understanding of the deeper psychoanalytic relationship to recognition as that which makes us subjects to one another rather than objects. . . . In our small-town segregated world, we live in communities of resistance, where even the small everyday gesture of porch sitting was linked to humanization."[9] This lesson, that one's humanity, within a racist society, is affirmed by simply sitting on a porch and acknowledging others in public space, provides insight into interviewees' interpretation of the past and their experiences in the present. When Whites look at them as if they do not belong, interviewees experience racial exclusion, but they also experience a refutation of place-based, humanity-affirming civility.[10]

As a refuge from Whiteness, Northeast Portland facilitated Black placemaking.[11] Black Portlanders established a community where they experienced joy, belonging, and connection. My focus here is not on Black cultural production, though Northeast was indeed a cultural hub. Instead, this chapter shows that residents and institutions created a place where young people traversed the neighborhood while feeling recognized and known. Rather than simply being tolerated as a perpetual other, they felt that their neighborhood belonged to them.

As they share memories of growing up in Northeast, some interviewees report that they were largely unaware of White racial dominance in Portland. Some were knowledgeable about the city's history of Black exclusion and community displacement. Others commented that city permitting policies and planning decisions hurt local Black-owned businesses. But in their daily interactions they did not see the perspectives and interests of Whites being placed center stage. We will see in subsequent chapters that, as Northeast neighborhoods became majority White, White interests and perspectives became reestablished in place. Neighborhood change did not simply introduce an unfamiliar culture; it redefined Black people as "bodies out of place" in a formerly protective part of the city.[12]

THIS WAS OURS

Interviewees remember Northeast Portland in the 1980s and 1990s as a place where they felt a sense of belonging they shared with other Black residents in the community. Layla (b. 1977), a nonprofit program coordinator, returns to Northeast every day for work but has not lived in the neighborhood since her early twenties. While describing childhood experiences in Northeast, Layla remembers feeling that "this was ours": "Fond memories. I still have friends to this day from those times, but I mean, it was a great experience. I had a great experience growing up in Portland. It was a very family-oriented, family-friendly, pretty diverse in Northeast Portland. Well, I mean at the time—well, I wouldn't say diverse; it was a lot of Black people in North and Northeast Portland. . . . Great memories, felt like this was ours, you know, everywhere you looked, there were Black businesses, Black people; it was a good time." Many shared Layla's feelings that "this was ours." Northeast was different from the rest of the city in that it did not "belong" to Whites. It was a place where Whiteness was not defined as the normative identity. Layla did not feel like an "other" there. As a young mother with little income in the late 1990s, Layla found no place she could afford in her home neighborhood, so she moved to the far east region of the city, often called "the Numbers." Later, when she was able to buy a house, Layla moved to a suburb north of the city. Layla certainly appreciates the amenities in the suburban town where she now lives: the houses are bigger and less expensive, and the schools are "amazing." But her suburban neighborhood does not offer the experience of belonging that she remembers in Northeast. "I lived in that house for ten years; I didn't know anybody in that community. Nobody came to talk to us, nothing, and we were the only Black family in that community the entire ten years that we were there. Didn't know no one, never spoke to us; it was horrible." After growing up in Northeast, Layla found that being the only Black family and having no relationship with neighbors was difficult. She never felt at home in her suburban neighborhood. However, at the time of her interview, Layla had just moved into a new house in a different suburban community. She was feeling optimistic about making a home there. A neighbor brought her homemade cookies, and a Black family that she knew moved in two doors down from her. As she considered her experience in each place, her time in Northeast Portland had special significance: "My favorite thing—I mean for me—was just it feeling like a family during the time that I was growing up, being able to go to school with my friends that were my neighbors that looked like me, and you know, Portland was a good place." If we put her comments in the context of the larger city, it is clear that Layla could not have had these experiences in any other part of Portland, then or now.

For many interviewees, the feeling of neighborhood belonging and support was linked to the development of close relationships with people who lived in the community. For others, feeling at home in

Northeast was associated with institutions and businesses where they felt welcome. Drew (b. 1984), a graduate student, remembers being free to roam the neighborhood with other kids and taking advantage of activities at Matt Dishman, a community center named for one of the first Black police officers in Portland.

> DREW: We would go to Matt Dishman, and we would swim there a lot, and we would play basketball there a lot, ping pong. Matt Dishman was awesome.
> SHANI: And you didn't have to have an adult with you?
> DREW: No, we never had anybody with us. I mean, nobody was really by themselves, so I think that we would have young people with us. But, as long as we went in there like a group, it was all good. And we would go in there deep and it was all good. So, I don't remember there ever being any restrictions or like, "Oh you guys can't come here." I don't remember that.

Drew felt at ease coming and going from Matt Dishman, as if the community center existed for his and his friends' use. There is a long and pervasive history of Black people being excluded or ejected from community pools.[13] But Drew did not worry that Whites were watching him or might call the police about a large group of Black boys in the pool. Other people mentioned the shops where they could go in and get what they wanted or needed without worry. For example, Veronica (b. 1989) recalled: "There used to be a drugstore on Thirtieth and Ainsworth on the corner where you can go in there and pay your bills and mail your letters and then get some Tylenol and get the meds for Grandma. It was just the neighborhood drugstore." The experience of familiarity when using amenities and shopping in stores differs greatly from interviewees' perceptions of exclusion and surveillance in the shops that have opened in recent years.

PLACE-BASED SELF-AFFIRMATION

Structured programs that were designed to support Black youth were also essential to interviewees' experience of being at home in Northeast. These programs helped to define the area as a place where Black people belonged. Self Enhancement Inc. (SEI) was established in 1981, first as a basketball program for teens and later as an organization offering academic and "comprehensive wraparound services" for students and their families.[14] A large service center was opened in Unthank Park in 1997. Zora (b. 1985), an administrative assistant and first-generation college graduate, described the role SEI played in her life: "They did everything. They gave us jobs in the summer. We were in college, they sent us care packages."

[SEI] did everything. They're the reason I went to college. I knew nothing about college. No one in my family had gone to college. They took me on the college tour where, you know, I realized that that was an option for me. They helped me apply for college. One of my coordinators at SEI did my FAFSA [Free Application for Federal Student Aid] every year for me. Like, I didn't even know my [PIN] when I got out of college, and we start paying stuff back, I was like, "What's my PIN number?" I'd never touched it; I had no idea what it looked like.

SEI facilitated Zora's college enrollment and experience in a way that resembles familial support. SEI, with its far-reaching programming and substantial physical structure, was initiated to serve Black Portlanders in Northeast.[15] In addition to the academic and social services it provides, SEI signifies a connection between Black young people and the neighborhood where it sits (increasingly, people who participate in SEI programs live outside of Northeast). While interviewees' specific experiences with SEI were varied (generally positive, but a few negative), the organization's role as an institution that helped affirm the belonging of Black people in Northeast Portland is undeniable.

While SEI continues to function today, there are many other programs that historically served a Black placemaking role. Founded in 1991, the House of Umoja served Black youth in Northeast and was modeled after a Philadelphia program whose mission was to provide "a sense of belonging, identity, and self-worth that was previously sought through gang membership."[16] The Black Education Center, founded in 1970, was a program and school that emphasized Black culture and history. Harriet (b. 1941), a former Black Education Center teacher and parent, describes a memorable aspect of the school program:

> They always had an evaluation at the end of the day where all the children would come together in a room, and teachers would be in there with them and they would say, "Did you act like an African person today?" Each person would stand. They would go down the chart and call the child's name. The child would stand up, and they would say, "Yes I did." If the students agreed, they would clap, or they would go like, "No, you didn't. No, you were saying something mean today to somebody or you were disrespectful." They had to know that they were going to be accountable at the end of the day for their behavior.

Harriet clarifies that asking "Did you act like an African person?" was equivalent to asking "Were you a good person today?" This pro-African perspective is indicative of the Black Liberation movement that developed in the 1960s. As an institution, the Black Education Center centered Blackness and the African diaspora in a way that contrasted with the normative position of Whiteness in the larger city. As interviewees moved through the neighborhood, Black-serving institutions like SEI, the Black Education Center, Talking Drum Bookstore, the House of Umoja, and the Urban League served as indicators that this was a place for them (figure 3.1).

Participation in Black, neighborhood-based community programming helped some interviewees develop a positive, place-based sense of self. As a teenager, David (b. 1965), who grew up in a working-class family, participated in a job program at the Black Education Center under the federal Comprehensive Employment and Training Act.[17] Harriet, the teacher quoted above, led the program, which David highlighted as a transformational experience: "Our job was unique because I wasn't working at a car wash or something. We went to a place to get educated about our community. To this day, Harriet is a person that— and that program—is what I really believe was the turning point in my life in terms of gaining the knowledge and the consciousness that I have right now about myself and this neighborhood and Black people in general. . . . She taught us about our community, about the Albina community." David continues to live in Northeast. Compared to most

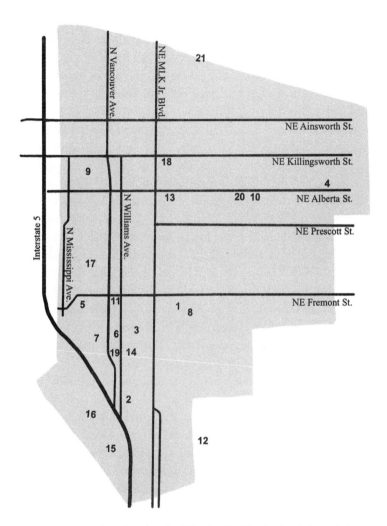

FIGURE 3.1. Map of Northeast Portland showing Black institutional places (1980s–present) that were mentioned in interviews.

1 Albina Head Start
2 Billy Webb Elks Lodge
3 Black Education Center
4 Black United Front
5 Boise-Eliot School
6 Dawson Park
7 Emanuel Hospital
8 Irving Park
9 Jefferson High School
10 Joe's Place & Solae's Lounge
11 Craigo's
12 Lloyd Center
13 Martin Luther King Jr. School
14 Matt Dishman Community Center
15 Memorial Coliseum & Moda Center
16 Portland Public School Headquarters
17 Self Enhancement Inc. & DeNorval Unthank Park
18 Talking Drum Bookstore
19 Urban League
20 House of Umoja
21 Woodlawn Park

other interviewees, he is less bothered by the demographic shift in the neighborhood. The neighborhood still feels like home to him. He explains: "I feel like it's the back of my hand. I feel like even though all the changes have came, I don't care. I care about the changes, but at the same time, I adapt to them. I still feel like Alberta's the street that I had my first job on. I still feel like MLK is the place where I had my first business on." A successful business owner who has benefited financially from neighborhood change, David is unusual in his relative acceptance of gentrification. But, like other interviewees, David associates the historically larger Black population in the neighborhood with the ability to be at home and more freely occupy space. After living in the majority White Kenton and Irvington neighborhoods, David's parents rented a home in a predominantly Black part of the Sabin neighborhood. David reflected on his experiences growing up there in the 1970s and early 1980s by listing the Black families that lived on his street. "We moved in the middle of middle school to the Sabin area, and then that neighborhood was much Blacker. That particular area was. Our next-door neighbor, my cross-street neighbors were [Black families] the Jones family. The Watkins. A lot of Black folks in the neighborhood." When I asked David to explain what it was like to spend his teen years in the Sabin neighborhood, he replied: "That neighborhood was fun. We had [a] great time. We had parks all around. We would. . . . There was enough Black folks to go to the different parks and everybody would be Black. There was enough Black folks for that. We'd have these big basketball tournaments. I was never part of those 'cause I was never a good basketball player. But, anyway, I watched them. There was enough Black folks where we could congregate, have skating rinks. That neighborhood was a great neighborhood." David's recollection that there were "enough Black folks where we could congregate" suggests that new possibilities emerged for socializing when Black people gathered in larger numbers and Whiteness was decentered. In the absence of a White majority, David and his neighbors avoided both passive and aggressive forms of interpersonal racism in public space. As Marcus Anthony Hunter and Zandria Robinson have written about Black urban "villages," Black residents of Northeast Portland "deliberately used their ability to densely occupy space to obscure the White gaze and develop an intricately dynamic lifeworld."[18]

Later in the 1980s, drugs and gangs began to shape the lives of many Northeast residents just a few years younger than David. In 1989, David was involved in a frightening altercation in front of his house.

> I was trying to get into my house and then this guy was running from these two guys. I had my groceries and my bag in my hand. . . . They ran onto my porch and there was this big old commotion. And for a second, I thought I was going to get shot because they were chasing him. He saw me, he reached up to grab me because he was scared, trying to get behind me. I figured he was trying to shield himself from bullets. I'm thinking, "They're going to start busting right now." So, I don't go in my house because I've got a newborn baby. I've got my wife in there. . . .

David ran to hide in the back of his house. When he returned several minutes later, the young men were gone, but so were his groceries and his bag. After describing this terrifying experience, David explains that there are some "good parts" of gentrification. "There are good parts of it. Now I can live in a place right next to the place where I got mugged and robbed without getting robbed and mugged because people down the street aren't shooting and selling drugs. But at the same time, I can't go to the park and see the basketball tournaments and things like that. That's why I say it's good and it's bad. It's not one thing. It's a variety of things." While David was one of only a few people in the sample who described positive aspects of gentrification, his unique perspective highlights the potential for conflicting responses to gentrification and White spacemaking.

Although many of the Black businesses that once operated in Northeast were closed in the 1970s, many people who grew up during the 1980s and 1990s feel that the neighborhood provided many of the institutional resources they needed. Sitting in a cafe near her home in Gresham (east of the Portland city boundaries), Bethany (b. 1981), who works as an office cleaner and childcare provider, described her childhood community: "It was a clean Black space. It was just—you wouldn't know that you were in this big White utopia from my experience. It was all Black. It was surrounded by Black. It was just Black. The White people, you know, they redlined a district for us. They weren't coming in, we weren't really going out. But within that there was everything. You had your stores, your schools. Everything was in there." A mother of three, Bethany has made it a priority to learn about the structural processes, like redlining, that confined most Black Portlanders to Northeast neighborhoods. Even with the knowledge that "they redlined a district for us," Bethany perceives Northeast as a Black place that provided for her.

Interviewees' sense of belonging was tied to the concentrated presence in the neighborhood of Black people and institutions. However, Blackness is not an essential characteristic. Rather, racial identification and categorization are achieved through dynamic social and cultural processes. For Damian (b. 1969), an educator, Black racial identity is complicated and unsettled. Nonetheless, his connection to Northeast as a historically Black neighborhood was evident and impactful. I first met Damian at a community event at the Billy Webb Elks Lodge for the Historic Black Williams Art Project, an art installation that memorialized the Black history of Northeast Portland (see chapter 6). When Damian sat in the folding chair to my left, I saw his light tan skin and straight brown hair and perceived him to be White. However, as community elders at the event stood to recount their memories of the neighborhood, Damian surreptitiously wiped away tears. This led me to revise my assessment of his race.

Later, I interviewed Damian, who racially identifies as "mixed," and asked about the Historic Black Williams Art Project event. He explained, "When I was there, I was really tearing up because I think mainly just thinking of my mom, thinking of the history in the neighborhood, and just how much I've lost, but seeing people that still. . . . It made me just really appreciate that my mom is still here, and I have someone I can talk with about what things were like." Damian elaborated: "Gosh, it felt like the world was ours, like Portland was ours. We could ride our bikes around. We rode over at the Coliseum all the time, and lots of kids in the neighborhood. Very diverse neighborhood. Facing our house to our left, there was a family from the Dominican Republic, next house over a Native American family and then to the right, Navajo family. Across the street were a Black family, and then the rest of the street, mostly Black. . . . It felt like it was a mostly Black neighborhood. It was." Like many other interviewees, Damian says he felt a sense of ownership and belonging as a young person in a "mostly Black" area of Northeast Portland. However, growing up with his Black mother and often absent White father, Damian struggled with his racial identity, explaining, "I don't know where to fit in." Today, Damian thinks people sometimes dismiss him as a new arrival in the neighborhood: "I think most people perceive me as White, even though I am mixed. I think the perception is probably I'm just another person coming in and capitalizing, that I wouldn't understand or I don't know the neighborhood." Damian's example reveals that feelings of ownership and belonging sometimes coexisted with struggles over racial identity. The experience of being at home in the neighborhood is not based on interviewees' authentic, essential, or settled racial identity; rather, it is attributed to a feeling that, unlike most of the city, the sidewalks, stores, and youth programs in Northeast existed for themselves and their community.

KNOWING AND BEING KNOWN

Interviewees felt at home in Northeast largely because the people who occupied public space in the neighborhood acknowledged and recognized them and their humanity. This contrasts sharply with their experience in public space after it became White space (chapter 5). For example, Malik (b. 1988), a teaching assistant with a bachelor's degree, attributed his ability to walk nine blocks to the barbershop in the late 1990s, when he was in sixth grade, to the fact that the community was Black and people recognized him as his mother's son. "Sometimes, when I think about it and I look back on it, because I used to live on Twenty-Second and Alberta—the barbershop was on Thirteenth and Alberta—I would be able to walk to the barbershop. That was the local barbershop. I could walk there by myself. Like, my mama let me walk to the barbershop when I was in sixth grade, and that's because the community that we were in was a Black community. She knew a lot of people; a lot of people knew her." Young Black boys and men like Malik are often perceived as a threat, and as potentially violent, in White-dominated spaces. By contrast, in Northeast, Malik's mother felt comfortable letting him walk in the neighborhood where he was recognized as the child he was.

This is a recurring theme: interviewees felt acknowledged and recognized in Northeast.[19] In addition, as young people, they were expected to speak to and show respect to neighborhood adults, who shared the responsibility of monitoring them.[20] For example, Shari's (b. 1973) recollections demonstrate that the front door was not the defining boundary of home. Even outside the house she shared with her family near NE Ainsworth Street, she was observed and acknowledged: "What I remember most about that neighborhood is that when you walked outside, like, I knew everybody, everybody knew me, everybody knew my brother. My brother would do something, and when my mom would come outside, they would sure let my mom know: 'Kevin was doing this,' or 'I seen him doing that.' Like, you couldn't get away with anything. They knew what time you were supposed to be home from school." Like many others, Shari recalled that her neighbors would observe her and her brother when they were outside. In this respect, neighbors shared the responsibility of caring for children. Shari said, "It was nice in the sense that it felt like home, even when you were outside, it felt like home, not just in the house." Eunice (b. 1963), an apartment building manager, averred that "When I was growing up I was surrounded by, I call them aunties, which was any Black woman that lived down the street." These comments are not just romantic recollections of a golden era. Shari and Eunice point to particular uses of public space in her community. Her neighbors enhanced the use value of the neighborhood by pooling and activating the resource of adult attention and care in public space.[21]

Tina (b. 1963), a healthcare administrator, remarks on the difference between her childhood experience and that of her grandchildren: "These kids don't even understand. They can't wrap their heads around that . . . everybody knew everybody." Tina continued:

My neighbor—because we grew up in an apartment complex—Ms. Reed, she lived upstairs, she was right across the hall. I remember my mom would go to work and stuff. [Ms. Reed would] sit on the sofa in the living room, have her front door open. We have our apartment door open because she could sit on her couch and look straight into the living room. She would babysit us. We tried to sneak our friends up the stairs. Ms. Reed would say, "I'm going to tell your mama" from the couch, from her apartment. We'd be, "Go back, go back, go back." You know what I'm saying? It was like that.

Tina's sense of being watched and cared for extended even further, beyond the apartment complex. When she and her brother rode bikes through the neighborhood, they not only passed familiar faces; they passed homes where they knew they were welcome:

> One thing about growing up in Northeast Portland was—you knew people at every block, every block. I'm talking about from where I grew up all the way down to the Columbia Villa. You know what I'm saying? If you were a kid and you were playing, because we used to ride our bikes everywhere. We'd be all over places we ain't got no business. . . . You knew houses. You could knock on the door, "Can I go to the bathroom?" You know what I'm saying? You can't do that now. . . .

The distance between Tina's apartment complex and Columbia Villa is nearly five miles.[22] Even in neighborhoods that were miles away she felt that people recognized her and would open their homes to her.[23] For Black people, particularly in a majority White city, a far-reaching Black community provides relief from White surveillance and the threat of White racial violence.[24] Knowing that the people in the houses they passed cared about them and would welcome them allowed Tina and her friends to have fun without experiencing the stress associated with the constant risk of racialized violence.[25]

An interconnected community in Northeast Portland was possible because most Black people in the city occupied a very small space. As Earl Wright and George Lipsitz write, Black people turned "segregation into congregation."[26] Rhonda (b. 1963), a teacher who grew up near Williams Avenue in the 1970s, surmises that her childhood was better than her grandchildren's because people in her community held her accountable for her actions: "I had a lot of people that had high expectations for me. They would love me up when I was doing the right thing. And get a message to my mother, I don't know how, before I got home when they saw me doing something wrong." Rhonda estimates that the circle of people who enforced this accountability went about ten blocks in every direction. The boundaries of the Black community were shaped by racial exclusion and containment. For example, there were few businesses Black people could comfortably patronize. As a result, people would often see their Black friends and neighbors when doing regular activities:

So, yeah, the accountability I mean, because there was only certain places that Black people could go in Portland. So, that circle was really small. You'd go up to Safeway, the Safeway that's by the Lloyd Center now. That was pretty much where the Black people shopped. And there was a Fred Meyers, that's now a police station.[27] But those were two grocery stores, when we wanted groceries, that we would go to. And so, you would run into people when you were shopping with your parent. And when you weren't shopping with your parent, you were running into people that just, "Aren't you Thelma's girl?"

Interviewees fondly recall being acknowledged, and in some cases reprimanded, by adults in the neighborhood. This may be an example of nostalgic misrecollection. As young people, they may not have been pleased with the prevalence of observant adults in public space. Nonetheless, the pertinent point is that in the Northeast community of their childhood, interviewees' Blackness was associated with recognition and belonging in place. By contrast, in the Northeast of today, and in the watching eyes of newcomers, Blackness marks them as outsiders in White space.

In the 1980s, gangs emerged in parts of Northeast, the first members having reportedly migrated from California. Subsequently, parts of Northeast were divided into separate gang-affiliated regions. The arrival of gangs did not eliminate the sense of being at home, but it did change the scale of homeplace. As I show later in this chapter, interviewees who came of age in the 1980s or later were less likely to say that they knew people in all regions of Northeast Portland. Younger people focus more on their relationships with neighbors on their own block, rather than in a ten-block or five-mile radius. In addition, by the 1990s the Black community in Northeast Portland was decreasing in size, and more White people were moving into the neighborhoods. For the youngest respondents, who grew up in the 1990s and early 2000s, feeling known in the community was tied to particular stores, community centers, or parks. Although the Black population in Northeast was shrinking by the late 1990s, the community was much larger than it is today. The greater concentration of Black people in the area continued to create opportunities for impromptu socializing in public space. Veronica (b. 1989), who works for a nonprofit, remembers the ease with which Black people could spontaneously get together. "Everything is just so different. In the summer, everyone would sit outside on their porch. So, when people would drive down Ainsworth, they would just say, 'Hey,' and they would stop. They would just stop. And then before you know it, there's like two or three people just—it wasn't planned, but they'd just stop and get out of the car and then you're hanging out. If you had kids, they would get out, and then you would play in the yard and run around. It was just such a community." In addition to the concentration of people, the built environment created opportunities to know and be known.[28] Neighbors watched children and greeted passersby from their front porch. They ran into each other on sidewalks. They met for impromptu gatherings in driveways and front yards. These features of the built environment are missing in many of the places where Black people have since moved. Displacement from the neighborhood has often been accompanied by the interruption of community life in public space.

DISTRESSED, BUT OURS

Despite many fond memories, interviewees did not claim that life in Northeast was perfect, and few people indicated that the past was altogether better than the present. There were difficulties and struggles. In addition to the increased presence of gangs and drugs in the late 1980s and 1990s, hundreds of abandoned houses were decaying throughout the neighborhood and many Black-owned businesses had closed.[29] Nonetheless, interviewees revealed a strong attachment to Northeast during this period.

Barry, introduced at the beginning of this chapter, described the eye-opening experience of moving from majority-White Kenton to majority-Black Woodlawn, where he felt recognized and at home. But Woodlawn was also the place where he was introduced to the gangs that operated in the Woodlawn Park. According to Barry, "once we moved to Northeast Portland, the area we moved to was a very heavily populated Blood gang territory, so it was very different, and Woodlawn Park was the park you just didn't go to after a certain time." Barry recalls one especially frightening night when he was rushing to get home before dark. His mother told him not to walk through the park but he decided to take a shortcut. Once he was in the park, several men approached him. "I remember them asking me, 'What set you from?' and all that, and I didn't know what they were talking about. I knew it was gangs, but I didn't know what I was supposed to say, what my response was supposed to be. I didn't know. So, I just kept walking, and they're all, 'You hear what I'm saying to you?!' I was terrified at this point, I just hurried up and tried to get away." As Barry quickly walked away, one man showed him his gun: "they didn't point it at me, but they pulled the gun out so I could see it. It was like, 'Don't walk through here,' type situation." Barry did not go into Woodlawn Park again at night, and he avoided it during the day for several months. He never told his mother about the incident.

But this was not the first time Barry was threatened with a gun. When he was eleven years old and still living in the Kenton neighborhood, Barry had his first encounter with the police when he and his White friend were caught "being dumb, bad kids," throwing rocks at their school. Barry explained: "We knew we were in trouble, and we were both running. And so, I turned and ran towards the bushes, and so I could still see my friend running, but they let him run, and they followed me and jumped out of their squad cars and pulled their guns on me and told me to come out of the bushes, or they were going to shoot me." While Barry's White friend ran away, the officers focused only on him. Two years earlier, when he was nine, Barry's mother told him how to respond when threatened by the police, but at the time he "just didn't understand any of it" and thought "why would they ever do that?" Still, he followed his mother's guidance. "I came out of the bushes with my hands up because I remember what my mom told me: 'Keep your hands up.' And then, when I could see from the bushes that they got the guns on me, I just thought they were going to shoot me so I came out with my hands up, shaking, crying, and afraid, and I said, 'We were both throwing them.' And they were like, 'We don't care about him. You keep your hands up.'" This was Barry's first realization that the police would treat him differently from his White friend. A couple of years earlier, this same White "friend" and neighbor called Barry a "n——," which led to a conflict in which the friend's parents called his mom "you Black bitch." Although he felt unsafe at Woodlawn Park at night, Barry did not define Woodlawn as a dangerous neighborhood and Kenton as a safe neighborhood. Hazards were present in both neighborhoods, but Barry felt at home among those who made a point of knowing him in Woodlawn.

Moreover, while some respondents did fear violence in the neighborhood, most did not fear local gang members, because they were relatives and classmates.[30] As Barry explained, "I had family members that I knew were in gangs, but they didn't bring that stuff around. . . . My mom didn't tolerate that." Shari explicitly parsed out the difference between local gang members and the threat of violence: "I wasn't really scared of the people that were, you know, gang banging, because I knew them, but the gunfire scared me. I got tired of hearing the gunfire."

Interviewees' comments reveal a coexistence of local gangs and place-based community. In the 1980s and 1990s, the enforcement of new spatial boundaries allowed these two features of the neighborhoods to coexist. Tom (b. 1982), now a nonprofit case manager, lived near Twenty-Second and Alberta. In the 1990s, he knew everyone on the block, but the boundaries of his neighborhood were sharply demarcated.

> I was a part of when gangs hit Portland, when drugs really hit Portland, but at that time, Northeast Portland was a community. We played outside, you know what I'm saying? Our friends were everybody that lived on our block. We spent the night at each other's house, so I thought it was cool, just because it was a sense of community back then. . . . We spent more time in that neighborhood, so like if you lived on Twenty-Second, we never went past Seventeenth, so everybody that lived from Eighteenth to Twenty-Fifth all played together.

Tom went on to explain that he never went past Seventeenth Street because that was the territory of a rival gang. Similarly, Barry said that once he went to middle school, he quickly learned: "if you're going to be walking in the area, just where to walk and where not to walk, and what streets to walk down and not walk down, and definitely at what time of night. And if you're going to ride your bike around, just where you ride, all of that played a part." Likewise, Terrence (b. 1973), a trucking company manager, said, "No. I didn't feel afraid, because I knew them all. I knew where I could go and where I couldn't go."

Some respondents who grew up in the 1980s and 1990s also recall public drug sales and adults struggling with addiction. However,
concerns about the local effects of drugs did not dissolve feelings of
attachment to the neighborhood. When she was a child, Miriam's
(b. 1976) parents struggled with addiction. The experience of having
drug-addicted and unreliable parents makes her more insistent on
the value of her connection with neighbors: "The space of when I was
growing up, the neighborhood was mostly Black. I tell people even
though my mom was on drugs, I don't feel like I was missing out on
parenting necessarily. I still had the strong sense of community. I still
had people who looked out for me." Miriam specifically describes a
neighbor, who regularly checked in on her and asked about her grades.
She later learned that he sold drugs. Still, his concern made a meaningful impression. Miriam explained, "even his presence was valuable
and important and impactful for the kids and the community."

Interviewees are clear-eyed about struggles, while insisting that
the neighborhood and its public spaces provided opportunities to
socialize without fear of White hostility. Drew spoke about this du-
ality. He explained that men who sold drugs on the corner near his
house disrupted his everyday life in the 1990s: "They were standing
there all day. And as a young person, you can walk past those dudes
and sometimes they'll leave you alone, sometimes they'll make fun
of you, sometimes. . . . You don't know what's going to happen, and
sometimes you just don't want to deal with that." Nonetheless, Drew
is exceedingly positive about growing up in Northeast. He recollects
that he and his friends would have great fun at Craigo's, the "ghetto
Walmart before Walmart," despite the presence of the outdoor drug
market. "We would get together as kids, and we would have our little
dollar or seventy-five cents, you could go to Craigo's and you would
be *on*. Just, those trips to go to Craigo's were just awesome memories.
There's also a lot of bad stuff at Craigo's, drugs and all that stuff there.
If you just avoid that and you don't participate in that—it doesn't
have the same meaning, because that stuff was everywhere." Drew
also mentions Unthank Park as a place where the complexity of the
neighborhood was on display. There were drug sales and "three rival
gangs in the park," but there were also parents playing with their kids,
people playing basketball, and children "playing checkers and braid-
ing gimp." Evoking Du Bois's double consciousness, Drew simulta-

neously explains how he experienced the park and how it looked to outsiders: "People who aren't from places like that, they kind of look, I believe, I assume, they look at the place. . . . If they were there, all they would see is the drug dealer and all they would see is the whatever, the 'scary group of Black men,' or whatever. But, they wouldn't see there's that and there's this other thing going on there, too. There's multiple things happening in the space at the same time."[31] Drew imagines outsiders, presumably White, who would look on the scene at Unthank Park and just see "the scary group of Black men." But in Northeast neighborhoods where few Whites were present, Black people could braid hair and do gimp without dealing with Whites watching and challenging their presence.[32]

LEAVING HOME

Although Portland, Oregon, is widely known as one of the Whitest cities in the United States, for most interviewees growing up in Portland did not mean growing up in White space. They grew up in an environment where White people were present but were not the dominant group in their daily interactions. Moreover, they understood this to be a positive aspect of their experience. The protection they experienced in Northeast became more apparent when interviewees left. In fact, interviewees who rarely traveled outside of Northeast said they did not realize that they lived in a majority White city until they approached adulthood. Rhonda (b. 1963) spent most of her childhood in Northeast with her mother and siblings. She didn't know that her neighborhood was any different from other parts of the city until she was a teenager. "I didn't realize Portland was as White as it was until probably 1983. I think it coincided with me learning how to drive. I'd go out to Clackamas Town Center. And I said, 'Mom there's so many White people in Portland now.' And she was cracking up. She's like, honey, there's always been. But my hub was so insulated that I didn't know that. I didn't know that Portland was that White." As Rhonda drove across the city to get to a mall in a suburb, she observed a world that looked quite different from the place where she grew up. It is noteworthy that Rhonda describes her neighborhood as an insulated hub. *Insulation* provides protection, and a *hub* is the center of important activity. These were two distinguishing features of Northeast for interviewees.

For many Black Portlanders who grew up in the 1970s, the first meaningful exposure to White space came when they were bused to majority White schools located in other parts of the city. Interviewees were often surprised and hurt by initial interactions in White schools. As Edward (b. 1961), a nonprofit program officer, describes his first day being bused in third grade, his anxiety about going to an unfamiliar school in a distant neighborhood is palpable. "Definitely culture shock. The first, the first day getting on a bus I remember being really scared, really nervous, and Mom forgot to give me some lunch money so I was thinking about that: 'Oh my goodness, how am I gonna get lunch?'" Edward got on the school bus at 7:00 a.m. so the driver could drop off Black students from Northeast at five different schools in Southwest Portland. He was relieved when he arrived at school and found that his mother, having realized her mistake, had driven there to drop off his lunch. However, his relief quickly turned to shock and anger when his new classmates rejected him on the playground: "So, they had a bus full of Black students integrating these schools. The very day we get there early you know and the kids are downstairs, are down on the playground playing kickball. And we thought like, 'Oh, can we play?' 'No, n—— get out of here.' We were like, 'What?!'" On the playground, Edward got into a physical fight with several of his new classmates on the first day of school. By fighting the students who insulted him, Edward aimed to show that he deserved respect. "Everybody's like, 'Oh my goodness, don't mess with them, they're beasts,' or whatever, you know? So, we had instant respect in the school. . . . Nobody messed with us." In this childhood experience in White space, Edward literally fought to prove that he was worthy of respect and safety. Being seen as "a beast" is not an ideal form of respect. In fact, it is equivalent to being treated as less than human. But in this White space, it appeared to Edward to be his only option apart from subordination.

It was not only the students who made busing difficult. Some teachers in the newly integrated schools also let Black students know they did not belong. Rita (b. 1962), who is now an elementary school teacher herself, reflected on her experience attending a school where nearly all of her peers were White. She strongly resented the argument that she would have more educational opportunity outside her home community. "There was nothing really affecting my learning until I moved into Kellogg [middle school in Southeast Portland], which is where I experienced having tomatoes thrown at me and teachers being frustrated because they didn't know how to respond to me. There was a lot of conflict there at the school. Like, what are we going to do with these kids type of thing? . . . I'll never forget that. It was as if it was being imposed on them." Educators conveyed to Rita that she and the other children from her neighborhood did not belong in their school, which had long functioned as a White space. In addition, she had traumatic experiences in the neighborhood surrounding the school. If she stayed after school for an event, Rita would have to wait for the public bus to go home. While she was waiting on the corner, White people yelled at her from cars and once threw tomatoes at her. In Rita's early experiences in White space, adults conveyed a clear message: this is not the place where you belong.

By contrast, Troy (b. 1972) had a positive experience as one of eight Black students who were bused to a majority White school when he was in third grade. Most teachers treated him well, and being in a White school made him feel more confident about himself, even as he felt the constant scrutiny of White classmates. "I began to like it, not because of the way they gawked at us, but because of feeling like an individual, feeling like I was good enough to be accepted. I had good grades. The teachers were fair. Had friends. It was different than my other school, but it was the same. . . ." Attending a majority White school helped Troy to think of himself as an individual and not "just a number or a statistic." With White classmates, he felt that he could be a unique human being, and that White educators couldn't write him off. Troy's experience at Humboldt, the school in his Northeast neighborhood, had been good. But he felt that his White teachers at the majority Black school looked at him and his friends as less capable than White students his age. "Poor kid, free lunch. It was just like, [low achievement] is what we expect from you, the Black kids. . . . The White teachers. The teachers, the school system, Portland Public Schools. . . . 'We don't expect you to have this and this and this.' I felt that. I felt that as a kid. I felt like I was embarrassed about my situation or I was embarrassed about the fact that you don't really believe that I can do this stuff." Moving to a new school allowed Troy to show himself that he could succeed academically and socially along with White peers.

Several interviewees who initially had negative experiences thought that they ultimately benefited from having attended better resourced, majority White schools, but this did not repair the damage that most experienced. Tina (b. 1963), a medical office manager, is especially interested in the long-term effects of the busing experience on herself and her fellow classmates.

> TINA: As a parent, I understand why my mother felt it was a benefit for us to be out there. With any benefit, with anything different, comes challenges. That's part of the challenge that we had to deal with. I should do a research paper on what happened to those kids because I'm one of them. I believe that it wasn't a good ending for a lot of people of color that had to endure that.
>
> SHANI: What do you mean?
>
> TINA: Emotionally.
>
> SHANI: People have emotional scars?
>
> TINA: That's the least. Total mental health issues because you had teachers who didn't want to teach you, totally ignored you. We're talking second grade. Okay? What do you do with that? . . . What do you do with the isolation of being in a classroom where kids won't even interact with you because they have been told all these horrible things about African Americans?

Tina said she got through the experience by maintaining tight relationships with other students who were bused from Northeast: "We learned early on to cling to each other."

Leaving Northeast for school was also how people learned that White Portlanders in other parts of the city looked down on their neighborhood. For example, when he attended a majority White high school, Edward's White friends were afraid to visit him in his neighborhood. "The neighborhood was all Black. It was not scary for Black folk, but you know, White folks rarely came around here. I used to have some girls, they would get off the bus and come over to the house, and they'd be like 'Oh my goodness.' . . . They'd say 'Wow.' I didn't think about it like that you know? She's like, 'Yeah, it's kind of scary over there.'" By connecting with White friends outside Northeast, Edward learned to see his neighborhood through outsiders' eyes: not as a familiar homeplace, but as a threatening environment.

SHANI: What was she scared by?

EDWARD: By the hood.

SHANI: Was it the buildings, the people?

EDWARD: No, just the Blackness, the Blackness, and you know, she had to walk from around the corner on Mississippi, around the corner to my house and would see five, six, seven Black folks outside.

Not only did his White classmates think his neighborhood was scary; what made it scary to them was the presence of people who, like him, were Black. Edward moved from attending a majority White middle school where he had to fight for respect to attending a White high school where he made friends and did well academically. Today he has a positive perspective on his educational experience: "If I look back on it, it was really good to be able to have that cultural experience, to be able to walk in the White world and still be able to walk in the Black world also." His experience in "the White world," while providing some structural advantages, also exposed Edward to racist aggression, both overt and passive.

The philosopher Charles Mills writes about the inseparability of race and space, noting the message conveyed to Black people: "You are what you are in part because you originate from a certain kind of space, and that space has those properties because it is inhabited by creatures like yourself."³³ This circular logic, connecting Black people and Black place, helps explain how interviewees learned to see Northeast from a White vantage point. Drew first experienced White perspectives on his neighborhood when his mother transferred him to a Catholic school in a White neighborhood. Drew, who is biracial, felt at home in his community, where he spent afternoons playing around the neighborhood with other kids his age. However, his new classmates at the Catholic school told him his neighborhood was a place that should be avoided. "We would go on field trips, and we would drive down Fremont, but we would always take a left on MLK; we would never go past MLK on Fremont. We'd be on the bus and people would be like, 'Yeah, my mom told me I can't go down there.' It was like the dark place in *The Lion King*." Being from a place his classmates denigrated made Drew reexamine himself, who he was, and what it meant to be from his neighborhood. "I was like, 'Damn, I live down there.' You know what I'm saying? So, I go down there all the time, it's not that bad. I mean, there's some shootings. A bunch of drugs being dealt, but besides that, there's some cool people down there. And so, I always felt like I had to switch up who I was in order to fit in, which isn't necessarily a very healthy coping mechanism." Drew and others experienced what Randol Contreras terms *spatial anguish*, which refers to the shame felt when outsiders fear, condemn, or ridicule one's place of residence.[34] While interviewees did not accept negative portrayals of Black people and Black place as accurate, they were distressed by the degradation they faced when they left Northeast and entered spaces that were predominantly White.[35]

Northeast Portland was a site of prolific Black placemaking. In chapter 2 I showed that life in Northeast was structured by policies and practices, including real estate discrimination and urban renewal. In this chapter my focus is on the agency of residents who made a community where they felt safety, ownership, and belonging. This was possible in part because the neighborhood provided a refuge from White watching. Residents could share public space without worrying about how Whites might perceive or respond to their presence.

Researchers tend to introduce Black urban neighborhoods by referencing familiar stereotypes about crime and distress. As the sociologist Mario Small writes, urban ethnographers often seek readers' sympathy by representing poor Black urbanites as "a problem first, and multi-dimensional human being a distant second."[36] Katherine McKittrick critiques this practice as a fetishization of Black people as those "without," who "inhabit spaces of otherness."[37] I reject this fetishization by examining the perspectives, diverse experiences, and placemaking practices of Black residents in majority Black sections of Northeast Portland.[38] To do this, I draw on McKittrick's theory of a "Black sense of place": "A Black sense of place might not be read as an authentication of Blackness, or a truth-telling conceptual device, or an offering of a 'better' place; rather, a Black sense of place locates the ways in which anti-Black violence in the Americas evidence protean plantation futures as spaces of encounter that hold in them useful anti-colonial practices and narratives." Rather than an essential, nostalgic, or idealistic perspective, a Black sense of place sees potential for humanity-affirming practice alongside a legacy of racial violence that continues to shape contemporary space and place. Racism structures social life, and Black agency resists and reimagines.

Although I asked participants about their individual experiences, some of the memories shared in this chapter likely reflect collective processes.[39] Over the years, people talk to each other about their experiences and recollections of Northeast Portland. Through these conversations, longtime Portland residents develop shared interpretations of what happened and what it means. They make collective decisions about what to remember and what to forget. Thus, even though I present each person's interpretation and experience as their own, their sensemaking also may reflect group-level processes. This does not make their memories less legitimate, but it does suggest that their perceptions of the past and their sense of group belonging may be co-constructed through the process of remembering.

When recollecting Northeast Portland in previous decades, interviewees describe a place where they felt they belonged. Within Portland, Northeast was one of the rare places where Whiteness, as a system of racial domination and exclusion, did not determine the rules of engagement.[40] Although interviewees rarely offered detailed accounts of intra-racial conflict in Northeast Portland, this does not mean that such conflict did not exist. Rather, it reflects the fact that my interview questions focused on participants' experience with urban change, not their relationships with other longtime residents.[41] The need to find a refuge from White space may be less apparent in cities like Chicago, New York, and Philadelphia, where Black and other non-White people live in larger numbers. But the social practices of people who live in these more diverse cities may also reflect an interest in creating a refuge within gentrifying, and increasingly White, central cities. Interviewees remember Northeast as a corner of the city where Black placemaking enabled home to extend far beyond the front door of their apartment or house. These memories are what is at stake when interviewees interpret the racial and economic shift that occurred between 1990 and 2010.

4

Making Sense of Neighborhood Change

Beyond Gentrification

Since the 1990s, Northeast Portland has been a site of racial and economic change, fueled by public investment and private development
as well as by community action and changing residential preferences.
By 2010, Northeast neighborhoods that were once majority Black had
become majority White. Most urban sociologists would interpret this
as a clear case of gentrification, whereby Black people are "priced out"
as housing prices increase. However, a close examination of the experiences of Northeast Portland's longtime Black residents makes clear
that gentrification is an inadequate framework for explaining how
Northeast neighborhoods changed. In many cases, gentrification and
White spacemaking are intertwined and reinforce each other. Nonetheless, conflating racial change and social class change, or examining
White spacemaking and gentrification as a single process, precludes
researchers' thoroughly investigating either process. By recognizing
these two interconnected (but not interchangeable) processes, researchers, activists, and policymakers can develop better responses
to both.

This chapter considers how longtime Black residents experienced
and made sense of demographic, social, and physical changes in
Northeast Portland. Urban neighborhoods are perpetually in flux. As
Sam Stein writes, "a city that never changes is probably not a city at
all."[1] Local residents often lament the changes that happen over time,

which can render their home neighborhoods unfamiliar.[2] But the transition of Black neighborhoods to White space is distinctive because it may represent the loss of homeplace, a place where Black people can recover from the injuries of everyday racism and "confront the issue of humanization."[3]

To understand the mechanisms of urban change, researchers typically examine political and economic conditions and study the activities of investors, developers, and community leaders. The analysis in this chapter, however, focuses on the experiences and perspectives of longtime Black residents, many of whom were not involved in formal efforts to "revitalize" Northeast Portland. Rather than providing a comprehensive account of how and why Northeast Portland became majority White and middle class, this chapter presents perspectives that are largely absent in urban research—those of longtime and former Black residents. These perspectives reveal the limits of the gentrification framework and the utility of White spacemaking. In particular, interviewees describe mechanisms of Black displacement and White emplacement that were explicitly racial/racist and that could not be attributed to the relationship between race and class. Feelings of cultural, social, and political displacement were shared by all of the interviewees, regardless of their social class status.

WHAT HAS CHANGED

Losing Community

When Drew (b. 1984) meets new people, he tries to explain how he feels about his hometown: "One of the ways that I've found to describe it . . . is I say, 'I'm from Portland, Oregon, but I can't go home.' And then people go, 'Why?' 'Because, my home is gone.' Every single thing that makes up where your home is . . . like you can go back to something, you can go back to a place that has all these separate meanings and a feeling of where things slow down and you can kind of relax and all this stuff. That place is gone." Drew's feelings of loss are so complete that he avoids the area: "The houses are structurally a lot the same, but the people are different, the vibe is different, the whole place is different. So, I don't really go over there." Barry (b. 1980) similarly associates changes in Northeast Portland with feelings of loss and alienation:

> BARRY: . . . there used be a hub, a community. We had a Black community that we knew, in this area this is where you're going to find the Black folks. We don't have that anymore and we've been just taken and just sprinkled all over the Portland Metro . . . there's no hub. There's no "that's where the Black community is."
>
> SHANI: So, why does that matter?
>
> BARRY: Security, safety, sense of belonging. Yeah, I think all of those things.

Like Barry and Drew, Tina (b. 1963) no longer lives in Northeast Portland. She rents an apartment in Southeast Portland. However, she owns a house in Northeast, which is occupied by her daughter. Tina drives to Northeast every day to work in a medical office. She describes her daily drive as "sad" because she does not know where to go to be in community with people she knew growing up: "I'm in Northeast Portland every day. I think I really get sad in the summertime when I'm driving around on this side of town. I remember where every other block, you're seeing somebody you knew. Now, it's just, where are we? I don't know where we are." By saying "I don't know where *we* are," Tina emphasizes her experience of connection with other Black people in Northeast. In particular, she misses the feeling of being together in public space. "I mean, in the summertime, I really get melancholy about that. It really affects me more in the summer . . . you want to go enjoy the sun and do something that gives you the warm and fuzzies. You don't get it. I think that's what I really get melancholy about all of this." Although physical displacement is a major concern for many Black Portlanders, those who have remained in the neighborhood, or own property there, nonetheless lament lost opportunities for congregation in public space. While Tina uses the term "gentrification" to describe change in Northeast, it is clear that she is primarily describing racial change and the loss of Black places. "The reality of it is gentrification is taking place across our nation. It's really not just here. I think it's more so a problem for us up here because we never had a whole bunch of us in the beginning. You know what I'm saying? We needed that. We needed to be able to see each

other and to be able to be there for each other on any kind of level."
Although Tina is a property owner who has not been physically displaced, she has deep feelings of cultural and social displacement that
followed Northeast Portland's transition to White space.

Others missed living in community with Black elders. For example,
Eunice (b. 1963) described a lost sense of responsibility for older residents: "[Now] you don't see any of the elders sitting on their porch,
and then you would go and say, 'Hey, are you okay? We're going to
the store. Do you need anything?' Or your uncle's going to mow their
lawn for them or check on them, 'I didn't see Ms. so-and-so today.
Go over there and knock on the door and see if she's okay.' That was
community." These nostalgic remembrances are a way for respondents to articulate what they want in the present. While recognizing
that Northeast Portland was disinvested and under-resourced, interviewees lamented the loss of humanity-affirming interactions that
emerged in public space.

The Freedom to Move?

Most respondents complained that Black people who once lived in
Northeast are now dispersed throughout the city. Scholars might interpret this as a positive change because it reflects lower levels of
racial segregation.[4] Moreover, since predominantly Black urban neighborhoods had developed through processes of racial exclusion and
discrimination, they might conclude that Black dispersion represents
greater freedom among Black people to live where they choose. But
as Miriam (b. 1976) explained, being able to move to other parts of
the city does not prevent one from being subjected to the violence
of White space in those "open" neighborhoods: "When we even talk
about gentrification, the freedom to live where you want, but do you
really have the freedom? Redlining isn't technically there anymore,
but you don't really have the freedom to live where you want or the
freedom to live in a community that's mostly Black if you want to and
that sense of feeling free in your place and space." Some interviewees
did associate gentrification with greater residential freedom. For example, Bethany (b. 1981) had a distinctively mixed view of gentrification. In chapter 3 I shared Bethany's recollection that "you had your

stores, your schools. Everything was in there" in segregated Albina. But she later described her current neighborhood in Gresham, east of the city limits, as having more commercial amenities than the Northeast of her youth.

> For me gentrification is terrible and great because we were all stuffed into that little area . . . and we only had like the two options for groceries. . . . You know what I'm saying, if you didn't have a car . . . I think out here you have more opportunities. Like my son can go work down the street at McDonalds. There [in Northeast], there's only one McDonalds and it's far. So, gentrification for me—[in Gresham] they went to a school that has a swimming pool and tennis courts and two tracks and summer programs and—so I don't know.

Since Bethany can no longer afford to live in Northeast Portland, she attributes her proximity to fast food chains and better resourced schools to gentrification-related displacement. Bethany suggests that gentrification is both "terrible and great." However, what she describes are not great things about gentrification itself. While gentrification (and White spacemaking) may have pushed her out of Northeast, what allowed Bethany to move into Gresham, with its grocery stores and well-resourced schools, was the attenuation of violent efforts to contain Black people in Northeast neighborhoods.

Despite having access to these amenities, Bethany explained that her moving away from Northeast also represented loss of community and community-based resources:

> I feel lost just because we had a lot of roots there and a lot of our programming was set up around that area. My sons when we were living over there were in the SEI program, but when we moved out here, it wasn't part of this experience. And a lot of kids gonna suffer for that. We live in a town where my kids would be getting ready to go to college and we don't have money for them to go to college. And since they weren't involved in those [SEI] programs, I don't think that they will go to college.

By living in Gresham, her children can go to a school with a pool, where higher education is normalized. Bethany indicates that if her sons had the family resources of many of their classmates, they would be going to college. But the programs that support racially and economically disadvantaged and first-generation college students, like SEI, are not available where she lives.[5] Bethany also told me that she was homeschooling one of her children because of racial discrimination in his school. Her new neighborhood provided some opportunity, but also exposed her family to the risks of White space and reduced her sons' access to opportunities designed to address racial disparities. Bethany's example illustrates how valuable resources, such as educational opportunities, are spatial, but they are also tied to racialized advantage and family wealth. Having the freedom to move to an area with more commercial and educational resources did not guarantee her access to those resources.

The Built Environment

Respondents also observed major changes in the built environment. Many understood these changes to represent a shift in the population the neighborhood was meant to serve. Tom (b. 1982) lamented that the spaces he associated with friends, family, and outdoor play had become new condominiums and entertainment venues. "If you look at all these new condos, those are where my—people I knew houses growing up, you know what I'm saying? . . . Everything is—you don't recognize it no more, those houses. They knock houses down and build restaurants and shops and all that stuff." Tom went to college on a basketball scholarship in the late 1990s, and was particularly struck by the built environment when he returned to Portland in the 2000s. "I moved back and I went to my old neighborhood, went to Alberta, it was totally different. Like, the corner where we used to play kickball in the grass, that's gone. Just on Mississippi, them were houses. They knocked down everybody's house and built crap. . . ." Zora (b. 1985) experienced these spatial transformations as an erasure of her past: "It's almost like going back to the neighborhood that I grew up in and that I was a kid in, it's like someone erased it with a pencil eraser and then drew their own picture. Like none of the things are there, none of the culture is there, none of the experiences are there." In addition to the erasure Zora describes in Northeast, the Gresham apartment complex where Zora now lives does not enable the type of community connection she remembers from her childhood in Northeast Portland. Specifically, her apartment building lacks shared public spaces where her daughter can easily socialize with other children: "There's just so much that doesn't happen anymore and mainly it's because of where we live. We're so spread out. I mean, even where I live right now, there's nowhere for her to play outside. I live on a busy street and outside is a parking lot, like a driveway and a parking lot, like there's no play place. So, when I do stuff with her, we have to leave and go to a park or that kind of thing. But when I was growing up, the neighborhood was the park." Zora is troubled by both what she lost by moving to Gresham and what she sees when she drives through Northeast Portland. Both aspects of her contemporary life signal the loss of home.

Historically, many Whites saw Northeast as a place where "no one" would want to live.[6] Because the transformation of the built environment coincided with an increase in the number of White residents, respondents understood the construction of new and renovated buildings as a remaking of the neighborhood for White preferences. Troy (b. 1972) grew up in Northeast Portland and now lives in Gresham. He works in property maintenance at a Northeast apartment complex. He explained that while Northeast was once avoided by Whites, it was transformed to resemble other popular and majority White neighborhoods: "They were telling White people that came to town, 'Don't go to Northeast Portland,' in the '80s and '90s. Then now, the whole area is remodeled. Two churches that I used to go to or have been around, they've torn down, and now they're new buildings and all this fancy stuff that are there. That's when we knew like, what's happening? Alberta looks like Hawthorne, and it's like, what's going on?" Troy's comments reflect a critique of White spacemaking. He describes the replacement of Black communal spaces like churches with buildings that mimic popular White-dominated commercial streets like Hawthorne. Interviewees varied in how they perceived the aesthetics of the new buildings. Many of the newer commercial and condominium buildings in Northeast are large, angular, and unlike the Craftsman, Foursquare, and bungalow homes that line most streets in Northeast (figure 4.1). Tom expressed his frustration about houses and open lots being turned into condos, but he nonetheless likes the look of many

FIGURE 4.1. A mixed-use development (completed in 2016) adjacent to a house that was built in 1903. The house, which is now occupied by medical offices, was the home of Reverend Eddie Cannon in the 1960s and 1970s (Millner, Abbott, and Galbraith, "Cornerstones of Community"). Photograph by author.

of the new buildings. "I think they're fresh. It looks like some California stuff, but it don't look like over here, so you got that on the corner, and then there's a raggedy house next to it, so eventually, they're gonna keep putting pressure on whoever got the raggedy house next to it so they can buy that and then build this, and then everything over here's gonna look like that." Tom's aesthetic appreciation of the contemporary "California" style structures was overshadowed by the sense that the new buildings were setting the standard for housing in the neighborhood that would put pressure on long-term residents to adjust to the new norms. Tom's critique fits well with both a gentrification and a White spacemaking analysis. He suggests that new buildings reflect a potentially racialized aesthetic that does not match what was there before. Simultaneously, he suggests that longtime residents might not have the financial resources to be able to maintain property up to the new standard. Others did not appreciate the style of new construction. For example, Tina said: "Visually, they're horrible. Visually, even the house structures don't even fit with the community. I mean, these box houses that don't even match with the landscape. It just blows me away how no one even considers that." Tom and Tina had opposing reactions to the style of the new buildings. But despite their differing tastes, Tina and Tom shared the perspective that new construction was redefining the built environment in ways that disregarded longtime residents. In their commentary, interviewees reveal concerns about gentrification and White spacemaking.

Another concern that emerged was that new buildings were tall, which reduced residents' access to the sun, a limited and valued resource during much of the year in Portland, Oregon. For example, Harriet (b. 1941) said: "I'm not saying that it was perfection before these people came in, but I'm saying that with the huge displacement it looks like a canyon. When you go down Williams the sun won't even shine down on the street anymore because of all these buildings. It just feels closed in and claustrophobic to me." Harriet treats the tall buildings and "displacement" as interchangeable. Her comment suggests an entanglement of the physical and the emotional. The built environment affected the way people felt as they moved through space.[7]

Interviewees also remarked that changes in the roadways signaled the remaking of space for White newcomers. Bike lanes and speed bumps alter the way drivers move through space, making them particularly noticeable to long-term residents. Looking back, Bilal (b. 1977), a construction worker, links speed bumps to the beginning of gentrification: "They didn't start to gentrify that area until about around the early nineties, so probably around '92. And one of the first things they did is they started to put speed bumps all over the place. They started to enforce laws that they never enforced before, traffic laws and things of that sort." Portland's traffic-calming program, which began installing speed bumps in 1992, was implemented citywide.[8] Nonetheless, from Bilal's perspective, the implementation of the program in Northeast Portland signified increased public interest in what happened on Northeast streets. Here, Bilal interprets controlling speed and greater law enforcement as evidence that newcomers and their supporters were "taking place" in Northeast Portland.[9]

Much the same as in previous studies, respondents perceived the construction of bike lanes as evidence that a neighborhood was being remade for Whites.[10] However, this was not because they associated bike riding with White culture. In fact, many respondents shared memories of biking in Northeast. Instead, bike lanes were a source of consternation because they indicated that the city government only became concerned about upgrading infrastructure and keeping bikers safe as more White people moved into the neighborhood.[11] In an exaggerated assertion, Derek claimed that bike lanes were taking over some Northeast streets: "You go on Williams, there's only one lane now [for cars]. There's 45 lanes of bikes. That ain't for us. We ain't riding bikes around here like that. . . . We rode bikes on the concrete, on the cement, on the sidewalk." Derek grew up on Northeast streets where there were few marked crosswalks and no bike lanes. Moreover, the neighborhoods where many Black people have moved in Gresham and the Numbers lack crosswalks, bike lanes, or even sidewalks. For interviewees, the city's focus on providing these amenities in neighborhoods as they become Whiter indicated that the city prioritized the safety and well-being of White residents and newcomers.

HOW DID CHANGE HAPPEN?

Priced Out

Depictions of racialized displacement tend to focus on long-term residents being priced out of neighborhoods as rents and property taxes increase. In most popular and scholarly accounts, racialized displacement and being "priced out" are flattened into a single gentrification narrative.[12] In the following sections, I show that interviewees attributed racial change in Northeast Portland to a variety of racial processes that do not fit within a "priced out" rubric. At the same time, many interviewees did attribute racial change in Northeast Portland at least in part to the rising cost of housing. Thus, before transitioning to focus on the racist mechanisms of White spacemaking and racial change, I describe interviewees' experiences and perceptions of racialized economic displacement.

Residents faced financial pressures, and some felt they had no choice but to leave their Northeast neighborhood. Many interviewees asserted that Black people had been dispersed throughout the city because they could not afford to stay in Northeast. For example, Malik (b. 1988), a teaching assistant, said: "Black people better get in where they fit. So, like wherever you can get in and you can pay rent there or own the property and you can actually afford it, you better get in there. There's no 'all right, let's wait and see if something better comes along' because it's not going to be something better come along because they're fixing everything every day in Portland, so the prices are going to go up for everything." Barry (b. 1980), a father of four, lamented his move from Northeast Portland to Gresham a few months before our interview. "I hated moving. Our family expanded. My wife was saying that we needed something bigger. I was like, 'We can make it work.' I just did not want to move, and the main reason was because we were the last Black family on this block. . . . We were the last Black family." For eight years, Barry and his family lived in a two-bedroom house that was subsidized by Portland Community Reinvestment Initiatives. When they arrived, four other Black families lived on the block, but the others had since left. "Slowly but surely. . . . Some are homeowners so they either sold their homes or rented them out. Some—just—they were there one minute and they were gone the next. You didn't know what happened. And so, I felt like moving was giving up. It was like they win. If we move out of here, then there's no more Black people in this block and I don't want to give them that." By leaving his block, Barry felt he had facilitated the neighborhood's transition to White space. He wanted to stay in part to affirm that the neighborhood was still a place for Black people. However, he could not find housing in Northeast that was both affordable and large enough for his growing family.

While Barry regretfully left Northeast, Terrence owns his Northeast home as well as three Northeast properties he rents to family members. The rental properties provide about 30 percent of his income. As a property owner, we might expect that Terrence would express a preference for more amenities and higher housing prices in his neighborhood.[13] Instead, he said that he worries that a park renovation might increase rents and displace more Black residents. "It hurts me so bad to see how this neighborhood has changed. . . . They wanna rebuild King Park, which is okay, but I know it's a bad idea, 'cause once you build a park, it brings up the value in the area." Terrence summarized past examples of amenities and new developments that facilitated displacement: "They built a park on the corner of 52nd and Prescott and right when they built the park, everyone that was renting had to move because the owners doubled their rent, and they did the same with the complex on 60th and Killingsworth . . . these families are gonna have to relocate after that, because they got a notice on December 31st that your rent was moving from $1,000.00 to $2,400.00." Terrence said he called a new apartment building in Inner Northeast "just to do some research" and was dismayed to learn that the rent for a one-bedroom apartment was $2,750. The person on the phone told Terrence about amenities in the area, including a new grocery store, and asked if he'd like to also hear about two-bedroom options: "And I was like, 'No. You're pushing the people out of the area that cannot afford the property' and just the racism that you see every day. . . . It's always a struggle." The assumption that landlords are always motivated by a desire to increase rents and maximize profits reflects a White spatial imaginary, which primarily views space as a means to generate exchange value.[14] Terrence profits from his property ownership, even as he expresses worry about the affordability of housing in Northeast. His professed commitment to making housing affordable may contradict his role in the housing market.[15] Still, his claim of focusing on neighborhood access instead of privatism is indicative of a Black spatial imaginary. At the end of the interview, when I asked Terrence what he hoped for the future, he said: "Hope for the future that [then Mayor] Ted Wheeler can put a rent control—they're gonna have to put a cap on it . . . and all these big condos they're building around, they gotta have a percentage for low income. They have to offer it."[16] As a middle-class property owner, his emphasis on making the neighborhood more affordable, rather than promoting policies that benefit the middle class, contradicts previous research on middle-class Black urbanites.[17] Moreover, his response to rising rents reflects his perspective that housing costs are a major mechanism of racialized displacement. However, being "priced out" is just one mechanism of racial change. In the sections that follow I identify major themes in interviewee accounts of Black displacement. They highlight mechanisms of change that are not dependent on economic processes and do not fit neatly within a gentrification analysis.

Serial Displacement

Most respondents understood demographic, cultural, and structural shifts in Northeast Portland to be part of a complex and enduring history of racialized serial displacement.[18] Nicole (b. 1961), a public administrator with a bachelor's degree, said the process of serial displacement "was like taking a scab off of a sore. Like every time it scabs over you take the scab off." Terrence (b. 1973) offered this account: "It goes way back. It goes back to the Vanport flood, which Mother Nature did that, but they moved our families into the Sacramento area, the Rose Garden [arena], [Memorial] Coliseum area, where my grandparents, my father, mother, they grew up, and then, they started building over there, buildings and stuff, buying out homes." Terrence further asserts that Black-owned businesses in Albina were limited in what they could sell, which restricted their success and permanency (discussed in more detail below). "They moved us to this area here and we have a couple nightclubs that can only sell beer and wine and then you start seeing all these coffee shops popping up, White owned, and it starts changing slowly and slowly and they started moving people out."[19] Here Terrence uses "they" loosely to represent White newcomers, the city government, and the Portland Development Commission as partners in Black displacement and White emplacement.[20]

One of the most cited displacement events in the interviews was the Vanport flood. Although the flood occurred in 1948, more than sixty-five years before the interviews took place, respondents understood the event to be highly relevant to Black experiences in the twenty-first century.[21] Layla (b. 1977) said she started to pay attention to changes in her neighborhood in the late 1990s when a friend returned to Portland after several years away and said, "This is not where I grew up at. What is going on?" Her friend helped her pay more attention to changes that she had barely noticed: "Then I started looking around and I'm like, 'Oh my gosh, she's right. We used to own this and that and this and that,' but it was just like little places here and there and then over time it was just like everything was just gone." As Layla was making sense of changes in Northeast, an acquaintance associated those changes with the Vanport flood. "I just remember someone saying, 'It's the same thing they did to us when we lived in Vanport.' They talked about the Vanport flooding and how they wanted to get us out of the area and all that and I'm just like 'wow.' It's like you're so worried about just the day-to-day and life and you don't realize that people have other agendas and that they're secretly behind your back trying to figure out ways to make things better for them and not thinking about us." The association between Vanport and contemporary Northeast Portland makes sense to Layla because she deduces that in both instances Black people were not wanted and [White] "people have other agendas" about the future of place. In both cases, White city elites endeavored to remake the spaces where Black people made their homes.

Many families who lived in central Albina in the 1950s, 1960s, or 1970s lost their homes to urban renewal projects, including the Memorial Coliseum, the I-5 highway, and the ill-fated Emmanuel Hospital expansion. Theresa (b. 1950) is a nonprofit leader who grew up in a middle-class family that owned their home. Losing the family home in the 1950s was a seminal experience in her childhood:

> I'm a child of that eminent domain that is practiced on African Americans quite regularly in Portland. . . . First my parents had bought a home in what is now the Memorial Coliseum, Portland Public Schools Headquarters Blanchard Center [this building was renamed in 2022 for the school district's first Black superintendent, Matthew Prophet, Jr.]. . . . And so, we were there. . . . All of that area was taken out [to be redeveloped] and we used to say, "If you want to make that a Memorial, it should be to all of the people that you pushed out using eminent domain, Black people, to create what you say is 'for the public's benefit.'" The first urban removal was here in Portland.

Theresa's experience with displacement in the mid-twentieth century is shared by many Black people in urban neighborhoods across the United States. As the Memorial Coliseum was being built in Portland in 1960, similar projects were happening in cities across the United States. Theresa's assertion that "the first urban removal" occurred in Portland is not accurate. However, it helps to convey that Theresa understands displacement to be emblematic of the Black Portland experience. It is noteworthy that Theresa says that the clearing of

neighborhoods occurred for "What you say is 'for the public's benefit.'" While the city claimed projects would benefit the "public," Black
Portlanders assert that the city's conceptualization of the "deserving
public" prioritizes White people.[22]

After losing their home, Theresa's family bought a home in Southeast Portland. They maneuvered around discriminatory realtors and
neighbors with the help of her father's Jewish colleague, who served
as an intermediary. Theresa spent part of her childhood in a White
neighborhood in Southeast Portland, near Reed College. She remembers that when she and her sister walked around her neighborhood,
White people stopped to ask "are you lost?" Despite these attempts
to undermine her belonging, an internal counternarrative to anti-
Blackness had already been built up by her parents and her early
childhood experiences. "So, our sense of ourselves certainly wasn't
supported by the attitudes or the feelings of Whites, but we were
so comfortable in who we were, we were able to transcend that. The
fact that I have those memories [of life before moving]. . . . We were
girded then just like they have to gird sons and daughters now, for the
meanness, the ignorance, of this utopia, if you will." By referring to
Portland as a "utopia," Theresa touches on a theme present in many
of the interviews—that Portland is a White utopia or "White folks'
Mecca." She interprets the serial displacement of Black residents as
a mechanism by which this White utopia is created and maintained.

> SHANI: Why do you say "utopia"?
> THERESA: Well, Portland is a utopia for some, the Northwest. I knew
> the history of "This is White land." This has always been a struggle
> here, then and now, about who gets to claim this space. You know?
> The neo-Nazis and White supremacists have always talked about
> homeland in the Northwest, and . . . it cuts through almost every-
> thing that I think about when Portland's called the wonderful, so
> perfectly planned. I know who was pushed out, relocated, dis-
> missed, marginalized, and it's always started with us.

Among urban planners, Portland is widely seen as a well-planned city
that fosters a high quality of life.[23] To Theresa, the city acquired this
reputation through a series of projects that relocated, displaced, and
dismissed people the city determined to be undesirable.

Ella (b. 1954), a retired teacher, saw herself and her family displaced from their home in 1961 to make way for the construction of the I-5 freeway. Ella resented the city's assertion that her family home was "blighted." In Ella's view, the PDC used unfair and arbitrary criteria to determine the condition of a home. When describing the context of her family's move, Ella referenced urban renewal projects, noting "in their audaciousness, PDC granted all this property and destroyed everything that was there. . . . We lost our church, our home, my dad's business and our community." "It was a beautiful community. I mean our next-door neighbors . . . their house was perfectly immaculate. He'd go out. He'd mow the lawn one way this way and one way that way. Horizontal, vertical, and diagonal. And then he'd go out with scissors to make sure it was perfect [laughs]—but these were blighted homes . . . hardwood floors, pocket doors in the living room, built-in china closet, it was beautiful. We lost that. I was an adult before I stopped dreaming about that house and that yard." Like Teresa, Ella refers to her family's displacement as "urban renewal/Negro removal because that's what it was about, getting rid of Black folks." Urban renewal disrupted the community life that gave Ella and Theresa a sense of identity in Black Portland. Ella and Theresa both grew up in the 1950s and 1960s and were raised in middle-class families.[24] But people from homeowning families who lived through urban renewal were not the only ones who saw recent changes as part of a longer process of serial displacement.

Younger residents, and those from lower-earning families that rented their homes, also made these connections between the past and the present. Zora (b. 1985), who spent much of her childhood in Northeast but moved around various Portland neighborhoods, explained that homeownership is rare in her family: "We never owned homes. I could name the people on one hand in my family generations back that have owned their homes. We just haven't owned anything. We moved a lot. I feel like it was because of rent increases." Although her family did not own their home and she was not alive during the urban renewal projects of the 1960s, Zora described displacement from Northeast Portland as part of a longer, repetitive history of serial displacement and of Whites determining where Black people in Portland could and could not live:

. . . when Black people came here, Oregon, Portland, White people who own whatever [said] you can live here. And they said, actually, we don't want you to live there anymore because we wanna live there. So, you can live here. Actually, that seems like a really cool place, how about you live here and we're gonna live there. Actually, one more time, I want you to live all the way out there so I can live right here because this place is actually really cool now. Like, repeatedly they have done that to our community.

Interviewees' accounts of racial change in Northeast Portland were grounded in the historical context and reflected a series of exclusionary events, including the racial exclusion law, the Vanport flood, housing discrimination, and urban renewal. They understood Black displacement in Northeast Portland to be a prolonged racial process that followed a well-established pattern of anti-Black racism.

It Was Planned

Several interviewees suggested that the transition of Northeast neighborhoods into White space was planned by the city and came to fruition through city policy. For example, Terrence (b. 1973) is a third-generation Portlander and a city employee. He still lives in Northeast Portland, but he finds it hurtful to see "nothing but White people, walking dogs, riding bikes" in his neighborhood because they evidenced the knowing removal of Black life and Black residents from Northeast Portland. He ties his observations of demographic change to his knowledge about structural racism. With strain in his voice, Terrence explained: "Because, because, it was planned. You can tell it was planned. Planned to come and raise the rent. Come and plan to try to buy people out. It was planned. You can tell it was planned . . . other people get opportunities—White people get opportunities that colored people don't. I might go ask for an apartment or something like that and get denied, but White person go, and get approved, and we got the same credit limit, the same credit score." Terrence's depiction of racial disparities in lending are well supported by research. Black borrowers are more likely to be denied standard loans and are more likely to be offered subprime loans than Whites with similar economic qualifications.[25]

Tom's (b. 1982) take on the planned displacement of Black residents reflects both gentrification and White spacemaking:

> The PDC decided to develop this community . . . they started planning for it to look like this over here 40, 50 years ago, and that's why they put in those provisions and those restrictions and redlined and got it to where people's property couldn't be improved. You couldn't make the necessary improvements! And then your property would be considered blighted, and then they could come and take your stuff. And then three White people move into the community, start a neighborhood association, and then say you gotta do certain stuff to this, and then the bank wouldn't give you [a loan]—I think all that stuff was planned, to me.

The phrase "it was planned" speaks to questions of intent. In these remarks Tom and Terrence reject the notion that the demographic shift in Northeast Portland was the accidental outcome of redevelopment efforts. They interpret neighborhood change from a standpoint that recognizes the reach of anti-Black racism, the power of White policymakers, and the appeal (to some) of White space.

The mayor's office, the PDC, and neighborhood associations had indeed produced multiple plans for Northeast Portland, including Model Cities, the 1993 Albina Plan, and the Interstate Corridor plan. However, interviewees did not identify specific plans for neighborhood change; rather, they described "the plan" in an abstract manner. For interviewees "the plan" referred to a broad effort to transform Northeast Portland. To Layla the plan was about removing Black people from the neighborhood. She proclaimed, "it's totally different now and [Black residents are] gone and *there was a plan* to make sure that they're gone and nobody cared. It's like it should be illegal I think to do this but it's not." Layla explained that the first time she heard about the plan was in the late 1990s, when she was eighteen and had an internship with the City of Portland. An older Black woman who worked in the office predicted major changes in the neighborhood where they both lived. "I remember her telling me, 'You know they've been having all these meetings. They're really going to try to take over

North/Northeast Portland.' I'm like, 'What are you talking about?' She's like, 'They meet about it all the time how they're going to take over.' And she used to tell me this and I'm thinking this lady doesn't know what she's talking about and [now] I'm just like, 'Okay.'" Layla rolls her eyes as she remembers what she thought of the woman's warning at age eighteen. At the time, Layla thought that the older woman was delusional. But Layla has come to think of that conversation as a wise prediction of what was to come. "And slowly but surely, I was observing and seeing, 'Okay, she's right.' They're slowly purchasing homes and taking . . . but it happened over such a long period of time that I don't think people were prepared and ready and all of a sudden you just looked up and everything had changed. So, it was something that was planned from what she told me and then looking back I'm like, 'Oh yeah, she was right.'" Now this plan makes sense to Layla because she deduces that city leaders saw potential in Northeast neighborhoods. "They realized that where the African-American community lived was good land . . . you know Moda Center [arena] and Lloyd Center [shopping mall] is right there, downtown, this is the perfect area for them to have and so they figured out a way to take over." Layla describes the transformation as a "takeover" because she believes that city elites set out to remake Northeast for the benefit of White people. Her concern was not just that the neighborhood was becoming increasingly White, but that city elites and White newcomers were redefining the neighborhood as White space, rather than working with longtime residents to make it better for everyone.

Unlike Layla, who argued that the city implemented a plan to take over the neighborhood from Black people, Malik (b. 1988) interpreted the city's plans as "innovation" and "progress," but, like Layla, he asserts that "when Black people are not a part of the innovation plan, that's a problem." "The elected officials that are here in Portland that represent the people of Portland, supposedly, they make up these new projects, so they start these new renovations or whatever, but they don't ever, like, conform to their communities where they're starting these projects . . . or for instance the people from the community don't know about the meetings because it's never really advertised as such. And then they'll come up with a plan, make a plan to expand, but the expansion means removing people from their place." Here Malik suggests that when the city claimed to make plans on behalf of a community, they ignored the priorities of those who lived there. Research on urban renewal projects in Portland suggests that the Portland Development Commission has a long history of making decisions without community input, but Black residents have repeatedly fought to have a voice in the process.[26] Still, Malik was unaware of his neighbors' participation. Instead, Malik observed that the city seemed to ignore the concerns of longtime residents when implementing its plans.

Missed Opportunity

Some interviewees, particularly men, maintained that contemporary Northeast Portland, with its renovated homes and flourishing businesses, "could have been ours" if they had only been given the chance. Black Portlanders missed the opportunity to develop a prosperous community because they were not provided with the public services or private investment that became available as the area transitioned to a gentrified White space. For example, Drew shared many good memories of hanging out in the neighborhood with his peers, but as an adult he avoids Northeast because it reminds him that he and his peers did not have the opportunity to live in a well-resourced neighborhood. "It's just really difficult for me to be in a place now, that has gotten so much investment and is now, quote unquote, thriving. . . . And you're like, 'No shit it's thriving. Because you guys pumped all this money into it.' To me, it's very simple and so, to me, that's kind of sinister and I just don't really like participating in it."[27]

While Drew says it is "simple" and "sinister," other respondents were perplexed by investment disparities. Malik (b. 1988) regularly takes morning walks around his Northeast Portland neighborhood. He compared his childhood recollections to what he sees today. He began, "a lot of the stuff that I felt like could've always. . . ." His voice trailed off and then he continued: "I remember like, 'why do all these buildings always look beat up?' I feel like the businesses in them who could never . . . I feel like the businesses never got refurbished or . . . just anything. It was never in the city's budget to prioritize, to make sure these Black businesses and these Black neighborhoods actually looked up to par. You know, cleaning up. Just small stuff, removing the graffiti, stuff that they're doing right now. They never did that when we were just predominantly Black families living there." Although Malik holds the city and its priorities responsible for these disparities, his tone is uncertain. He seems unsure about who was responsible for past neglect and current investment.

An underlying question—"why couldn't we have what they have?"—was evoked by many interviewees as they tried to make sense of prosperity in Northeast. For example, in the focus group, participants sought to explain why White people seemed more empowered to buy property and own businesses. Kelvin (b. 1989) moved away from Portland for several years as a teen. He described his experience visiting Northeast between 2005 and 2010. "Every time I came back to visit, it just got progressively more distant and distant as far as the Black neighborhood and Black community goes. Now when I see it, I just have questions. I always wonder 'cause I don't necessarily think that it's just that White people make significantly more money than us. So, I question, are they just living off of less?" Derek (b. 1984) countered: "They're putting their money together, though." Kelvin continued, "I just want to ask, 'How can you afford this place? You work at a coffee shop.'" While Kelvin speculates that there may be a difference in how White people spend, Derek adds that White people are working collectively and "putting their money together" in order to invest. Later, during an interview, Derek elaborated: "I just feel like history was snatched away. It looks like that could have been us. You know what I mean? I feel like that could have been, if we put our mind to it, we could have had all these thriving businesses and everything, if we just put our money together like that." Without knowledge of systemic processes that produce racial disparities in lending, salaries, and opportunities to build wealth, Derek and Kelvin can only identify individual and cultural explanations for racial inequality.

Other participants offered more structural justifications for missed opportunities. For example, Tom suggests that disparities in lending help explain why the neighborhood was less resourced when it was largely Black. "They [White people] are more likely to get a loan to do the necessary improvements on their home, so just like they redlined this community forever, which meant people couldn't go and get—couldn't get loans on their houses, but then they'll sell it to a White person. The White person can go get all the money they want to do the—fix it, do the renovations that you just wouldn't let the person that was in there before do." As these examples show, interviewees largely offered racial rather than economic explanations for missed opportunities—specifically, that Black people did not get the economic opportunities that were granted to Whites, or that Black people are not "putting their money together" like Whites. When they say "that could have been us," interviewees are talking about racial change, and specifically the transformation of historically Black places that have become White space, not just social class change. The fact that it was usually men who shared thoughts about what "could have been" may reflect hegemonic norms about men as economic providers.[28] Men of all ages lamented that they did not have the economic opportunities that would facilitate the establishment of a well-resourced community and a well-maintained built environment. Men were also more likely to say that Black property owners should not sell. For example, speaking about his late mother's house, Edward (born 1961) proclaimed, "I'm putting my stake in the ground and all, this is my property, I'm never gonna sell, I'm gonna rent it out, gonna make money that way with it, just missed opportunities, just heck of missed opportunities and the community you know, could have stayed in here."

Social Control and Black Displacement

There is a long and documented history of police targeting Black residents in Portland, as they do throughout the United States.[29] In addition, for decades, some business owners have accused the city and other government entities of aggressively sanctioning businesses that serve Black clientele until they are forced to close. Some interviewees attributed neighborhood change in Northeast Portland to police practices and state-led, racialized social control. Interviewees assert that, over decades, the cumulative effects of racial violence in policing and the unequal treatment of Black-serving businesses contributed to Black displacement and ultimately to White spacemaking.

INCARCERATION AND RACIAL BANISHMENT

Efforts to "improve" or "revitalize" a neighborhood often involve excluding or removing people who are perceived to be a threat to the neighborhood's ascent.[30] This is how Bilal (b. 1977) understood the process of neighborhood change in Northeast Portland. He explained, "They made it as livable of a place and as safe as a place for the White people that they could. That meant moving out a lot of the quote-unquote 'riff raff.'" A few interviewees mentioned incarceration as a mechanism by which residents were removed from Northeast neighborhoods. Incarceration rates increased dramatically in Oregon during the 1980s and 1990s, as they did across the United States. The growth of prisons and incarceration in Oregon followed the passage of Measure 11 in 1994, which established mandatory minimum sentences with no chance of parole and required children as young as fifteen to be tried as adults for some crimes.[31] In Oregon, Black people make up 2 percent of the population and 9 percent of those who are incarcerated.[32] Interviewees shared that their mothers, fathers, sons, and brothers had been incarcerated. In addition to removing people from the neighborhood, incarceration disrupts community life and the connection of people to place.[33]

Along with incarceration, police and courts had another tool at their disposal. In 1992, Portland's city council passed an ordinance to create Drug Free Zones (DFZ) in downtown Portland.[34] In 1997, two additional zones were established, both in Northeast Portland. The zones were located in regions of the city with high numbers of drug-related arrests. After the ordinance was passed, people who were arrested for a drug-related crime outdoors in one of those zones could be prohibited from entering the zone without approval for up to ninety days. Those who were convicted could be excluded from the zone for one year. Excluded people could live, work, and attend school in the DFZ, but they could not move freely in public space.

The district attorney who created the ordinance said it was founded on the idea that "constitutional rights are not absolute."[35] In 1999, 3,700 expulsions were issued in Portland's exclusion zones.[36] Most of the exclusions issued in court went to Whites, but the majority of those issued by police went to "minorities."[37] People excluded after an arrest may have never been prosecuted or convicted of any crime. Unless they received a special variance, excluded individuals could be arrested if observed by police in the zone, regardless of what they were doing at the time. In contrast, people who were engaged in drug use or trade in other parts of the city, or inside their homes, were not at risk of exclusion.

In their book *Banishment,* the sociologist Katherine Beckett and the geographer Steve Herbert note that exclusion ordinances are increasingly common and are typically implemented "in contested urban spaces where gentrification is on the horizon."[38] Bethany (b. 1981), who lives in Gresham with her young sons, said she "started paying attention" to changes in her neighborhood in high school after her friend was shot by police. In 1998 or 1999, Bethany realized that some of her peers had disappeared from the neighborhood. Asking around, she learned that they had been excluded: "When you got in trouble for something inside the redline, they'd banish you outside the redline so you weren't allowed to come in the district. That's what your judgment was, like when you went to court. They were like you're not allowed to come past 82nd . . .—they'd start moving us out that way." Recognizing that Black people were historically contained in Northeast Portland, Bethany describes her childhood neighborhood as "inside the redline." By stating "they'd start moving us out that way" Bethany depicts the exclusion ordinance as a potential mechanism of racialized displacement.

The Drug Free Zone ordinance was repeatedly challenged in court, and maligned as racially unjust by activists, civil rights groups, and the local press.[39] In 2007, then Mayor Tom Potter decided not to seek renewal of the exclusion ordinance after a report he commissioned showed clear racial disparities in who was excluded among those who were arrested for excludable offenses. African Americans who were arrested, in any zone, for an excludable crime (1,015 total) were issued exclusions 68 percent of the time, while Whites who were similarly arrested (756 total) were issued exclusions 54 percent of the time. The report only examines racial disparities in exclusion, not arrest. However, its authors call for additional research to examine "the fact that African-Americans are being *arrested* with far more frequency than any other race."

Although she knew few details about the Drug Free Zone ordinance, Bethany made sense of the policy through her own experience, both as a teen in the 1990s and as a mother in 2017. "So, say my 11-year-old got in trouble right now and he went to court. What they would say is, 'Well, since you're causing so much trouble, you can't come past this line. You have to be out in the numbers.' And so, if they said that to my kid, obviously I'm going to have to either move over there or provide him a place to live over there or just move completely. So that was the beginning of it." While the ordinance did not require excluded people to move out of the DFZ, it did make their lives much more difficult. They were at risk of being arrested whenever they left their house. Although Bethany misunderstood the details of the ordinance, her comments demonstrate that exclusion had the potential to disrupt a person's relationship to a place.

The plausible connection between the Drug Free Zone ordinance and racialized displacement is particularly evident in the city's arguments for keeping the ordinance in place. In 1999, when the ordinance was challenged in court on the basis of double jeopardy (punishing excluded people twice), the city argued that exclusion was not a form of punishment, but a civic effort to improve neighborhoods: "The ordinances are intended to address certain societal problems created by drug use—*the problems of declining property values* [emphasis added] and quality of life that occur in specific neighborhoods that have a disproportionate number of drug-related crimes."[40] In this statement, city representatives suggest that social problems found in the Drug Free Zones were not caused by unemployment, discrimination, or disinvestment, but were "created by drug use." The statement also suggests that the way to resolve challenges in "specific neighborhoods" is to remove the people city representatives perceived to be the problem. Additionally, this statement confounds "drug use" and "drug-related crime." Drug use is quantified as "crime" through police action, arrest, and incarceration, all of which disproportionately target Black people.

The city's argument also references "the problems of declining property values." Property values are closely tied to the racial makeup of a neighborhood. For example, the value of an average house in a White urban neighborhood is appraised as three times higher than a similar house in a Black or Latinx neighborhood.[41] Moreover, racial inequality in home appraisals is stark and growing over time. In the racialized US housing market, neighborhoods that lose Black residents increase in value, while those that gain Black people decrease in value.[42] Thus, one potentially effective way to increase property values in a neighborhood is to change the demographics of the people living there. In summary, the city's strategy of increasing property values by enforcing the Drug Free Zone ordinance is interrelated with mechanisms of racial change and White spacemaking.

LICENSING AND THE SURVEILLANCE OF BLACK-SERVING VENUES

Some interviewees stated that public officials helped displace the Black community by thwarting the success of Black-owned and Black-serving businesses in Portland. As Layla put it, "they don't want us here. They clearly don't. Every business that we try to have gets shut down." For decades, the Oregon Liquor Control Commission (OLCC) has placed strict restrictions on businesses that serve Black clientele, particularly after violent incidents occur near the business.[43] Bars and clubs that do not follow the OLCC restrictions are at risk of losing their liquor license or being closed down altogether.

One interviewee, Tom (b. 1982), described his own experiences trying to open a nightclub in another part of the city. Not long after it opened, someone was shot near his club. Although the people involved had not been at his business, OLCC representatives visited Tom and said that he would have to implement a number of restrictions if he wanted to remain in business. Tom reached for his phone to find the detailed list of restrictions. "I couldn't play hip hop anymore. I'll show you. . . ." Tom read aloud from the OLCC letter, which stated that patrons could not wear clothing that is "known to be associated with gang membership, including, but not limited to, athletic jerseys, with the exception of game-day attire for local events . . . torn or ragged clothing, casual sweatpants or track suits, headwear of any kind." According to Tom, the letter also stipulated that he not sell alcohol before 9 p.m. and that the bar must close by 11:30 p.m., "which is a bunch of bullshit that I couldn't do, so I just closed."

Tom's experience with OLCC is not uncommon. Black business owners have repeatedly accused the OLCC of racial discrimination, and many have sued.[44] One court complaint alleged that OLCC and the city were leading a campaign "intended to thwart Black-owned clubs or clubs that played hip-hop and catered to the Black community."[45] While Black-owned clubs were closed when shootings occurred nearby, the complaint listed four White-owned, White-serving clubs that were not closed after one or multiple nearby shootings.

This case was dismissed in 2019. According to an article in *The Orego-nian*, the judge ruled that "statistical evidence [showing] that the city in the last decade had pressed the state to immediately suspend the liquor license of half of the nightclubs owned by African Americans while taking action against only a fraction of all other nightclubs in town—wasn't sufficient for the discrimination claim."[46] Another suit, still awaiting litigation, alleged "unconscionable, illegal conduct creat-ing insurmountable obstacles to success of Black club owners catering to Black people and clubs offering entertainment and playing music appealing to Black people."[47]

Although Tom's club was not located in Northeast, his first-person experience is demonstrative of a common understanding among in-terviewees that Portland officials endeavored to prevent Black people from congregating for social purposes in the city. Moreover, as the demographics in Northeast changed, Black residents saw that a dif-ferent set of rules applied to White business owners.[48] A 1992 *Orego-nian* article reports that OLCC closely watched and documented in-fractions near one Black-owned bar: "Many involved simple assaults, early morning noise, shouting, honking, tires squealing and loud car stereos."[49] Some interviewees, including Terrence (b. 1973), claimed that OLCC was much more lenient with, and supportive of, White-owned bars. "On every corner, there's a bar now. They wouldn't give our Black owners liquor permits at all. On 18th Ave, Solae's, it was Joe's Place. It was the last-standing Black club and he could only sell beer and wine. As soon as he leased it out to White people, they gave them a full liquor license."[50] Solae's, a jazz bar that opened in 2015, was lauded by some journalists as a "return to old Alberta." Joe's Place, one of Northeast's longest-running Black-owned bars, once occupied the same address.[51] But not long after Solae's opened, the city attempted to impose a 10 p.m. curfew.[52] In late 2015, the bar was forced to close because of unpaid noise violation fees. Solae's closed permanently in 2018.

The discrimination suits allege that in addition to placing restric-tions on Black-serving businesses, OLCC and police discourage other venues from hosting hip-hop events, which would likely attract a Black audience. Hosting a hip-hop event at a club would require permission from OLCC and the police, as well as extra security. If these require-ments were not met, the club would risk losing its liquor license. Staff at one downtown club reported that maintaining a primarily White clientele was "the only way to avoid undue harassment and scrutiny by the Portland Police, OLCC, Fire Marshall and other city entities." In the witness reports, a White promoter recounted a police officer saying "if we stopped playing hip hop our problems would go away . . . they also mentioned that if we stopped selling Hennessy, we wouldn't have as many issues."[53] The police officer encouraged the promoter to stop selling Hennessy because it is a drink that is often associated with Black people.[54] Tom described the disparities he saw between hip-hop events and other musical performances: "On a night that it's just a regular [White] concert, it's real simple. You walk through. You get in. . . . You go on a night if it's a hip-hop artist or a Black artist, the whole police force is there. They're standing all in the door. They make you go through metal detectors and all kind of crap." Tom explained that while he was working as a promoter, if he or a club owner did not follow the restrictions associated with hosting hip-hop artists, OLCC would threaten the venue, which would then cancel the event out of fear of losing their liquor license. This practice of penalizing venues for hosting rap and R&B events has also been documented in Oakland,[55] where the proportion of downtown nightclubs owned by Black people decreased from 55 percent (80 percent of clubs were owned by people of color) to 36 percent between 2001 and 2016, while White-owned venues increased from 20 percent to 61 percent. Researchers Erin McElroy and Alex Werth conclude that most rap and R&B venues closed not because of increasing rents, but because of "intense surveillance and prosecution by the city."[56]

A similar pattern was observed in a small midwestern city where the sociologist Charles Gallagher served as an expert witness in a racial discrimination case.[57] Based on a review of internal documents, Gallagher determined that city officials understood the presence of Black and Latino business owners and patrons to devalue the city's waterfront. City council members hoped to turn the area into a tourist attraction for the larger cities nearby.[58] In order to make the waterfront more attractive to tourists, city council members set out to remove non-White business owners from the area. Echoing the discriminatory language used in Portland, one bar owner was instructed to "not sell Hennessy" and to enforce a strict dress code in order to discourage Black clientele from consuming on the waterfront. Gallagher makes the following assessment of city practices, which he calls "re-Whitening": "White city officials hyper-policed minority owned bars, used racist and ethnocentric language to describe racial minorities in their work as government officials, enforced a zero-tolerance policy for minority bars, but not White-owned bars, and worked in concert with city council to target bars whose owners were racial minorities with the intent of shutting down these minority owned establishments." Gallagher writes that city elites succeeded in closing all of the minority-owned restaurants through licensing and inspection codes and zoning ordinances. Restaurants were replaced by establishments that were almost entirely White owned. And the city broke ground on a $50 million riverfront development project. Gallagher contends that city elites "colluded to reestablish a White space by using ostensibly race neutral legal measures to target, shut down and push out non-White establishments." Gallagher insists that what he uncovered in his analysis was not gentrification. It was "in effect a hostile takeover of non-White spaces by elite Whites in order to re-segregate and 're-Whiten.'" Likewise, many of the processes described in this chapter do not accord with typical definitions of gentrification, but instead suggest that city agencies enforced the rules differently for Black people.

Researchers tend to attribute the racial outcomes of gentrification to the association between race and class. While interviewees did suggest that some Black longtime residents were priced out of the neighborhood, other potential mechanisms of neighborhood change, including racialized policing and surveillance of Black social actors and Black-owned businesses, do not easily fit within the gentrification framework. Other concerns echoed by respondents, including racialized serial displacement, are also incongruent with the economic focus of gentrification. Instead, they show how Black longtime residents make sense of the physical, social, cultural, and economic changes they observe in their everyday lives. Their experiences reveal a sense of loss and offer an alternative to interpretations of neighborhood change that prioritize economic processes over anti-Black racism.

5   Life in White Space

THIS IS NOT FOR US

In 2005, Devon (b. 1985) left Portland to enroll at an HBCU in Texas. ¹⁰⁹ Reflecting on his time in college, Devon smiled and proclaimed, "That was like heaven on earth."

> My first day, I sat on the Student Center steps on the main strip. And I missed my first two classes. I just sat, and I was culture shocked. I saw Black people. And they just kept coming. And I was amazed. I'm like, "I've never seen so many that are my age, and they keep coming. Is this a video game? Is somebody just throwing, simulating Black people?" They just kept . . . I was like, "Oh my God." And then I realized . . . I mean, I knew Portland was White. But I was like, "Damn, Portland is White."

Before that day, the largest group of Black people Devon had seen in one place was at the Vanport Classic, a football game between Grambling State and Portland State in 2002. He imagined that the 16,000 people at the game were "pretty much every Black person in the Portland metro area."

Devon grew up in Northeast Portland and, like many of the people introduced in chapter 3, he did not initially realize that he lived in a majority White city. By the early 2000s, the Black population in Northeast was shrinking and more White people were moving in. In high school, he played sports against majority White schools. By the time he left for college, he increasingly experienced Portland as White space. He was struck by the contrast between his home city and his new college environment.

> It was empowering just to see Black people running everything on the campus. But not just the campus, in the neighborhood . . . you go to the grocery store, it's all Black. You go to the bank, it's all Black. You go to the car wash. Everywhere you go, it's all Black. And I remember, after my first semester, coming home for Christmas and getting off the plane. And then I realized that I didn't think about racism for three months. I realized that I felt comfortable being in my own skin. I didn't think about White people, didn't think about racism, didn't think about prejudice one time while I was down there. And that just blew my mind. And then it just kind of let me know how we should not be in Portland. This is not for us.

Devon further compared his experiences of racialized exclusion in Portland to his recollections of Texas:

> It's not constant, but it happens enough for you to notice it. . . . I'm in New Seasons [grocery store in Portland] in the line, and they're talking, and they're all perky to one person, and they get to me, and they looking down, and not making eye contact. [I say,] "Hey, how you doing?" And their whole energy changes. . . . Because I've experienced the opposite of what I'm experiencing here, I know that it could be better, and it should be better. But it's not, because we're here, and there's a lot of White people, and they're not comfortable with Black people. And if they don't say it, they'll show it.

Devon and his wife recently purchased a house in North Portland, about four miles from his childhood home, where they live with their two children. Although Devon dreams of moving back to Texas, his wife wants to stay near family in Portland, and he feels "kind of rooted." This experience of feeling simultaneously rooted and excluded in contemporary Northeast Portland is the focus of this chapter. Moreover, I demonstrate that middle-class property owners and working-class renters shared similar experiences of racialized exclusion in Northeast Portland, thereby revealing the limitations of gentrification as a framework for analyzing neighborhood change.

For many people who grew up in Northeast in the late twentieth century, it is upsetting to spend time there today. For example, Devon remarks on the current state of his old neighborhood, now a popular shopping area and tourist destination: "It's gross. It's nasty. It's just weird. It doesn't even. . . . It just feels like an out-of-body experience." Today, instead of being a refuge from Whiteness, most interviewees experience contemporary Northeast Portland as White space where they are subjected to persistent surveillance and exclusion. In the neighborhood's retail spaces, Whiteness is centered, and Blackness is marginalized. Strikingly, upper middle-class property owners and lower-income renters share similar experiences with surveillance, exclusion, and marginalization in public space.

WHITE WATCHING

Tina (b. 1963) is relieved that the subsidized apartment complex where she grew up in the 1970s remains intact in the Boise neighborhood, "because my kids and my grandkids can see where I grew up at." Tina's own grandparents grew up in Louisiana and Mississippi. After migrating from Mississippi, Tina's paternal grandmother lived in a house just off North Mississippi Avenue, now a popular five-block commercial strip that, according to the *New York Times*, "delivers a hipster experience as reliably as the rain."[1] Tina, who lives in Southeast Portland, did not remember the exact address of her grandparents' old house but set out to find it on a whim one afternoon. "I remember I was coming back [to Northeast] for a meeting. I was coming from Interstate [Avenue]. I remember my grandmother lived off of Mississippi. I have just snippet memories of playing out there. I said, 'I'm going down to the street, and I want to see if I can find the house.' That's what I told myself, right. I'm driving slow and I'm looking. I know I had to go down a little bit, pass the old Boys' Club." Driving through the neighborhood, Tina reminisced about buildings from her childhood. She remembered playing in the Boys' Club, where girls were not allowed. She and her friends once snuck in and played until someone noticed them and kicked them out. She was not exactly sure what her grandmother's house looked like, so she drove slowly down the block.

> I'm driving down the street, down Mississippi. I'm just trying to force my mind to remember the house, right? I'm driving real slow. I'm just looking. I know it's on the right-hand side. I'm like, "I just really want to just know what house it is," because I have snippet memories of it. Then all of a sudden, my mind went from what my mission was to all these White people looking at me like I was getting ready to do a damn drive-by. I'm looking like, "What the hell are they looking at me for?" Then I thought: Wow, they're looking at me like, you're out of place. Why are you driving down the street?

In this moment, Tina experienced herself both as a person trying to revisit memories from her childhood and, through the eyes of watching Whites, as a person who did not belong and was "out of place."[2] This is what W. E. B. Du Bois called the double consciousness: "the sense of always looking at one's self through the eyes of others."[3] Moreover, in her grandmother's neighborhood, Tina experiences what the sociologist Elijah Anderson describes as the risk of "social, if not physical, jeopardy" in White space, where her offense was conducting herself "in ordinary ways in public while being Black at the same time."[4]

In their study of Black experiences in White colleges, Joe Feagin and colleagues apply the term "hate stare" to Whites' "negative or hateful glances and actions that imply an unspoken question, 'Why are you here?'"[5] But it would be a mistake to interpret the looks Tina experienced in her grandparents' former neighborhood as necessarily hateful. It is unlikely that the White Portlanders were motivated by hate. Instead, they were silently asserting their sense of who belongs. They normalize Whiteness in space, while simultaneously marginalizing Blackness. Rather than a hate stare, I use the term *White watching* to refer to the racial appraisal and ocular interrogation some Whites perform when Black people enter White space.

White watching is similar to, but not the same as, the White gaze. The White gaze refers to the normalization and centering of White perspectives in American culture and society. The White gaze may lead a Black person to dress, style her hair, or speak with the perceptions of her White observers in mind. The White gaze leads Black creators to automatically imagine a White audience when making art and literature.[6] The White gaze names the taken-for-granted perspective that the White audience is *the* audience. The White gaze also represents internalized surveillance. Black people know that their behavior is being judged according to a White norm and learn to adjust their behavior accordingly. In contrast, White watching does not silently hold Black people to a White standard of behavior. Through White watching, White people actively assess Black behavior according to an arbitrary standard that functions to treat Black people as outsiders and thereby limit Black autonomy and deny Black humanity. The standard of behavior is still grounded in Whiteness, but White watching incriminates Black people for doing things that White people do without notice.

People with varied social status, from upper middle-class property owners to low-earning renters, describe very similar experiences with White watching in Northeast Portland. Lawrence (b. 1952), a retired educator with a master's degree, speaks at length about exclusionary comments and facial expressions during our interview in the living room of his large home in an upper middle-class suburb.[7] Lawrence moved to the large house so that he could better care for a relative with a chronic illness. Although he lives fifteen miles from Northeast Portland, Lawrence travels there almost every day because he volunteers with a local nonprofit. He also owns and maintains nine rental properties that were left to him and his wife by his father-in-law. The houses, which were purchased in the 1960s and 1970s, are occupied entirely by White tenants. Lawrence has benefited financially from gentrification, but he nonetheless feels slighted by the new residents who are remaking the area as White space.

> I don't have any problem with gentrification, except for the fact that many of the people, I won't say all, but many of the people that are over there, the way they treat those people of color who actually live there or own property there. It's like a "What are you doing here?" type of attitude. I don't know if that's intentional or learned, or what, but the subjective part of that to me is it's kind of an insult, a slap in the face to folks, particularly when you've given a sacrifice in the area.

Lawrence explains that when he goes to check on his rental properties, neighbors stare at him with bewilderment. Some have gone so far
as to ask, "Can I help you?" Lawrence attributes these interactions to
the new residents' failure "to assimilate" to a multicultural world. He
laments that, when it comes to integrated life, "we [Black people] are
the only ones that's really making a sacrifice many times."

Revealing his role as a landlord, Lawrence calls the offending residents "clientele," explaining, "the clientele of people who are moving to that neighborhood have their own views: 'That is mine. You
don't belong here. Why are you here?'" Landlords are typically regarded as agents of neighborhood exclusion. The fact that Lawrence
feels racially marginalized by his prospective tenants indicates the
import of race as a status that can shape interactions as much as social class does.[8]

Lawrence notes that White people in Northeast are most suspicious when they first encounter him. Once he engages in conversation and explains his presence in the neighborhood, the interaction
changes. "Now, I have some good neighbors in some of the houses,
but others, if they haven't seen you for the first—when they get to
know you, they're fine, but it's like the initial observance or connection of seeing someone that is of color that is over there: it's work that
needs to be worked on." To help people get to know him, Lawrence
tries to break the ice and "make them talk," because "you can tell they
have a type of subtle perception." This observation, that White people
are fine with Lawrence once they talk with him, is indicative of what
Anderson calls the "dance" that middle-class Black people must do to
be accepted in White space.[9]

In part, Lawrence holds the city responsible for his mistreatment
and proclaims that "the city says they're working on it." City-supported
neighborhood associations, he supposes, should help new White residents learn how to coexist with Black people. For Lawrence, being
watched by Whites is especially upsetting because it is accompanied
by what he sees as a disregard for the history of the place. He explains,
"what bothers me is just the fact that the population that is there does
not seem to have a connection, or doesn't want a connection, with
those that have been there before, so those of us that go over there
feel like outsiders." The problem is not just that people look at Law-

rence as if he does not belong, but that they seem to have no regard for the significance of the area to longtime residents.

It is not only the middle-class property owners who feel compelled to prove that they belong in White space. Sitting at a large round table in a deserted Southwest Portland diner, Bilal (b. 1977), a construction worker, shares very similar thoughts about his interactions with Whites in Northeast.

> It bothers me that I don't have my neighborhood anymore. It bothers me that I can't go to Northeast Portland and feel comfortable anymore. It almost feels like it was a hostile takeover, the way that they look at you and the way that they treat you now when you go over there—it's just—it's kind of insulting. The hipsters walking around like they've been there for twenty years . . . the way that they look at you, the smugness of some of 'em, just the disdain that some White people look at you with. What are you doing over here? That type of thing. It's insulting.

Lawrence and Bilal have very different life histories and connections to Northeast, but both describe their experience in the neighborhood as "insulting." Unlike Lawrence, Bilal does not own property in the neighborhood. Lawrence is twenty-five years older than Bilal. Lawrence began a professional career immediately after high school, then went to college and began a second professional career. Bilal joined a gang and began dealing drugs in high school during the 1990s. After his friend was killed by police, Bilal moved to California for several years and then returned to Portland to find that "everything had changed."

Like Lawrence, Bilal feels that at first glance White people do not see him the way he sees himself, but "if they have a conversation with me—they seem to—it seems to open up their eyes as to the person that I am." Although he is not a middle-class professional, Bilal does "the dance" to help Whites understand him as he understands himself, as fully human.[10] While Lawrence blames the city, Bilal blames Whites' perceptions on the state of Black Portland. "The Black community here is just not as advanced as some other Black communities are. I'm probably sure that it's probably more advanced [in Philadelphia] because there's more Black people in Philadelphia. I know that it's probably like that in Atlanta, but it just, it's just slow here and so the expectations that they have of you here are just less." According to Bilal, when there are many examples of Black economic success in a place, such as Philadelphia, Atlanta, or his former home of Los Angeles, Whites are likely to perceive a Black stranger as a potentially successful person rather than as a stereotype. Although Lawrence and Bilal offer different explanations for White behavior in Northeast Portland, both feel prejudged by the White people they encounter in the neighborhood. Elijah Anderson has pointed out that middle-class Black people go to great lengths to prove that the "ghetto stereotype does not apply to them" and that they are worthy of "decent treatment and trustworthy relations."[11] Bilal's story shows that it is not just middle-class Black people who do "the dance" in White space. In fact, the ghetto stereotype, a dehumanizing and demonizing trope, is not wholly applicable to any person.[12] As Candice Jenkins notes, "public Blackness operates as a perceptual case of mistaken identity for rich, middle class, and poor alike."[13]

Moreover, the argument that White people mistreat middle-class Black people because they misread their class status minimizes and oversimplifies the role of anti-Blackness in these interactions. Black people are treated with suspicion in White space not just because Whites assume that they are poor or "ghetto," but because they perceive Black people through a lens of anti-Blackness. There is ample evidence that Black people, regardless of class performance or credentials, are routinely presumed to be incompetent and untrustworthy.[14] White people, whether middle class or poor, are not subjected to the same scrutiny.

Interviewees did not have the same experiences with White watching in all Portland neighborhoods, which demonstrates the interconnectedness of race and space. For example, Derek (b. 1985), a reentry counselor who grew up near Alberta, had experienced White watching in Belmont, another majority White area that is promoted to tourists as a hipster hotspot, but not in downtown Portland. "That's what Mississippi and Alberta reminds me of now—Belmont. How it's just predominantly—When I walked on Belmont one time, I was walking, they looked at me like I wasn't supposed to be there. I don't know what it is, wherever I go [on Mississippi and Alberta] now it feels like I'm not supposed to be there. They make me feel that way, it's weird, but downtown I don't feel that way for some reason. I don't know why." Like Derek, most people associated White watching with tourist-friendly commercial strips in majority White residential neighborhoods, such as Mississippi Avenue, Belmont, or NW Twenty-Third Avenue.[15] Downtown Portland, while still majority White, was generally experienced as a more diverse and welcoming space.

White watching was more hurtful in Northeast because of the connection people had to the area as a Black place and a refuge from Whiteness. Micky (b. 1995) lives in Northeast and works at a youth advocacy organization in downtown Portland. Like Derek, he agreed that White people did not give him the same exclusionary looks downtown (specifically, the Pearl District), but if they did, it would not have the same effect because he did not have the same connection to the neighborhood. "I think it hurts even more so . . . in the Albina and Alberta area because it's like they look at you like you don't belong. Like you haven't lived here your entire life. So yeah, they'll look at my grandma in the Albina neighborhood like she don't belong, or why are you here? when she was born there and continues to live there. So, I think it has a greater impact than if you go somewhere in the Pearl or Lake "No Negro" or something like that." Lake "No Negro" is a reference to Lake Oswego, a Portland suburb that has a reputation of persistent racial exclusion. Micky claims that feeling excluded in Lake Oswego or downtown Portland would feel less hurtful because he never experienced those places as home.

Micky explained two aspects of White watching: detached disregard and persistent surveillance. He recounted a time when neighbors made a noise complaint to police about a going-away party his grandmother hosted for a friend.[16] The police came and told his grandmother what volume level was acceptable. The police received a second complaint and they made another visit even though, he said, the volume had not increased. "And so there's like this mixture of the White people not fucking with us, like not talking to us, not acknowledging us, not saying anything. But, also, when it comes to things like the noise complaint or my grandma's tree was like over someone's yard or something. And they'll complain about that, but will never talk to you actually in person." In addition to being watched by Whites, some interviewees describe being ignored and unacknowledged in public space.[17] Miriam (b. 1976), a high school graduate and community organizer, said she largely avoided Alberta Street and only visited long-standing shops and the Black United Fund. Otherwise, the lack of civility she experienced while walking on the street made her feel disconnected from her childhood neighborhood. "There's no sense of connection or even people saying hello or walking on one side of the sidewalk [to allow you to pass]. I have a cousin from LA, and he came to town, and he calls Alberta the place where White people don't see you. We were walking down the street, and people weren't looking. He reached out and he was like, 'Hello, hi,' and no one would look up or say hi or anything. So that's his running [joke], like, 'That's the street where the White people don't see you.'" Miriam's interactions on Alberta, which lacked the civility of recognition and acknowledgment, occurred in a place where she spent time growing up. While Miriam had similar experiences on other commercial streets in White, tourist-friendly neighborhoods, like NW Twenty-Third Avenue, the effect was different, she said, because "I don't have a connection to that place."

Some people connected White watching in Northeast with the knowing and conscious takeover of Black space. Layla (b. 1977) travels to her office in Northeast every day. She contrasts her childhood experiences to today.

> Growing up, you were used to walking around, seeing people, they speak to you, I mean it was just different. It was like family. You could talk to people and have conversations. Now it's like they'll just side-eye you. . . . It's not friendly, even though they've taken over and they're here, they're not friendly. It's almost like they're looking at us like, "Why are you here? This is ours now." It's not like they came but they want to build with us. It's like they came in to take over and they did.

In Vancouver, Washington, the suburb where Layla now lives, residents sometimes look at her as if she does not belong. However, to Layla, this does not have the same meaning it has in Northeast. "It's like you get the side-eye [in Northeast] because, I think, these people know. They know that yeah, 'this used to be theirs and now we're here,' and it's almost like an awkward-type side-eye or whatever, where in Vancouver, it's like we came over to their spot so. . . ." New residents' redefinition of the meaning of that place made Layla feel uncomfortable and disoriented: "It's just weird. It's a weird feeling."

For Saul (b. 1985), a middle school teacher with a bachelor's degree who now lives in Gresham, seeing White people feeling at ease in Northeast was an alarming signal that Whites owned the neighborhood and that he may not be safe. "Seeing White people jogging at night, that's scary to me. It's just not what it used to be. I feel like they have come in and taken over, so now they feel oh, it's theirs, right? . . . I feel more uncomfortable now that . . . White people are comfortable because I don't know how they're going to see me." Saul wondered if he could still claim Northeast Portland as his home since Whiteness had been reasserted in place.

> The things that I've learned just make me cautious about White people coming into the neighborhoods, taking over, and feeling that sense of entitlement. I was in that neighborhood before that, right? And so, I know the history of this place, but that doesn't mean they won't call the cops, and it doesn't mean the cops won't believe them. And so that's just like . . . it feels weird being in that neighborhood now, just because it's like I don't. . . . Do I belong here anymore? Is this . . . can I say that I grew up in this area?

He is "vigilant" in public space because a White person watching him might think "there's a Black man walking down the street. I got to call the police."[18] The risk of interpersonal racism and racialized police violence was pronounced in a place that had once functioned as a refuge from interpersonal racism.

THE BLACK SPATIAL IMAGINARY

Interviewees were not bothered by racial exclusion in Northeast simply because it revealed Whites' stereotypes and narrow perceptions about who belonged in the Northeast. It also disrupted the sense of community they wanted to have with their neighbors. When Layla laments that new arrivals did not "want to build with us," it is evident that building community was important to her. When Whites look

at Layla as if she does not belong, they exclude her from the center
of place-based community life. George Lipsitz argues that communal values are integral to the Black spatial imaginary that developed
among Black Americans in response to systemic discrimination and
constrained residential opportunities.[19] Unable to control the exchange value of their homes, segregated Black communities instead
focused on strengthening use value by relying on each other and using
public space in new ways.[20]

Drew (b. 1984) suggests that changes in his neighborhood in the
late 1990s threatened the viability of communal life. In Drew's view,
the problem with the new residents was not that they were White.
In fact, Drew's White mother purposely raised her biracial sons in
a Black community, despite the objections of Whites in her social
circle. Drew's concern is that the new residents did not participate in
the existing communal place-based practices; moreover, he observed
White newcomers creating exclusionary connections with other new
White residents. "As new people moved in, they would just go from
their house to their car and leave. Now that house was no longer a
part of the neighborhood. Does that make sense? And so, you see that
happening, but then, who would they rock with? They would rock
with the other new people." Most interviewees' sense of exclusion and
disregard in the neighborhood is tied to both gentrification and White
spacemaking. However, Evelyn is one interviewee who experienced a
lack of acknowledgment and civility in White space but did not share
the often concomitant negative feelings about gentrification. I interviewed Evelyn (b. 1950), a retired city administrator in the home near
Killingsworth Street she had bought more than forty years before.
She remembers Mississippi Avenue having just six businesses in the
1970s: a grocery store, a couple of taverns, a building supply place,
and a bowling alley. She appreciates the enlivened commercial strip
on Mississippi; however, she does not feel comfortable making use of
it because the White people she sees there do not acknowledge her
and treat her as if she does not belong.

> I like seeing all the stuff that's going on down there, but I feel de-
> tached, because people don't even. . . . I don't know if this is a cultural
> thing, but African Americans, I don't care if you know somebody or
> not, you speak, and you can have a conversation, or acknowledge

somebody. And most of the White people don't do that unless they know you. They'll talk with you if they know you, but just to even acknowledge that you're there, unless you say something specifically to them. So, that's the thing that I'm not used to, and I think it's a cultural thing. . . . I can sit on the porch, and as they walk by back and forth, I could say hi and they'll try to avoid making eye contact, look down, or do something else. . . . When I go into an all-White environment, not only do I not feel like I belong, there's like this sense of "you don't belong, we're not even going to acknowledge that you're in the room."

Generally, Evelyn was not opposed to the changes in her neighborhood: "Change is good. You just adjust." Her experience in Northeast Portland was relatively unusual in that she did not feel the same unbridled attachment to the neighborhood. She was born in a small town in eastern Oregon and moved to Portland in third grade in the 1950s. Although her social circle in eastern Oregon had been a small, very close-knit community of Black families, her Portland peers teased her, saying that she sounded and acted White. It took several years for this bullying to stop. Eventually, Northeast Portland became home and a place where her children grew up fully immersed with the "neighborhood kids" in the 1980s and 1990s. Still, her connection to communal life in Northeast may have been affected by her initial experiences in the area. It is telling that someone who has a complicated history with Northeast Portland, and who does not feel hurt by gentrification, still felt the loss of civility and acknowledgment when spaces became majority White. Evelyn's case suggests that the experience of racial exclusion that accompanies the neighborhood's transition into White space can exist independent of negative feelings about gentrification.

THE RETAIL EXPERIENCE

Discrimination

Racial discrimination in retail settings is so widely recognized that it is simply called "shopping while Black." Black shoppers are often followed around stores by suspicious employees, and they may receive

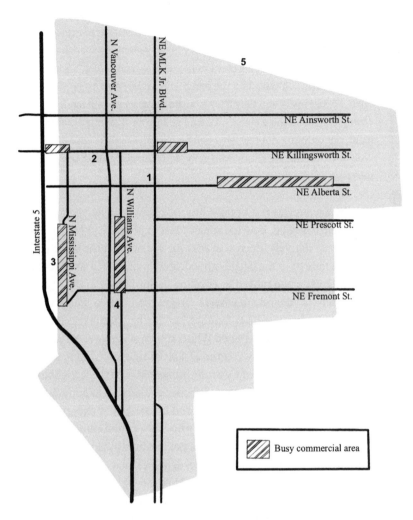

FIGURE 5.1. Map of busy commercial streets in post-2015 Northeast Portland.
1   Alberta Commons   4   New Seasons
2   Chapel Pub   5   Tough Luck Bar
3   Miss Delta's Restaurant

less assistance with their shopping endeavors than Whites.[21] When I asked if they shopped in the retail establishments on Northeast streets like Alberta, Mississippi, Vancouver, or Williams, interviewees volunteered experiences of discrimination or fear of discrimination (figure 5.1). Tina (b. 1963), a hospital administrator, said that her greetings in shops are often countered with "dryness" or surveillance: "I'll make a joke and say, 'You ain't got to watch me. I got money. I'm cool. Trust me, I'm cool.' I'll say that. I'll call them out on it because it's like enough is enough. I'm not going to tolerate that. . . . I don't really do much shopping [in Northeast]. Number one, it's overly priced. . . . Then two, I'm not going to spend my dollars where I don't feel like my person is being appreciated." Shari (b. 1973), who teaches financial literacy classes in a social service organization, recently moved back to Northeast Portland with her three teenagers after a subsidized unit became available. She discouraged her children from shopping in stores that were not welcoming: "I don't really do much on Mississippi at all and I don't like how the business owners on Mississippi treat the kids. I tell my kids, 'You deserve to be here.' Now, my kids go to the store and I tell them to stop spending money where you don't feel comfortable. . . . People in the store treat the kids like they're stealing when they just walk in the store. They're following them." Dawn (b. 1982), a social worker, was hesitant to shop on Mississippi and Alberta because she did not want to face discrimination. "My mom had worked in retail for years so she understood the value of greeting people at the door and giving them space and time to look around then coming back and checking in, but that's just not what we get when we go in those stores. And then to turn around and see a White person walk in the door and have that experience that we would hope to have, it just doesn't feel good." Dawn's mother enjoyed shopping in small boutiques, especially those that sold fabric and craft supplies. Dawn said that while her mother also noticed their differential treatment, she told her daughter, "I'm from here. I have the right to be in here. I'm gonna go shop." In contrast to her mother's claim on the neighborhood, Dawn felt uncomfortable and "hyperaware" in retail stores. "I'm gonna get irritated because I'm going to be hypersensitive or hyperaware of what's happening around me, and when I say what's happening around me, it's like if I walk into a store, I'm constantly checking to make sure my hands aren't in my purse, and I'm curious to know how people are greeting me. And it's not every store on Alberta, but there are some shops where it just doesn't feel comfortable." Dawn adds, "it was almost like we were either invisible, like people just didn't care to see us, or they would see us and just be on us, just to make sure that we weren't going to take anything."

With her concern about how the White retail staff might see her, Dawn has learned to police her own body to counter the threat of discrimination. By refusing to put her hands in her purse, Dawn reinforces the norms of White space, which interpret her as a likely criminal. Dawn explained that she learned these practices from her mother and grandmother.

> My grandmother always taught my mom and my mom always taught me that when you walk into places like, any store, don't ever put your hand in your purse. If I have to refill my lip gloss, don't do it in the middle of the store. Go outside and do it because you don't want to give anybody the impression that you're taking something. And it's something that I still hold to this day. I will just refuse to get my phone or anything in the store 'cause I don't want there to ever be any confusion.

Dawn integrated what she learned from her mother and grandmother with her own experience in stores. Some scholars have argued that Black people respond negatively to gentrification because their knowledge of past racism fosters cynicism about neighborhood changes in the present.[22] Although interviewees are knowledgeable about historical racism, their perspectives on neighborhood change were largely shaped by their own racialized experiences in Northeast as it became White space.[23]

Not for Us

While many people discuss discrimination in retail establishments, a more pronounced theme is that shops and restaurants in the neighborhood are "not for us." Gentrification researchers have established that Black residents often feel excluded and uncomfortable in the retail spaces in gentrifying neighborhoods, but scholars offer a limited account of why this is the case.[24] Existing explanations tend to rely on a class-based argument—that is, Black people feel uncomfortable in new retail establishments because they cannot afford to buy available products. In fact, in some studies, the terms *Black* and *low-income* are used interchangeably.[25] One clear problem with this approach is that it ignores social class variation among Black people.

Additionally, by focusing on class-based explanations, researchers underemphasize how racialized retail theming and exclusionary interactions in White space shape Black retail experiences.[26] Retail establishments, along with developers, real estate agents, and local organizations, work to symbolically redefine neighborhoods through retail theming. In her New York study, Sara Martucci finds that retail actors observe changing themes in the aesthetics in gentrifying neighborhoods, and apply those themes in their own businesses.[27] "Theming and neighborhood identity," Martucci notes, "often rely on the exclusion of existing residents and the inclusion and attraction of new visitors and residents." In his study of Venice Beach, California, Andrew Deener describes this exclusionary demarcation of a neighborhood as "symbolic ownership."[28] Like Venice Beach, California, and Williamsburg, Brooklyn, Northeast Portland is themed as a White bohemian neighborhood that eschews name brands and national chain stores. Retail stores, including coffee shops, restaurants, and boutiques, sell handmade, often locally produced and design-oriented products.

Like some previous studies, I do find that interviewees mention the cost of goods and services when depicting exclusionary changes in local stores. However, interviewees' statements about cost are often as much about the centrality of White bohemian taste in the retail offerings as they are about affordability. When people talk about increasing costs, they do so in a way that points to the transformation of the neighborhood into White space. For example, Edward (b. 1961) gave this account of the changing retail landscape.

> New Seasons [a natural foods grocery store, similar to Whole Foods] versus Safeway, you know Black folks can go to Safeway instead of go to New Seasons. You know they're building things for the *White taste*, the *White culture*, that's what they want in here you know. I think all those high rises over there, they're putting in—and they're charging an exorbitant amount of money for those rentals, you know? It's like Black folks can't afford that.

Edward owns a home and a rental property and could afford to live in a newly built apartment building. He is correct that Black people are less likely to be able to afford high-rent luxury apartments. On average, Black families in Portland, and in the United States, earn less and have approximately one-tenth the wealth of the average White family. Still, in his reference to White taste and White culture, it is clear that Edward's point is not only about the lack of affordable retail or housing in the neighborhood, but also about changes that are designed to appeal to White consumers and to transition the neighborhood into White space.

New shops and restaurants in gentrifying and Whitening neighborhoods are not simply "neighborhood improvements"; they reflect particular tastes, which are connected to race *and* class. When interviewees say that shops were "for them" and "not for us," they're not just referring to affordability; they are explaining that they experience these shops as White space.[29] For example, Elias (b. 1991), a writer and artist, described the changes he observed at the bar next to his childhood home. First, he explained that the bar was previously racialized as a Black place: "They probably would never call it a dive bar because it was a bar that mostly Black people went to, so they'd probably call it a hood bar. It's a low-key place. . . ." When the bar mostly served Black people, Elias notes, "they" would have considered it a "hood bar." Here, "they" seems to refer to the dominant perspective that defines mainstream, or White, meanings of space and place. Dive bars are unglamorous, outdated, and cheap, but their supposed authenticity is appealing to some middle-class Whites, while White patrons tend to avoid and disparage similarly "low-key" Black-serving bars as "hood."

After the owner sold the bar, it became a pizza place. Now Elias "hardly ever sees" Black people there. He attributes this shift to intentional changes in the store:

> It's something about the way it's marketed, it's something about the way they changed the coloring. It's something about the whole. . . . There's so many unspoken things that we understand . . . It's not that Black people don't enjoy pizza. It's not that Black people don't enjoy plants. But when the plant store goes in, we also know it's not actually for us, it's not that we can't give them their money, of course, capitalism accepts everybody's credit cards, but it's something about the marketing, the visuals, the manner in which these things go up.

The feeling that new establishments are "not for us" was common among interviewees.[30] Interviewees did not suggest that Black people avoided retail establishments because they were angry about the mere presence of White people who had "invaded" their neighborhood. Instead, they described the way cultural markers signify that new bars, restaurants, and shops are remaking Northeast for middle-class Whites.[31]

When I asked Layla (b. 1977) if she shopped in the boutiques on commercial streets like Mississippi, Alberta, and Williams, she explained that the items in the store did not appeal to her and seemed to be explicitly directed toward White taste.

> I mean, I eat on Mississippi sometimes at some of the restaurants, but the shops, no. They're weird. They're not my style of stuff. I mean a lot of the shops are like shops where maybe they've made their own things, and you go in and buy little trinkets that people have made. I'm just saying, I've walked in and I'm just like, "Who is buying this?" Or shops where you can buy incense or candles or stuff. I'm not into that type of stuff . . . a lot of the shops are like—I guess I would say they're more items and things that are geared towards them.

The products Layla describes—candles, incense, handmade trinkets— are certainly not appealing to all White people. However, they are consonant with the bohemian and artistic themes that were communicated by Whites who claimed symbolic ownership of Northeast neighborhoods. Layla was also not interested in the stores selling secondhand children's clothing that have opened in recent years. These upscale consignment shops, which sell only boutique children's clothes and will not consign goods from mid-range and discount stores like Carters, Old Navy, or Target, appeal to some parents' taste for high-end goods and their eco-conscious repudiation of fast fashion. Layla understands these stores to be targeting White consumers. "I mean, because you know, in the Black community I don't know whose child was wearing that stuff. No, I'm not going in there and buying—that's just how we are. Put a Target over here, and I'll go to Target or something." Although it is not necessarily true that no Black person would shop in the upscale consignment shops, in Layla's view stores like these were established to attract White people, not people like herself. Earlier in the chapter, Layla offered the following assessment: "It's not like they came and they want to build with us. It's like they came in to take over, and they did." Shops that served bohemian, White, middle-class tastes were a symbol of this process, because they were intended to attract clientele that facilitated the establishment of White space.[32] Layla explains: "I would just like to see more Black-owned businesses over there that are for us that we would feel comfortable going into, that if we go into, we're not being followed around or looked at or thinking that we're going to steal something because that's kind of the vibe you get over there." Layla's wish for more places that were non-discriminatory and prioritized (her interpretation of) Black taste diverges from analyses that presume high prices are the primary mechanism of neighborhood exclusion.

For many interviewees, the transition to White space is tied to an awareness that local retail establishments appealed to the tastes and preferences of new White residents rather than long-term Black residents. But some interviewees did like the products sold in neighborhood boutiques. For example, Dawn said, "I've been into a couple of shops; it's not that the clothes don't look good. I think the clothes look great. I just am not gonna pay that much money for a T-shirt." While Dawn is clearly commenting on the affordability of items, she is also defining herself as dissimilar from someone who would pay $200 for a simple shirt. In fact, the garments in many of the Northeast boutiques are very simple, oversized shirts and dresses whose high prices often reflect that the items were made locally or using "eco-friendly" materials. While people of any race or ethnicity might find the aesthetics of these garments appealing, upper middle-class Whites are more likely to be connected to the social networks that prioritize the consumption of such goods.[33] By appealing to this type of consumption, retail stores facilitate the performance of a particular bohemian middle-class White aesthetic, while excluding non-Whites and those whose incomes would not accommodate such spending.

Symbolic Disownment

Symbolic ownership, Andrew Deener writes, is the "process by which individuals and organizations work to control the aesthetic presentation, public perception, and social and economic utility of a social space."[34] In chapter 2, I note that organizations like the Alberta Arts District assert symbolic ownership over Northeast by branding it as a bohemian and art-centered neighborhood, consistent with the popular slogan "Keep Portland Weird."[35] As Northeast neighborhoods were branded as a hipster hot spot, long-term Black residents simultaneously experienced the removal of the symbolic evidence that Northeast was once a Black place and a refuge from Whiteness.[36]

Zora (b. 1985) explained how she feels when driving through the neighborhood where she grew up. "It feels weird. It's painful to drive down those streets and to just see those people so happy and excited by all the doggie shops and expensive ice cream parlors and restaurants and food, or clothing places, like, they look so happy, and it's almost like you don't even know you just ripped all that stuff from someone else, and they are sad for your happiness. That's what it looks like; that's what it feels like." Zora also said she lacked access to much of the retail in Northeast because she could not afford many of the products sold in the stores. Clearly, the degree to which people felt excluded by new retail was influenced by income and class status. Still, similar to higher-earning and property-owning interviewees, Zora attributed her discomfort in the neighborhood to cultural displacement, rather than just affordability.

Some interviewees' comments about neighborhood change did suggest feelings of resentment. However, these feelings did not reveal a general sense of racial hostility. Interviewees did not express a general dislike of White people. Rather, they are bothered by White watching and White racial dominance in place. Interviewees resented the assertion of racial marginality in a space that had once centered Black life. For example, when I asked Tom (b. 1982) if he shopped on commercial strips in Northeast, he had a ready answer.

> TOM: They turned people's houses into freakin' bars! Because—they didn't let us—so I don't know. They didn't let us improve our community ourselves. They came and took it over and made it theirs. This ain't even our neighborhood no more, so I'm not about to give 'em none of my money.
>
> SHANI: Do you ever walk by and think, "That looks like something I would want?"
>
> TOM: Nope. I'm still pissed.

Similarly, Rhonda (b. 1963), an elementary school teacher, explained that she avoided Northeast shops to protest systemic racism: "I don't mind just having people that are White owning businesses. I don't think there's anything wrong with that. The systems that undermine Black entrepreneurs, and Black businesses is what I was fighting against. And so, for me—and then there's some places I can't afford to shop either—but the systems that were at play, that moved a lot of Black businesses out. Yeah, so I kind of fought against that for a long time. I wouldn't patron any of the restaurants up and down Mississippi or Alberta." The new neighborhood identity, at least the one asserted by some dominant actors, also rendered Black people invisible. For example, Nicole (b. 1961) liked one boutique on Williams Avenue, which she described as "the one store that you walk in that you don't need anything in there, but you want everything—the $75 candles." But she attributed her general avoidance of boutiques to the lack of Black people in the marketing materials of the local business association.

> In general, no [I don't shop on Williams Avenue], and in fact the business association, the Williams Vancouver Business Association, has a brochure out that does not have any Black people in it. I called them or put it on . . . I tweeted it or something. I put it on Nextdoor, or I can't remember where I put it on. I might have put it on Facebook. I said, "Interesting. This is a business association in a historically Black neighborhood that doesn't have any photos of Black people in it. They've completely erased our image, our presence just through photographs. How rude is that?"

In part, the feeling of exclusion in the neighborhood was a visual experience. People read into visual representations of who lived in the neighborhood and what people did there. Eunice (b. 1963), a property manager in Gresham, shared her dismay that a chapel where many Black families held funeral services had been turned into a pub. "Across from Jefferson High School, there used to be a place called Little Chapel of the Chimes. That's where all of the Black people, for the most part, would go and have their services for their family members. It's now called the Chapel Pub. Right? That's some of that Portland shit. That's it, right there! That's why they keep Portland

FIGURE 5.2. Tough Luck Bar & Restaurant. Photograph by author.

weird and all that." With irritation in her voice, Eunice asserted that this transformation of a sacred site into a most secular place was fundamentally disrespectful to the people it once served. She also connects this act of disrespecting long-term Black residents to the city's bohemian slogan, "Keep Portland Weird." Eunice then proclaimed, "they never intended for us to be here. This is the White folks' mecca."

Like Eunice and Nicole, Nevil (b. 1981), a public administrator with a bachelor's degree, expressed irritation that the names of some new businesses seemed to disrespect or disregard the Black people who once made up the majority of the neighborhood's residents. Nevil, who still lives in Northeast, responded to the opening of a restaurant called Tough Luck in the Woodlawn neighborhood (figure 5.2).

There's different kinds of luck, right. There's hard luck. You heard about a hard luck case, it's like the world happened to you. Tough luck case seems a little bit different to me. It's like, you had a chance at it, and you didn't do anything with it. I feel still real unhappy that they decided to make any reference to luck in their title. . . . Without understanding their politics or their approach to the world, I'm inclined to think that it might be an insensitive jab at those that came before them, and it doesn't sit well with me.

Another source of contention was Miss Delta, a restaurant on Mississippi Avenue that sells soul food staples like collard greens, black-eyed peas, and macaroni and cheese (figure 5.3). While a few people mentioned the restaurant as a place where they like to eat, others found it distressing that the restaurant served "Black food" but presented itself as White space. For example, in the focus group, participants had the following conversation.

> ZORA: Oh my gosh, Mississippi is the worst.
> DEREK: They have a place called Miss Delta there, right? It bothers me because not only did they move us out, but they're making our food and stuff like that. It's not even run by Black people.
> BRIDGET: It's very misleading. There was someone that I know that went there because they thought that it was a Black-owned restaurant. It was not.
> DEREK: Yeah, that's crazy.
> JAROD: Yeah, and they had only pictures of White people on the walls.

FIGURE 5.3. Miss Delta restaurant. Photograph by author.

LEAH: We went in there, and you think, "Oh, this is kind of Southern style." I just about sat down, and I looked around and I was like, "All the pictures in here are fifties-style White people." They're black-and-white pictures. To me, that was a horrible time from the fifties to the seventies. Horrible. The buzz cut, the rolled-up sleeve, White T-shirt.

KEVIN: *Grease.*

Jarod said he and a friend offered to provide the restaurant with photographs of Black people who lived in the neighborhood between the 1950s and 1970s, but the server said he did not have contact information for the owner. Rita added, "You kind of get the impression that it's intentional to only capture a certain population, and they're a part of the gentrification." Later, in a one-on-one interview, Derek further explained his discomfort about Miss Delta. "You've seen *Do the Right Thing*, right? Do you remember when he was. . . . The pizza place where he was in there and he was selling all these pizzas in the Black community but then he looked on the wall, and he said, 'We buy all this, why there ain't no Black people on this wall?' That's what I felt like when I went to Miss Delta. They serving our food but they don't have us on there, so it's like they're disregarding us but selling our food." For White people, especially those who live in White space, seeing photos depicting only White people on the wall likely seems normal and unremarkable. Moreover, Whites can look at images of White people from the 1950s and feel nostalgic for bygone days, like those depicted in the film *Grease.* But to many Black people, images of White people in the mid-twentieth century evoke thoughts of Jim Crow laws and racial violence. By lining the walls exclusively with images of White people, the restaurant presents itself as White space, ignoring the history and perspective of long-term Black residents.

Interestingly, one person who was happy to shop on commercial streets in Northeast Portland was Damian, the "mixed" man who is often perceived as White.

SHANI: Do you like shopping on Williams and Vancouver and Mississippi, Alberta?

DAMIAN: I do. I know a lot of people that don't. I do. Part of it is because when we were on Albina [Avenue], right off Mississippi, there was business all up and down Mississippi; it's just there weren't restaurants. There was one barbecue place, Grandfather's, and there was a little ma and pop's grocery store. There wasn't much to walk to, but I was excited when things started coming in, like, "Oh, there's stuff to walk to now." For me, I've always been okay with it.

SHANI: Who isn't okay with it?

DAMIAN: Some of my coworkers who grew up in the area. "I refuse to shop over there" because of all the stuff, redlining, and all the stuff that did happen.

While it is unwise to generalize from this one case, it is noteworthy that Damian did not experience White watching, the looks of distrust and suspicion shared by other interviewees. He did not share stories of discrimination in retail stores and on sidewalks. Damian felt quite connected to the neighborhood as a Black place and felt emotional about losing Black place in Northeast neighborhoods. However, these feelings were not intertwined with the interpersonal experience of racial exclusion and discrimination in the White space of the present day. It is this distinct combination of loss of Black place and racial exclusion in White space that defined the experience of most interviewees.

The "upgrading" of urban neighborhoods is not simply the replacement of the old with the new. It involves moving marginalized groups from the localized center back to the margin. This has largely been understood as the arrival of upper middle-class newcomers and the displacement of poor and working-class residents. But, in many contexts, neighborhood change has racial significance that cannot be fully understood through a gentrification analysis. The relation between White and Black people in Northeast Portland is one of place-based domination and resistance. Some White people have always been present in Northeast, but it was the centering of Whiteness in the neighborhood that distressed interviewees. The impact of this shift is particularly great because Northeast was the only historically Black area in the city and it provided a refuge from interpersonal racism in an overwhelmingly White city. Moreover, the salience of race, more than class, is strong in Northeast Portland because newcomers are almost always White, and some of the Black people experiencing exclusion are middle class.

There has been an ongoing debate among researchers about whether neighborhood "upgrading" hurts or benefits long-term residents of urban neighborhoods. However, this question has largely been examined through an economic lens, which equates benefit or harm to financial gain or hardship. In historically Black neighborhoods, urban sociologists have paid little attention to Black residents' everyday experience with neighborhood change. As a result, researchers presume that long-term Black residents simply cannot afford to shop in gentrifying neighborhoods. Others mistakenly assert that Black residents who begrudge an influx of White newcomers are demonstrating racial hostility and avowing anti-White sentiment.[37] In Northeast Portland, "upgrading" was concurrent with the establishment of White space. Interviewees report that life in White space involves White watching, diminished civility in public space, and the erasure of Black histories. For these reasons, most interviewees experienced racial change as a negative and harmful process, even while some of them benefited financially from gentrification.

6 Claiming Black Place

Possibilities and Contradictions

Today, Portland's longtime residents live in a city that is markedly different from the one they remember from the late twentieth century. Although change is a constant feature of city life, only in the last thirty years has change resulted in the eradication of Portland's majority Black neighborhoods. In contemporary Portland, there is no neighborhood where one can go to reliably find groups of Black people being social in public space. Much of the city, including commercial streets in Northeast Portland, function as White space, where Whiteness operates as the normative, unmarked identity. These conditions led many interviewees to seek out and create Black place in Portland. Black people who visit or move to Portland also notice this characteristic of the city. For example, during one of my research visits, my Lyft driver, a Black woman in her fifties and a recent transplant to Portland, said, "the only thing I don't like is that it's hard to find *us*. Honestly, when I see one of us on the street, I almost want to say 'Hey! Where do you live?!'" The impact of the scarcity of Black place is great for longtime residents, particularly those who once experienced Northeast Portland as a homeplace.

Black places can provide a refuge from White space and White watching. Therefore, living in a city that lacks a Black neighborhood may heighten the effects of residents' exposure to interpersonal anti-Black racism in their everyday lives. For longtime residents, Portland is not an inherently "White city." Rather, most interviewees understood the pervasiveness of White space to be the result of a prolonged effort to define and redefine Portland as a city where middle-class White people can prosper and live comfortably. Only recently have efforts to "revitalize" and remake Northeast neighborhoods as White space been successful.

In this chapter I examine two means by which longtime residents have responded to the disruption of Black place. First, in their social lives, interviewees describe efforts to create and seek out settings where they are with other Black people, or where Whiteness is not centered. Second, through collective action some Black Portlanders have worked to challenge mechanisms of economic, social, and cultural displacement. However, a contradiction is intrinsic to much of this work. Even as long-term residents insist that Northeast Portland should be understood and experienced as a historically Black place, public entities like the Portland Development Commission simultaneously draw on these claims to inject the neighborhood with authenticity and socially desirable "diversity."[1] Moreover, because longtime residents must work with the city to enact change in the urban development process, that change continues to be undergirded by neoliberal definitions of "neighborhood improvement" that promote diversity and make incremental adjustments while failing to address the racist underpinnings of property valuation and capitalist urban development.

INDIVIDUAL EXPERIENCE

Seeking and Making Black Place

In chapter 5 I shared interviewees' experience with interpersonal White racism, primarily in public space. Interviewees explained that most White people they encountered were fine "once they get to know you," and most had White friends or acquaintances they met at work or school. Interviewees did not exclude White people from their social networks. Still, many looked for social settings where Whiteness was not normalized, mostly through relationships with other Black people. Zora (b. 1985) explained her decision to socialize with other Black people as a strategy to avoid racial discrimination and other differential treatment in White space. Zora said that when she was among other Black people she felt freer to experience human connection, without thinking about the dehumanizing effects of White space: "I'm not thinking about my natural hair. I'm not thinking about that I'm probably about to misuse this word. I'm not thinking about that I'm laughing loud . . . I'm not thinking about how I'm using up this White space or whatever." Zora did not have to worry about White watching when surrounded by other Black people. "It's like, you wanna be at a place where you can just be yourself, you don't have to think about how different you are, you don't have to have micro-aggressions come across your lap." Zora explained that while she spent time thinking about her behavior in relation to dominant racial norms, particularly at her workplace, her White coworkers benefit from their obliviousness to those norms: "The thing about the opposite end of that is like, White people and their privilege, they're so used to having privilege even though they don't know it. I don't think they think about that stuff. Like, we're constantly thinking about how we fit into a space and I don't think they're ever thinking about that. It's tiring." The regulation of the speech, hair, behavior, and pedigree of Black people in White space, via White watching, supports White supremacy by asserting that Whiteness is the "benchmark of normativity."[2] At the same time, White people are less likely to be penalized for failing to meet hegemonic expectations.

The act of maneuvering and responding to the norms of White space is what makes Zora and others aware of their subordinate status in the racial hierarchy. Saul (b. 1985) offered further explanation: "It's a comfort thing, right? Lets you know you're not by yourself. You might not really know who that person is, you don't necessarily know what they've gone through, but having darker skin in America unites people, just in a way of you know there's some type of struggle they've gone through."[3]

Saul met most of his friends through a training program for Black teachers. Other interviewees remained friends with the Black people they grew up with. Several women mentioned book clubs with other Black women or regular meet-ups at restaurants, while other interviewees spent most of their free time with family members. Although several interviewees described close friendships with Whites, most preferred to socialize with Black people or non-White people.

Nearly all of the interviewees said they purposely sought out Black social events such as those organized by institutions like SEI, the Urban League, fraternities and sororities, and Black churches. Some interviewees prioritized events that targeted people who grew up in Portland. SEI employee Edward (b. 1961) called the SEI building and Unthank Park "the beacon," and asserted that in those places "we got a place to centrally gather, we have activities over here . . . man it feels good to come out and kick it in the park and do all this stuff that, you know, we used to do." Shari (b. 1973), who recently moved from Gresham to Northeast Portland after waiting several years to access subsidized housing, said, "my neighborhood is very White, so I have to intentionally put myself in environments where I can see people like me. That's why I feel like I have strong connections to programs like the Urban League, or even SEI, to where I can see my own reflection." Given huge phenotypic variation among people who identify as Black, it is intriguing that "look like me" and "my own reflection" are such common refrains. I interpret this choice of words in two ways. First, Black people have internalized the norms of the racial system, which can render within-group variation illegible. Second, the reference to looking at one's reflection is analogous to the act of looking in a mirror, the meeting of eyes, and the recognition of one's humanity in the reflection. These comments suggest that humanity-affirming interactions were uncommon in White-dominated public space; therefore, Shari looked for "her reflection" in Black neighborhood organizations and events.

Most interviewees regularly attended Good in the Hood, a summer event that was created by parents at a local Catholic school in the early 1990s. The event, which includes a marketplace, food courts, live music, and a resource fair, is organized by a rotating group of Black volunteers. Terrence, a Good in the Hood volunteer, contends that the event is an opportunity to create and share culture and to access resources, such as healthcare information, that are less accessible to Black people. Good in the Hood is also about making and experiencing Black place. When I attended the event in the summer of 2017, I found an environment that was rare in Portland—food trucks served soul food, vendors sold Afrocentric clothing and skin care products, a DJ played 1980s and 1990s R&B, and most of the people strolling around informational tables were Black. That year, a White supremacist group sent a letter threatening to turn Good in the Hood into a "bloodbath."[4] In spite of this threat and the ensuing news coverage, Whiteness was not centered at the event. The public place created by Good in the Hood only exists in Portland on specific days and at specific events. For people who grew up in Portland, Good in the Hood and SEI events are opportunities to reconnect with other Black people, including those they knew growing up.

Although there were few specific places where former residents of Albina could reconnect, they did so when they could. Some interviewees looked for events on Facebook and Meetup. The Black community that originated in Northeast Portland did not disappear when the neighborhood became majority White and middle class. As Tina (b. 1963) explains, it changed form: "This is what I tell people of color here, well, we used to have a community, a brick and mortar, broader community, the building, the structure. We don't have that anymore. We carry our community with us. When we connect, that's our community because we don't have a place anymore." The events where people found other Black Portlanders are examples of what Japonica Brown-Saracino calls "ambient community," or community that persists even as it becomes disconnected from a particular space.[5] Tina identifies concerts as opportunities to find Black community:

I keep my hands in Black, predominantly Black community events because that's all we have. Where Black people come together in this city, my age, is at concerts. That's when we see everybody. It's like a family reunion. They got the Ohio Players coming up, Chanté Moore or whatever. They got the Commodores coming up. It's going to be a family. We go to these things to see each other. We go to see the music too but it's our family reunion . . . because we know we here but we can't find each other.

Some informants, particularly women over fifty, said they did not know how to find many of the people they knew while growing up in Northeast Portland. Events were a way to reestablish formerly place-based connections. Tina continued: "We would always say, 'We need to get together because I don't know where you at. Where you at, girl? Where you been?' And all that stuff, then it's like, 'wow, we got to have a reunion at a funeral or a community event.' Good in the Hood, the

Gathering, Juneteenth, Summer in September—which is no longer—
I'm just saying, that's it." For some longtime residents, these inten-
tionally Black-focused events were essential for temporarily creating
Black place in Portland.

In contrast, other interviewees, especially those in their twenties
and thirties, said they had little problem finding Black place in Portland, if not in Northeast. Perhaps this has to do with the greater reli-
ance of younger people on social media or their experiences growing
up in the late 1990s and 2000s, when Black people had already begun
to disperse from Northeast neighborhoods. They may be more accustomed to looking for, and making, Black place. For example, Micky
(b. 1995), one of the youngest interviewees, said it was Black newcomers who complained about the lack of Black place in Portland. "I hear
this from a lot of transplants, 'there's so many White people. There are
no Black people here, there are no people of color, there are no spaces
for us, there is nothing but White people.' And I think for me, since
I grew up around Black people and I know where the Black people
are and I know how to interact, that it's not this big thing for me."
Micky claims that he can find Black people "wherever I want them
to be," including at Black cultural events at Portland State University
and Portland Community College. Compared to older people, Micky
may be more accustomed to having to look for Black place in White
spaces. Also, younger interviewees spoke more broadly about socializing with other Black people, in contrast to older interviewees who
specifically wanted to connect with the people they knew in Albina.
Although the specifics of their experience varied, there was a shared
understanding that Black community life in Portland did not end after
Northeast gentrified and became White space. Interviewees shared a
commitment to finding, making, and spending time in Black place.

COLLECTIVE ACTION

Historic Black Williams Art Project

In addition to efforts to socialize and spend time with other Black
people, there have also been collective struggles to reassert Black
place in the built environment. The Historic Black Williams Art Proj-

ect uses art to communicate Northeast Portland's history as a historically Black community. Thirty mounted signs and ten sidewalk tiles
were installed on Williams Avenue in 2017. Each piece of art, and the
accompanying text, tells a story about people, events, activities, and
institutions from Northeast Portland's Black history. The installation
on Williams Avenue is similar to projects in other cities that use cultural symbols and heritage markers to imbue a neighborhood with
particular cultural meanings. In Chicago, Michelle Boyd finds that
middle-class community leaders claimed Bronzeville's Black heritage
in order to "legitimize African Americans' right to remain in space
that was designated for revitalization."[6] Black community leaders in
Chicago told an especially positive story about Bronzeville that emphasized the middle class, self-sufficiency, entrepreneurship, and cultural innovation, while minimizing the problems of segregation and
poverty. This story was used to make Bronzeville heritage appealing
to investors, while asserting that Black people should have a right to
control the future of the neighborhood. In Washington, DC, Derek
Hyra finds that White preservationists use heritage markers as a form
of Black branding that makes historically Black neighborhoods attractive to White newcomers who seek cultural authenticity.[7] In Chicago
and Washington, DC, residents and preservationists depict certain
Black neighborhoods as uniquely desirable and worthy of investment
because they are both "authentic" and exceptions to stereotypical
depictions.

    In contrast to these examples from other cities, the Historic Black
Williams Art Project was installed after the area had already become
predominantly White and middle class. Moreover, in contrast to Chicago and Washington, DC, which have multiple Black neighborhoods,
Northeast Portland had been the only Black area in the city. In Portland, Black people use art to assert their right to have any Black place
in Portland at all. The Historic Black Williams Art Project emerged
from conflict surrounding the development of a traffic safety project on North Williams Avenue. The Portland Bureau of Transportation (PBOT) organized a meeting for business owners, residents, and
neighborhood association representatives, who would make recommendations for the project.

    Longtime residents expressed concern to the PBOT that eigh-
teen of the twenty-two members of the stakeholder committee were

White. Simultaneously, a contingent of (mostly White) cyclists were pushing for more bike infrastructure. The PBOT decided to delay the planning process in order to hold more community meetings with longtime residents. In July 2011, PBOT held its first public meeting for the project. Attendees discussed plans to reduce traffic lanes from two to one and add a new bike lane on Williams Avenue. At one meeting, Michelle DePass, a Black woman who grew up in Northeast, raised concerns about the plans to change the spatial arrangement of Williams Avenue. "We have an issue of racism and of the history of this neighborhood. I think if we're trying to skirt around that we're not going to get very far. We really need to address some of the underlying, systemic issues that have happened over the last 60 years. I've seen it happen from a front row seat in this neighborhood. It's going to be very difficult to move forward and do a plan that suits all of these stakeholders until we address the history that has happened." This comment reflected widespread apprehension among longtime residents about the remaking of North Williams Avenue for the use of White newcomers and the lack of Black participation in the planning process. Once these concerns were mentioned, Donna Maxey, another Black longtime resident in attendance, elaborated on why it is important to consider history before making any decisions about the project. "Before you can get into the racial issue, you have to get into the history. This has been going on since the [19]20s here in Portland and so this is just a continuation of it. You can go ahead and move forward on this, or we can really come to grips with it and have an open discussion that makes Portland move forward in a different manner." These two women, and others, were compelled to reframe the project as one that was not only about safety, but also about race and spacemaking. They associated the street safety project with the long history of urban renewal and racialized displacement in Northeast neighborhoods. They saw the safety project as an opportunity to incorporate the concerns of longtime residents into the neighborhood planning process.[8]

Some of the White people in attendance were open to discussing racism and the history of the neighborhood, but others thought race was irrelevant to the planning process. For example, one White meeting attendee said: "I came here for a discussion of the safety issues. I'm worried I might offend people with this statement . . . but I honestly don't understand how a safety campaign on Williams is an issue of gentrification or racism." Sharon Maxwell-Hendricks, a Black woman who owns a general contracting business, told meeting attendees that when the neighborhood was majority Black, the city was not as concerned with keeping the residents safe: "You say you want it 'safe' for everybody, how come it wasn't safe 10 years ago? That's part of the whole racism thing . . . we wanted safe streets back then; but now that the bicyclists want to have safe streets then it's all about the bicyclists getting safe streets." Maxwell-Hendricks questioned why, now that it is majority White, public officials seemed more focused on making the roads safe. Maxey reinforced this point: "Years of people being told, you don't count, you don't matter . . . but now that there's a group of people who's coming in that look like the people who are the power brokers—now it's important. That's the anger. That's the hurt."[9] References to dog walkers and "cyclists" reflect the shared language used to discuss what some Black residents experience as a "takeover" by White newcomers in Northeast Portland. These comments are not about the mere presence of White people. Nor do they indicate that bike riding or dog walking are exclusively White cultural practices. Rather, references to cyclists and dog walkers speak to the ways middle-class Whites "symbolically appropriate public space" and enact new spatial norms in the process of "taking space."[10]

To help engage more longtime residents in the planning process, the planning committee was expanded to include twelve non-White members. The committee added a new project goal—"To honor the history of North Williams Avenue through elements of the transportation project"—and recommended that the PBOT fund "a public art installation developed by the community that honors the rich history of the neighborhood as a center for Portland's African American community." An RFP was issued for the project, and fifteen artists submitted proposals. The winning submission came from Cleo Davis and Kayin Talton Davis, married artists who owned a print shop.[11] The two designed thirty signs and ten sidewalk tiles that would be installed on North Williams Avenue.

On a Saturday afternoon, I attended an opening event for the Williams Avenue Project, advertised as a "Black community preview." The event was held at the Billy Webb Elks Lodge, which has been a Black community space since the early 1900s.[12] Inside, round tables were set up in the middle of a large multipurpose room. The round tables were reserved and were labeled with name cards. Dozens of chairs were arranged around the back and sides of the room. A buffet lunch was served on long tables near the entrance.

The pieces of art that would later be installed on North Williams Avenue were hung up on the wall in the back of the room. Before the event began, attendees walked around perusing the art, pointing and talking about the places and people they observed in the signs. Almost everyone in the room was Black, apart from a young White journalist and one older couple. The tables at the center of the room were eventually populated by elders, many of whom were helped to their seats as they pushed walkers or rode in powered wheelchairs.

Joyce Harris, a longtime community leader (see chapter 2), walked to a microphone at the front of the room and began the formal program. Invoking images of White spacemaking, she reminded the audience that "North Williams Avenue is in here (pointing to her heart). No matter how many dogs they walk." She explained to the attendees why it was important to see historical images of Black Portlanders on North Williams Avenue:

> Images, visuals are important to maintain the memories. This occasion is almost like a ritual. Unity, community, and what's the last one? Love. Sankofa is a symbol that means we have to go back and fetch it to move it forward.[13] Ashe—so be it. We are gathered here to honor the memories of those who built Williams and made us a strong community. . . . We honor ourselves because we are part of the legacy. We use our voices. We remember and we tell our children. Calling out names and pouring libations.

As she spoke, she poured a liquid onto a plant and stated the names of Black residents and community leaders who had died in recent years.

Some interviewees saw the Historic Black Williams Art Project as a first step in working with White newcomers to make a place where Black people could continue to feel at home. In chapter 5, Lawrence explained that newcomers treated him as if he did not belong and seemed disinterested in learning about the history of Black people who lived in the neighborhood before them: "people that are coming over there are not very well-connected, or [don't] want to be connected, because they come with the mindset that, 'This is mine now and that's history. It's over.'" He saw the Black Williams Art project as a partial solution to that problem. "There are projects going on. . . . They're trying to do the Williams Avenue Project, which they're putting these little historical, metal . . . different people going up on Williams Avenue so people can have a connection. They're like metal rods with pictures, silhouettes of history. They're trying to do that as a vehicle to try and get people to become a little bit more aware that the neighborhood that you're living in, there was a history here before you got here, and it needs to be appreciated." However, while he thought it could make (White) newcomers more conscious, he thought that the one-way communication of the project was inadequate.

> SHANI: Do you think that's an effective strategy?
> LAWRENCE: It's one. It is one way. But I don't know, there has to be a combination of things. It has to be dialogue. I think dialogue is one of the key things there. The visual things are good too, but . . . I don't know.

Although he was optimistic, Lawrence wanted White newcomers not only to see art, but to interact with longtime residents and hear about their experience.

The Historic Black Williams Art Project may counteract cultural displacement by asserting that streets and buildings are imbued with Black cultural meanings. Moreover, longtime residents who see the art along Williams Avenue may be reminded that Black people had rich and varied experiences there. This is what Troy liked about the project: "I like the fact that these are the areas that we were pushed out of. These were traditionally, historically Black, Black businesses. There were good things happening. They were strong Black communities, jazz clubs and bakeries and delis and all that stuff, and we got pushed out for the Memorial Coliseum. We got pushed out for Emanuel Hospital. They tore all those Black houses down and built all those and pushed us, pushed us, pushed us. It's nice to be remembered. . . ." Previous research reveals that heritage markers can be used to tell a particularly positive story about a neighborhood's Black history. For example, Boyd finds that Black elites used nostalgic narratives about middle-class Black community to advance a revitalization agenda that was symbolically inclusive, but privileged more affluent residents. Similarly, some of the art installed on Williams Avenue celebrates middle-class business owners. However, the Williams Project art also recounts racialized exclusion and working-class life.[14] For example, the art memorializes wartime migration, the Vanport flood, displacement caused by the failed Emmanuel Hospital project, and Portland's Black Panthers. The art commemorates places that likely served working-class residents, including the Knott Street Boxing Club, Tropicana BBQ, and Corner Pocket Pool Hall.[15]

While Troy thinks the markers may be beneficial to longtime residents because they remind them of "good things happening," he maintains that the benefits of the Historic Black Williams Art Project are limited because it does not help people return to, or stay in, their homes and neighborhoods: "At the same time it's bitter. Those folks that are pushed out don't get anything. They don't get their house back. They don't get money to buy a new house in the neighborhood. . . . It's nice for historical purposes and people don't forget, but at the same time it's still empty because you don't get your stuff back. You're no longer the owner in that neighborhood, and your wealth has been diminished for the course of your life and your family's life." As Troy stresses, projects like the Historic Black Williams Art Project do not slow or stop the physical displacement of Black people from Northeast neighborhoods. If the size of the Black population continues to shrink, there may be no Black people there in the near future. If that happens, the art along Williams Avenue will be a monument to the past, rather than a celebration of Black life in Northeast Portland.

Another potential benefit of the Historic Black Williams Art Project is that it brought people together and created momentary Black place. The opening event at Billy Webb Elks Lodge and another event at Dawson Park created an opportunity to be in community with people who once shared neighborhood streets and blocks. Damian, who was present at the opening event, longed to reconnect with people he saw in Northeast neighborhoods while growing up.

DAMIAN: I wish the old neighborhood was still visible.
SHANI: What would that be? What's an example of what you would see?
DAMIAN: People that I remember growing up. People that showed up at the [Historic Williams Avenue] event, I don't even know. I don't

even know where to find people that I grew up with. I do see some people just through Facebook and just generally here and there, Jefferson football games, that sort of thing.

Like Good in the Hood, the Historic Williams event momentarily created Black place. Damian wanted to find a way to recreate that experience in his everyday life. "It definitely feels like the community I grew up in is no longer around. How do we connect people more often? That's what I would like to see more moving forward, events to connect people. Like I said, I really appreciated just hearing old stories and just old memories, and keeping those alive. Going forward, how do we keep that alive? Also, keep connected, too. We can keep old stories alive, but how do we get new ones?" Damian is interested not only in maintaining Portland's Black history, but also in building Black futures. Without reliably Black places, he wonders how to make new stories that are not rooted in the norms of White space.

The Historic Black Williams Art Project and other Black heritage markers have contradictory implications. On the one hand, these projects answer a call from longtime Black residents to remember and document Black place in Northeast Portland. They may force White newcomers to acknowledge the presence and history of Black life in a neighborhood that increasingly functions as White space. Additionally, seeing heritage markers may remind longtime residents that they belong in Northeast Portland, even as they experience White watching and feel that they're "not supposed" to be there. At the same time, heritage markers do not redistribute economic resources or fundamentally restructure political power. Heritage markers may also be used to commodify Black culture and appeal to tourists and White newcomers' desire for "edgy" authenticity.[16]

Alberta Commons: Contesting Revitalization

In 2018, a new commercial development opened at Alberta Street and MLK Boulevard, a major intersection in Northeast Portland's King neighborhood. On the surface, the complex, known as Alberta Commons, looks like developments that have helped to gentrify historically Black neighborhoods throughout the United States. Alberta

Commons was developed by a large privately owned company that bought the land at low cost and then benefited from a tax abatement program.[17] However, a closer examination of Alberta Commons reveals a story of Black residents and leaders working to compel the city to implement a more equitable development program so that Black people, particularly poor Black people, could continue to make a home in Northeast Portland. While previous studies suggest that middle-class Black homeowners tend to advocate for policies and programs that ultimately benefit other middle-class homeowners, I find that middle-class property owners called for policy changes that would make Northeast more accessible to low-income Black residents.

In November 2013, the Portland Development Commission reached an agreement to sell a 1.8-acre vacant lot at the corner of Martin Luther King Boulevard and Alberta Street to Majestic Realty, a California-based real estate developer that claims to be "the largest privately owned industrial developer in the U.S." The property, which was appraised at $2.9 million in 2012, was sold for $502,160 to Majestic Realty, which planned to develop a shopping center and grocery store. The PDC had been working for several years to develop the site, but had failed to find what it considered to be an ideal "anchor" tenant. Calling the neighborhood "a food desert," the PDC described the development as a necessary addition to the neighborhood. Although the grocery store initially asked to be unnamed, it was soon revealed to be Trader Joe's.[18]

Local press described the sale of the property to Majestic as a "major subsidy," a "discount," and a "public incentive." The PDC claimed that low sale price was necessary in order to attract the "right" tenant; as such, the PDC insisted that the development would not be possible without a "bargain on the land."[19] Some active members of the local neighborhood association, most of whom were White, opposed the project, saying that the area was not a food desert since another grocery store had opened nearby in 2013. According to news coverage, some White residents also opposed the decision to sell the property at such a low cost.[20]

Soon after the deal was announced, a multiracial group demonstrated on the corner of Alberta and MLK opposing the deal as "a giveaway to the 1%." Protesters argued the project would likely contribute to gentrification and the displacement of long-term neighborhood residents. In December 2013, the Portland African American Leadership Forum (PAALF) wrote an open letter, addressed to then Mayor Charlie Hales and PDC leadership, opposing the project.[21] PAALF is an organization founded in 2009 to promote "the revitalization and sustainability of a vibrant African American community." Many of those involved in writing the letter were participants in PAALF's leadership development program. The letter was supported both by well-established leaders and by a diverse group of Black Portlanders (including long-term residents and transplants) who were motivated to develop their leadership skills. Published in its entirety in *The Oregonian*, the letter read in part: "Our opposition is rooted in the well-documented and ongoing attempt to profit from development in inner N/NE Portland at the expense of Black and low-income individuals. Rather than invest in proven methods to stop displacement and empower the African American community, the Portland Development Commission (PDC) and City of Portland have consistently supported projects that have displaced existing residents and attracted wealthier ones in their place." The letter writers argued that the decision to sell the property for $502,160 was consistent with the city's record of displacing and disempowering vulnerable community members.[22] Further, they insisted that what Northeast Portland needed was affordable housing; therefore, building a Trader Joe's without attached housing represented the continuation of past projects that prioritized profit over people. The open letter called on the mayor and PDC to meet the following (abbreviated) demands:

1. Suspend all further TIF funded development.
2. Suspend the development of the property until a sufficient amount of affordable housing is incorporated and an independent, community-controlled body can negotiate a legally binding community benefits agreement.
3. Publicly endorse the position that Legacy Emmanuel Hospital must relinquish the still vacant property and bequeath it to the African American Community in the form of a community land trust.

PAALF argued that, after years of promises, the city had failed to implement policies and practices that would help long-term residents to thrive in the rapidly changing neighborhood. Instead, the letter asserts, the PDC and mayor's office had repeatedly supported projects that enabled economic elites, like Majestic Realty, to profit from the transformation of Northeast neighborhoods.[23]

Alberta Commons: Media Framing

While the open letter stressed affordable housing and called on city leaders to recognize and respond to PDC's long history of supporting projects that facilitate Black displacement, the local and national press contended that Trader Joe's—and its appeal to White people—was the crux of the debate about the development. This narrative even appeared in the monologue of Conan O'Brien's late-night cable show in February 2014. O'Brien joked, "In Portland, Oregon, a group of African Americans are protesting a Trader Joe's because they say it will attract too many White people, which is ironic because Portland is the Native American word for too many White people." O'Brien's commentary, which highlights Portland's reputation as America's Whitest city, delegitimizes Black residents' protests and echoes the themes in national news coverage.[24] Several opinion pieces appeared in the national press about Black people opposing Trader Joe's, some arguing that it was "racist" (i.e., anti-White) for Black people to hinder the development.

This media framing also shaped the way some Black Portlanders understood the ordeal. For instance, Tom (b. 1982) expressed strong disagreement with efforts to halt the Alberta Commons development. Tom defined himself as a civically active member of Portland's Black community, stating that "if it's got anything to do with community and Black people here in Portland, I'm involved with it in some way." For example, he regularly volunteered with Good in the Hood. However, Tom was not involved with PAALF and learned about the Alberta Commons development from local media. Given the content of Tom's interview, we might expect that he would be aligned with the opposition to the Alberta Commons development. Tom observed that White people have had more access to mortgage lending than Black people have; he shared his personal experiences with White watching and racial discrimination; and he suggested that when White people moved into Northeast neighborhoods, they joined neighborhood associations and established new norms that longtime residents were then required to follow. He also critiqued the PDC, asking, "why didn't the PDC decide to improve our neighborhoods with us still remaining in our neighborhoods?" It seems likely that he would oppose PDC's plan to give Majestic Realty a "bargain on the land." However, Tom's framing of the issue, as being primarily about Black people opposing Trader Joe's, closely matched that found in the local and national press:

> TOM: Why the hell you all don't want Trader Joe's over here?
>
> SHANI: I don't know. Tell me.
>
> TOM: That's what I wanna—it made no sense. This is my thing, so let's go over that real quick before we get out of here.
>
> SHANI: Yeah, sounds good.
>
> TOM: Why make a big old stink and a big old fuss about some White people putting a White store in their White neighborhood? You don't even live over here, so all the people that were sitting there and making all that noise and, "Don't build this," you don't even live over here. Why do you care? It ain't your neighborhood.

By saying that PAALF was "making all that noise," Tom mimics the language in *The Oregonian*. For example, one article notes that while there were "plenty of arguments against the deal," "the *loudest* complaints came from PAALF" (emphasis added). Referring to PAALF as "the loudest"—instead of, for example, "the most persistent"— evokes enduring stereotypes that define Black people as loud and unruly and "making all that noise."

Tom's second point, "you don't even live over here," also echoes the coverage in *The Oregonian*. For example, the article claiming that PAALF had the "loudest complaints" includes no quotes from PAALF members, but does include quotes from two "residents" who supported the development. Both of the residents are White women, but they are not identified as such.[25] For example, one White woman who said she had lived in the King Neighborhood for eleven years made the following statement: "This [opposition to the development] is not what the neighborhood people want. This is terrible. I moved here when there were gunshots out the window. . . . I appreciate that [PAALF] is trying to talk about the origins of gentrification. That's really essential, but they can't stand up and say, 'As residents of the . . . neighborhood, this is what we want.' The residents of the . . . neighborhood want this to happen." By portraying White supporters as "residents" and "neighborhood people" who represent local perspectives on the matter, this reporting implies that those opposed to the project were non-residents who therefore do not have a claim to the neighborhood. This excerpt reveals how White space is demarcated and sustained in local media coverage through colorblind reporting. By quoting Whites, and calling them "residents," the article conveys a clear message about who has the right to say what "the neighborhood" wants. Although some PAALF members do live near the corner of NE Alberta and MLK Boulevard, the article does not scrutinize the assertion that none do.

Moreover, the phrase "I moved here when there were gunshots out the window" reveals the cunning methods by which some White newcomers simultaneously claim authenticity, take credit for improving the neighborhood, and assert the right to control its future. Additionally, this "resident" asserts that it is "important to talk about the origins of gentrification," then rejects PAALF's demands for change. This resembles the findings in Meghan Burke's research about politically progressive Whites in a racially diverse neighborhood. Instead of taking collective action for social and racial justice in their neighborhood, Burke finds that progressive, diversity-seeking Whites prioritized "individualized, consumption-driven actions and those that keep the community safe and intact for the interests of Whites and homeowners."[26]

Given how the issue was discussed in the local and national media, it is not surprising that Tom thinks PAALF's efforts amounted to "a lot of foolishness." He continued: "Build the store. People gonna get some groceries, man. Like, I think that we put a lot of energy into stuff that has nothing to do with nothing." Tom called on community leaders to put their energy into improving schools and funding arts programs. Astonishingly, Tom said that he would support PAALF if they advocated for affordable housing for Black Portlanders:

> TOM: Now, if they're building some affordable housing with a priority on placing Black families, instead of building Trader Joe's, that makes sense.

SHANI: Okay, and that's not what they were—?

TOM: No, and the people that was building Trader Joe's was Colas Construction, which is Black folks, so you took that whole thing out of—you took that away from them.

This comment is remarkable because Tom strongly disagreed with opposition to the development, but he says he would support the opposition if they did exactly what they were in fact trying to do. Building more affordable housing for longtime residents was a major goal of those who contested the Alberta Commons project. Tom is an unusual case, and no other interviewees shared his strong negative stance. Nonetheless, I share it in order to acknowledge the reality of disagreement and conflict among long-term Black residents. More important, his example indicates how media framing shapes the way the public understands and responds to debates about urban development.

Alberta Commons: Policy Results

Wanting to avoid controversy, Trader Joe's withdrew their plan to open the store in the Northeast Portland location. However, then Mayor Charlie Hales was eager to persuade the grocery chain to return and was willing to negotiate with Black community leaders in order to defuse their opposition.[27] During these negotiations, PAALF representatives focused on affordable housing and also promoted a "right to return" policy that would give housing priority to people who had previously been displaced from the neighborhood.[28] The city maintained that a one-story retail development was the only option for the corner of NE Alberta and MLK Boulevard because the lot was not suitable for building multilevel housing. In March 2014, the mayor pledged to spend $20 million in Tax Increment Financing on affordable housing to "begin to address the ongoing threat of displacement and gentrification." Later, this amount was increased to $90 million. In addition, PDC agreed to lend SEI and PAALF funds to purchase the family home of Avel Gordly, Oregon's first Black woman state senator, and develop it as a center for Black leadership and civic engagement.[29]

The Portland Housing Bureau organized a series of community forums to help determine how to spend allocated funds. An oversight committee included church leaders, community members, and an urban planning professor. They drew on community recommendations to develop the North/Northeast Neighborhood Housing Strategy.[30] Notably absent from the committee were any developers, bankers, and realtors. The Housing Strategy includes the following objectives: Preventing Displacement, Promoting Homeownership, Creating Rental Homes, and Land Banking. Another element of the Housing Strategy is the N/NE preference policy, which gives current and former residents, and their descendants, priority access to both subsidized rental housing and homeownership programs. Applicants received additional preference points if they lived in specific "identified areas" where city plans and eminent domain facilitated gentrification and displacement. Preference points help determine applicants' place on long waiting lists for housing.[31]

The money allocated by the mayor funded the construction of six multi-family rental housing buildings between 2015 and 2022, totaling 413 rental units. At least another 348 units are planned. All of these units are designated "affordable housing" and the average income of tenants is 22 percent of the area median. One hundred and ten new home buyers were identified through the preference policy and received home-buying subsidies and assistance.[32] Eighty-five percent of preference policy home buyers are Black. Seventy percent of home buyers earn less than 80 percent of median area income.[33] The allocated funds were also used to provide 158 interest-free home repair loans and 821 home repair grants between 2015 and 2021. About two-thirds of these grants, and one-half of the loans, went to Black households.[34]

The demand for housing under the preference policy far outpaces supply, and the waiting list is long. For example, more than 5,000 people have applied for fewer than 500 rental homes. A survey of residents (N = 98) who accessed housing through the preference policy reveals that 84 percent of respondents were Black and 65 percent had lived in N/NE Portland for their entire lives. Moreover, 80 percent of survey participants reported that "their connection to the neighborhood was their primary motivation for applying" for housing through the preference policy. Eighty-seven percent of respondents said "I belong in this neighborhood," and 91 percent said "the history of this neighborhood matters to me."

However, 37 percent of survey respondents agreed that there is "a lot of prejudice in the neighborhood." The report summarizes respondents' recommendations for improving the well-being of those who benefited from the preference policy, given that the area has been altered by gentrification and White spacemaking. Residents asked for more affordable stores, as well as more organized activities, like potlucks, to help "restore community" with other residents. Residents also asked for support with the difficulties that ensue when a neighborhood becomes White space. Specifically, they made the following recommendation: "Elevate Black identity in the neighborhood while bolstering multi-racial relations through events that honor the community's history. Engage in the neighborhood to address racial bias, cross-cultural communication and handle conflicts escalated by racial difference."[35] These recommendations suggest that residents perceived the preference policy as an opportunity to recreate homeplace in Northeast Portland.

When I spoke with Miriam (b. 1976), who helped write PAALF's open letter, she was certain that her efforts had helped produce meaningful change. She exclaimed, "all of the money right now that you see funneled into a focus on affordable housing and the PDC acknowledging past wrongs is a direct result of that work." "The open letter and all the pushback was saying that PDC needed to acknowledge the historical wrong, that we needed to look at how we spend TIF funds, that there needed to be a focus on affordable housing. That was one of the big pushbacks around that space. It wasn't about Trader Joe's, it was really about how is PDC spending public money and giving a discount to a large corporation instead of investing in community solutions." Miriam indicated that PAALF played an important role in winning additional dollars for affordable housing and creating the preference policy. This was affirmed by Nicole (b. 1961), who works in city government and helps implement the preference policy. When I asked how the policy came to be, Nicole replied: "I don't know if you were here during the PAALF Trader Joe's. . . . The protest was about not having affordable housing that was promised. . . . The housing [that was promised with past urban renewal projects] never materialized! Every place there were African-Americans there was some project being done and promises were made. I think PAALF was not worried about the store. They were worried about the process in which there's no public participation." By challenging the Alberta Commons development, PAALF and other residents instigated a housing program that would benefit people who may not have otherwise been able to live in Northeast Portland. My intention here is not to evaluate the effectiveness of the N/NE Housing Strategy as a solution for the problems of housing affordability and displacement. Instead, this example shows that a group of Black leaders and aspiring leaders successfully leveraged a key moment in the revitalization process to push back on development plans.

The people who challenged the Alberta Commons development included both middle-class and working-class people. Thus, the Alberta Commons dispute provides an example of Black middle-class people promoting efforts that explicitly benefited their less advantaged neighbors. This contrasts with research in other cities, where middle-class Black residents promoted policies and programs that primarily benefited middle-class homeowners. In fact, some scholars dismiss the notion that Black community members from different class backgrounds might work together to collectively advance Black well-being.[36] However, in majority White cities where White space is especially pervasive, the importance of Black collective identity may be greater than it is for Black residents of Chicago, Harlem, and Washington, DC. Black racial identity may become more salient in White space; therefore, cross-class organizing may be more feasible in cities like Portland.[37]

Alberta Commons: Making Black Place?

The Alberta Commons shopping center that opened in 2018 was in many ways identical to the project that was proposed in 2013. The project was developed by Majestic Realty and built by Colas Construction (whose founder is Haitian American). Majestic Realty successfully acquired land at a significantly reduced price and benefited from a tax abatement program. Instead of Trader Joe's, the primary tenant is a different grocery chain, Natural Grocers. The adjacent shopping center includes a variety of shops and offices. While much of the project was completed according to the initial plan, some features of Alberta Commons were influenced by the demands of PAALF and other Black leaders and activists. For example, PDC implemented a community benefits agreement that includes a minority hiring program at Natural Grocers, a commitment to hiring minority building contractors, and an affordable tenanting program for local, minority-owned businesses.

In chapter 5, interviewees reported feeling out of place in many of the shops that have opened in Northeast Portland. Some shared a wish for more Black-owned businesses in Northeast Portland. For example, Derek (b. 1984) said he felt "great" when he walked into Sweet Jam, a Black-owned soul food restaurant that opened in a Portland suburb in 2016: "I feel like there's something that's actually made for me and people like me." He hoped to see more places like Sweet Jam in Northeast Portland:

> DEREK: Sweet Jam is out in Beaverton. When I think of African Americans opening up businesses, why not try to open up one in Northeast Portland where we used to be? Why are we moving out to Beaverton? That's all I think about.
>
> SHANI: Why would it be better to build something in Northeast?
>
> DEREK: To try to get back, I don't want to say what was taken from us, but just have some type of diversity there. I don't feel like it's diversity anymore like it used to be. It's not diversified. It's one specific race that's running everything right there.

Sweet Jam offered Derek a temporary sense of belonging. Not long after my interview with Derek, a second Sweet Jam did open in Northeast, on MLK Boulevard. However, after several months in operation, both locations closed. Seeing new Black-owned businesses in Northeast Portland also made Layla (b. 1977) feel more optimistic about the future: "I feel like it could come back to the community. And I'm not saying it needs to be all Black the way it was before, but it needs to be enough Black where people still feel like a sense of community and then the White people that are here, we need to embrace each other." Black-owned businesses in Northeast signaled to Layla that place-based community was still possible. Layla and Derek longed for Black-owned businesses that would unsettle White space.

In a small way, the Alberta Commons development responds to the desires of people like Layla and Derek. Some of the retail spaces in Alberta Commons are occupied by Black-owned businesses. Cason's

Fine Meats is operated by Theotis Cason, who grew up in Northeast Portland and has operated butcher shops in various North and Northeast storefronts since the 1980s. Several interviewees said that they had appreciated having meat markets in Northeast Portland in past decades. Another store is Champion's Barbershop, which had operated at a different location on MLK Boulevard since 2008. The third Black-owned business is Greenhaus, a boutique that sells "artisancrafted goods and gifts, priced for real life." Like Solae's Lounge and Sweet Jam restaurant, these establishments might help longtime Black residents feel more at home in Northeast Portland. However, their existence does not disrupt the structural mechanisms of racial inequality and White supremacy.

In the context of gentrifying historically Black neighborhoods, there is sometimes a push to promote Black-owned business as a way to ensure that Black people benefit from the economic revitalization of a community. Black-owned businesses are cited as a way to keep Black wealth within the Black community. And neoliberal ideas of individual success and achievement point to entrepreneurship and business ownership as the solution to racial inequality. However, entrepreneurship often provides economic benefit to a select few without disrupting the systemic mechanisms of racial, economic, or gender inequality. An increase in Black-owned businesses may help grow the Black middle and upper class and reduce unemployment; however, if these businesses rely on processes that extract profit through exploitation (e.g., by paying low wages and selling cheaply made products), they fail to challenge key mechanisms of racial inequality. Rather than looking to Black-owned business as the solution to economic and political inequities, I suggest that Black-owned businesses could function as Black places that provide a reprieve from White space. They may help improve everyday experiences of place for some Black residents.

The Community Benefits Agreement at Alberta Commons also stipulated that two large murals be installed on the brick walls of the building. One member of the art selection committee explained that the murals are "designed to send out the message that African Americans exist in this community."[38] Two Black men were selected to create the murals, which depict the history and imagined future of Northeast Portland as a Black place. Arvie Smith, a man in his seventies who lived in Northeast Portland for more than forty years, asked longtime residents what they wanted to see in the work (figure 6.1). In a promotional video, Smith recounted: "They said we want something beautiful. We want something hopeful and I wanted to tell the truth about the neighborhood. The jazz in Portland. All these people came from the South and brought their music with them. Just below the

FIGURE 6.1. "Still We Rise" by Arvie Smith. The following artist's statement is provided at Arvie Smith's request: "Starting with the Vanport Flood of 1948, this work tells the story of the upward struggle of the Albina neighborhood residents. Despite the systematic dismantling of the neighborhood by the local government and housing market, the community forged ahead to maintain unity with resilience, determination, and hope. The historic events, landmarks, and resolve depicted in the mural include the legendary jazz scene, property redlining, police brutality, human struggle, and the ravaging of Black spaces through 'urban renewal.' Inspired by the words of Maya Angelou in her poem 'Still I Rise,' the nobleness of the human spirit, and the resolve to move beyond a 'past rooted in pain,' the artist created the central figure pointing to the 'Still We Rise' flag to encourage strength, pride, and hope for future generations. Let this work be held as a landmark at the core of this historic neighborhood that is so rapidly changing structurally, socially, and economically. Let this work capture the rich culture and history of Albina and inspire identity, pride, and unity."

FIGURE 6.2. "Until We Get There" by Mehran Heard, a.k.a. Eatcho. For more about this artwork see https://racc.org/2018/04/02/new-murals-celebrate-portlands-african-american-history-and-future/.

jazz musicians, people coming out of Vanport. Which for me is a metaphor for the uphill climb that Black people have to make in order to survive here in Portland." The second artist, Mehran Heard, a transplant to Portland, said in the same video that the mural's location in a recently gentrified area influenced his design. "I wanted to show the world what I saw as a minority and where it would be [if it was] up to us." Hearn said he wanted the murals to move beyond a portrayal of tragic things that have happened to Black people to imagine what is possible in the future (figure 6.2).

Some interviewees suggested that White newcomers were able to deny the right of Black people to occupy Northeast neighborhoods because they did not know the area's Black history. Projects like the Alberta Commons murals could affirm Black residents' experiences and counter newcomers' perception that Northeast was formerly empty and ripe for development. Murals are one way to reclaim space and inform newcomers about the Black history of Northeast neighborhoods.[39] At the same time, the murals at Alberta Commons draw on Black history to produce a cultural resource that facilitates tourism, development, and profitmaking. This process of using Blackness to attach aesthetic value to the neighborhood is evident in the promotion of Alberta Commons as a tourist destination on the Travel Oregon website: "The large murals at the corner of North Vancouver Avenue and Northeast Alberta Street depicting themes including Black cowboys, civil rights heroes and other iconic Black figures. Shoppers can find artisan-crafted and salvaged vintage goods. . . ."[40] In addition to depicting the past and imagining the future, the murals, and their representations of Black life, are used to appeal to (typically White) newcomers and tourists.[41] The interdisciplinary scholar Brandi Summers refers to this process as "Black aesthetic emplacement," when Blackness is articulated in ways that "accrue a value that is not necessarily extended to Black bodies." Black aesthetic emplacement also produces authenticity, which facilitates gentrification by appealing to White middle-class tastes for "real" cultural experiences. Moreover, the murals might help newcomers feel less like they're participating in racialized displacement by providing symbols of Blackness, even as the Black population declines.[42]

In 2017 the Portland Development Commission changed its name to Prosper Portland. According to a press release, this name change represented "the agency's shift toward more inclusive economic development."[43] A PDC employee I interviewed explained that the name change was meant to distance the organization from its reputation as an entity that demolishes neighborhoods while displacing and disempowering residents, "because we felt that PDC has a lot of negativity because of the urban renewal district and in the past . . . a disregard of the culture and the community . . . there's a lot of resentment from people in that community because of the impact that urban renewal had."

Prosper Portland did not just change its name; it also changed the way it communicates about the work it does. Prosper Portland now mentions urban renewal, racialized displacement, and past discrimination in much of their marketing and communications. In recent years, Prosper Portland has promoted itself as an organization on the cutting edge of equitable urban development. For example, a PDC project manager wrote for the Brookings Institution about its "shared value approach":

The pivot toward the shared value approach has its roots in the city's racist history: Discriminatory practices from the 1950s to the 1980s, such as redlining, destabilized communities of color and people who were not landowners. Prosper Portland's own subsequent urban renewal efforts, while focused on the preservation of Portland's neighborhoods and a lively downtown, also created conditions ripe for gentrification. Those conditions pushed lower-income households, frequently people of color, to more affordable areas of east Portland at the outer fringe of the city.[44]

It is noteworthy that this statement, while implicitly acknowledging histories of racialized exclusion, offers only economic explanations for persistent racial inequity. Racial displacement is depicted as an unfortunate set of events that ended in the 1980s, thereby obscuring the enduring problem of systemic racism.

In their marketing efforts, Prosper Portland emphasizes Alberta Commons as the exemplar of equitable development. Prosper Portland now markets itself as a reformed organization that values Black participation and promotes multiculturalism.[45] The Alberta Commons marketing materials disclose a theory of change undergirding Prosper Portland's "equitable urban development" work. According to the Alberta Commons Press Kit, Black business owners "understand the role they play in lifting up other members of their community and inspiring them to recognize and pursue their dreams."[46] The three Black-owned businesses at Alberta Commons were reportedly committed to providing training and mentorship to prospective Black entrepreneurs. This articulation represents racial inequality as an individual problem that can be remedied via training, mentorship, and inspiration, rather than as a systemic and structural reality that will persist without deep and far-reaching change.

Much of the language used by Prosper Portland's leadership reflects the work of Black activists to pressure the city to make amends for its role in serial displacement and racialized dispossession. Prosper Portland insists that it "holds [itself] accountable to Portland's communities of color and others our work has negatively impacted." But as Sara Ahmed argues, these "antiracist speech acts" are "nonperformative." This is to say that a proclamation of antiracism does not necessarily "do what it says" it does. In fact, Ahmed argues that antiracist statements often work to entrench inequality because the mere existence of the statement is offered as evidence that the problem (racism, injustice) has been resolved, "as if by saying that we 'do it' means that's no longer what we do."[47] Recognizing past racism and claiming to be antiracist can absolve organizations, even as they engage in practices that maintain White supremacy.

The fact that Alberta Commons was developed by providing public incentives to Majestic Realty—a private company with $70–100 million in yearly earnings, a strikingly homogeneous panel of White male leaders, and a billionaire president who supports right-wing political candidates—reveals the limits of anti-racist speech acts.[48] Moreover, in its work in Northeast Portland, Prosper Portland has not challenged the racial logic that motivates Black displacement from the 1950s to the current day. This logic defines White spaces as most desirable and property in White space as most valuable. As such, efforts to "improve a neighborhood" that do not consider the racialization of space and the racial meanings intrinsic to "revitalization" are likely to produce familiar patterns of Black displacement and White enrichment.

7   Conclusion

At Home in Black Place

Longtime Black residents felt at home in Northeast Portland in the late twentieth century. But by 2015 most of the people I interviewed experienced Northeast Portland as White space. Through facial expressions and direct questioning, White people challenged the presence of Black people in Northeast neighborhoods. Many public places in Portland, and in the United States, operate as White space, including but not limited to parks, swimming pools, restaurants, coffee shops, office buildings, universities, and neighborhood sidewalks. The exclusionary character of White space mirrors the inherently exclusionary nature of Whiteness—the boundaries of Whiteness have been strictly enforced by White people and by the law.[1] Similarly, the exclusionary rules of White space are imposed such that Black people are routinely sanctioned for being "out of place."[2]

Interviewees felt at home in some Northeast Portland neighborhoods, which they experienced as Black place even though these neighborhoods were never exclusively Black. Through Black placemaking, they experienced joy, human connection, play, and cultural affirmation within a space that was demarcated by racial oppression. Racial segregation was imposed by banks, developers, realtors, neighborhood associations, and White homeowners. For most of the twentieth century, Northeast Portland was the only place most Black people were allowed to live. But it was also the only place that functioned apart from the interpersonal violence of White space. For this reason, the racial transformation that took place in Northeast Portland has led to feelings of loss among long-term residents. But these residents do not simply lament the loss of a once "vibrant" and entrepreneurial Black community; they lament the loss of Black place, a homeplace, a refuge from Whiteness.

As Blackness is not characterized by exclusion, neither is Black place predicated on racial exclusion. Moreover, Black place is not simply where Black people are or where Black culture is prominent. Black place is where Black people can form communities, hold events, and build relationships while not contending with interpersonal racist oppression. Black place can emerge in racially and ethnically diverse contexts. Indeed, indigenous, Latin American, Asian, and White people were present in Northeast Portland when interviewees experienced it as Black place. Black place does not signify the absence or marginalization of non-Black people; rather, Black placemaking occurs in the absence of White supremacist interactions. Without White watching and the rules of White space, Black residents can inscribe places with "their own interpretations, meaning, and cultural significance."[3]

Some scholars dismiss Black people's descriptions of being at home in Black place as romantic nostalgia or "regrettable pining for a mythical past."[4] These dismissals reflect a willful disregard of Black people's everyday experience of anti-Black racism.[5] Critical urban researchers often assume that the primary urban conflict is between the poor, who are struggling to survive, and the rich, who seek to profit through urban development. When work in this vein mentions racism, it is discussed as an entirely structural or historical phenomenon that helps to determine who is rich and who is poor. These scholars cannot envision differently positioned Black people affirming each other's humanity, even as other forms of intra-racial conflict (e.g., colorism, classism, patriarchy, heterosexism) might persist.[6] Instead of simply dismissing these remarks as misguided nostalgia, I interpret them as representative of respondents' yearning for refuge from the dehumanizing effects of White racism. To be clear, Black place does not shield Black people from the structural racism that pervades the real estate market, banking, education, employment, healthcare, or policing. However, it can provide respite from the constant surveillance and harmful interpersonal interactions that characterize life in White space.

WHITE SPACEMAKING AND GENTRIFICATION

For decades, studies about White migration into formerly Black, Latinx, or Asian neighborhoods has been subsumed into gentrification research, even as gentrification was defined essentially as social class change. This practice mimics popular understandings of gentrification as neighborhood change that attracts high-status people and displaces lower-status people. In this conceptualization, status references both race and class—i.e., high status is White and middle class, and low status is working class, poor, and/or non-White. This paradigm conflates race and class and limits our ability to consider how race and class function as interlocking systems of oppression.[7]

While gentrification prioritizes social class change, White spacemaking emphasizes racial change. White spacemaking describes the reassertion of White racial dominance in space. Through White spacemaking, neighborhoods are reconfigured to make White newcomers feel that the neighborhood exists for them. Simultaneously, practices of surveillance and exclusion are established to remind non-White people that they do not belong. The painful influence of White spacemaking was palpable in interviewees' accounts of being viewed with suspicion and disregard in public space. They described being "vigilant" and "hyperaware" of how they were perceived in public space. Moreover, in Northeast Portland this feeling of being under surveillance and on alert was provoked by a place that had previously felt like home.

Gentrification research often depicts developers, city officials, landlords, and investors as racially neutral actors who impact the wellbeing of poor, working-class, and unhoused people, many of whom are non-White. In contrast, White spacemaking explicitly considers the agency of White social actors. It describes the public interactions through which White residents, business owners, and others reestablish Whiteness as normative in space. This more focused racial analysis highlights the direct relationship between White advantage and Black disadvantage. White spacemaking stresses the relational nature of race and space. The esteem and profitability of White neighbor-hoods is contingent on the denigration and undervaluation of Black neighborhoods. Even when Black property owners benefit from gen-trification and White spacemaking through rents or increasing prop-erty values, their own status in the housing market and in public space remains degraded. Simultaneously, White people in the present and future benefit from the ongoing hyper-valuing of Whiteness and prop-erty in White neighborhoods.[8]

The study of White spacemaking is no more important than the study of gentrification. However, the effects of (White) gentrification cannot be fully understood in a historically Black neighborhood with-out considering the making of White space. To be most effective, re-search and activism around these two processes should happen simul-taneously. In cities throughout the world, poor, working-class, and some middle-class people struggle to find and afford adequate hous-ing while investors and developers maneuver to profit from property. In recent years, the inaccessibility of housing has reached crisis level in Portland. The people struggling are a multiracial and multiethnic group, many of whom are White. However, the conditions that shape experiences and outcomes of poor White people and poor Black people are not identical. Attempts to unite around shared economic exploita-tion may falter if doing so ignores the very real experience of racial-ized oppression in White space. Understanding how race and class (and gender and sexuality) work together to shape the experiences and outcomes of differently situated social actors requires that race and class be treated as equally important, interlocking social systems.[9]

Some gendered patterns emerged in respondents' experiences with White spacemaking and the loss of Black place. For example, men expressed disappointment about missing the opportunity to de-velop economically thriving neighborhoods in Northeast when those neighborhoods were still majority Black. Men also spoke about the risks of being seen as a threat after neighborhoods became White space. In contrast, women were more likely to express sadness about losing regular contact with their friends and neighbors. Across gender, respondents shared experiences with White watching. These findings raise questions about how race, class, and gender intersect to shape placemaking and experiences of belonging.[10] I did not ask interview-ees about their romantic or sexual relationships. Although my data do not provide insights about sexuality and the experience of racialized neighborhood change, it is a topic that warrants further study.[11]

WHITE WATCHING: EVERYDAY EXPERIENCE IN WHITE SPACE

White watching is a necessary addition to discussions of contemporary racism in space. Through White watching, Black people become aware that they are under constant surveillance. Interviewees report experiencing White watching on streets and in stores within majority White and middle-class residential areas. It is noteworthy that interviewees reported that they did not experience White watching in downtown Portland, which has some racial diversity but is still majority White. For example, one interviewee, an avid reader, said he felt at home at Powell's, the famous downtown Portland bookstore. Downtown Portland may provide a "cosmopolitan canopy," a multiracial space characterized by civility.[12] Another possibility is that because downtown is mainly a place for doing business, rather than making one's home (and profiting from homeownership), White space is less strictly enforced. In either case, the dominant racial hierarchy remains in effect in downtown institutions. Black people may still be required to prove that they belong in exclusive downtown spaces.[13] However, my respondents did not experience it as White space.[14]

White watching further draws our attention to White agency in reproducing White supremacy. It is a microprocess of racial exclusion that contributes to meso- and macro-level inequality and racial domination.[15] Interviewees' experience with White watching reveals that hatred is not required for White people to participate in Black exclusion. In fact, many are likely unaware of the looks of contempt or interrogation with which they respond to Black people in White space. Even if these responses are involuntary, I do not assume that they simply reflect "unconscious bias" that is inconsistent with their worldview. Their responses to Black people in White space may reflect their perceptions about who belongs in their "nice" neighborhood. These may be the same beliefs that shape decisions about where to live and where to send their children to school. These residential and school choices reinforce the racial order by protecting White space, and the resources and hyper-valuation therein.

CULTURE AND WHITE SPACE

The racialization of space is also achieved through culture. In retail establishments, the music played, the art or photographs on the wall, the products available for purchase, and the interior and exterior aesthetics all say something about who belongs.[16] However, discerning the role of culture in the racialization of space is not as simple as demarcating some culture as "White" and other culture as "Black." As several interviewees noted, Black people often enjoy activities and interests that are deemed "White," such as biking, crafting, and gardening. Yet when places to do these activities appear in gentrifying and Whitening neighborhoods, longtime Black residents may feel unwelcome. White watching explains part of this phenomenon. If Black people are surveilled in these spaces, we would expect them to feel unwelcome and culturally displaced. Existing research on this topic tends to rely on class distinctions to explain how longtime Black residents are excluded or marginalized in space.[17] This approach, again, reflects a conflation of race and class. Questions about how culture itself functions to exclude on the basis of race warrant further study.[18]

EVERYDAY RACISM IS STILL RACISM

When studying racism, contemporary sociologists often focus on how systemic inequalities in housing, schooling, employment, banking, health, and incarceration produce disparate opportunities and outcomes. Sociologists assert that racial domination is not carried out by individuals who are filled with hate toward Black people. Rather, racism is reproduced through systemic processes that advantage Whites and disadvantage non-Whites. This turn toward social structure is necessary because it explains how racial inequality and oppression persists even as many White people claim to support racial equality.[19] Still, as Barbara Combs asserts, "everyday racism is still racism." While it may have less impact on socioeconomic inequality, interpersonal racism in everyday life affects people in meaningful ways. Exposure to discrimination causes stress that is associated with poorer mental and physical health.[20] For example, a longitudinal study of

Black youth found that living in a majority White setting was associated with higher average depressive symptoms. Moreover, this association "was fully explained by higher perceived racial discrimination in the predominantly White areas."[21] Everyday racism reproduces White supremacy by continually defining Black people as out of place.

Restaurants, bars, cookouts, and concerts can provide Black place for people who are seeking to reconnect with old friends and escape from the hostility of White space. However, city and state officials sometimes use aggressive policing, inequitable rule enforcement, and harassment to deter Black people from congregating in public space. These practices are often justified by racial stereotypes about Black criminality. In addition to preventing Black people from finding refuge and running businesses, the disruption and dispersion of Black place may also expedite White spacemaking.[22] Therefore, explicitly protecting the rights of Black people to congregate without harassment and undue surveillance is one necessary step toward making majority White cities more hospitable to Black residents.

Throughout the United States, Black people are seeking and making Black place. This is not a form of resegregation; it is an effort to find an escape from the White dominance that characterizes the larger society. It is often the case that Black people congregate to address some perceived challenge—to promote wealth accumulation, to talk about experiences with racism, to learn about Black history, or to promote entrepreneurship. While all of these projects have value, we should also acknowledge the potential benefit of Black place for the sake of Black place. Especially in parts of the country where White space is difficult to escape, Black place—a park meetup, a book club, or a bar—allows people to simply live.

Postscript

I interviewed Black Portlanders between 2017 and 2019. My analysis prioritizes the perspectives of the interviewees. In the main text
I avoided writing about anything that took place after 2019. Here, I
briefly describe several recent events that raise new questions about
the research I present in this book.

In 2020 Portland was the site of intense and prolonged protests
and counter-protests during the months following the murder of
George Floyd. Those involved included (racially diverse) racial justice
activists and (mostly White) anarchists, as well as White supremacists
and the national guard.[1] Given the timing of my research, I did not
ask interviewees about the protests. However, based on their comments about White support for Black Lives Matter, I suspect that interviewees might not have considered the 2020 protests as indicative of a broader commitment to eradicate White racial dominance
in Portland.

Several interviewees mentioned Portland's reputation as perfectly
planned and primed for middle-class White enjoyment; however, the
city may be losing this status.[2] Many businesses that closed in 2020
never reopened. As of 2024, downtown foot traffic is down 30 percent
from 2020.[3] The population of unhoused people increased by 63 percent between 2015 and 2023.[4] And Portland's opioid overdose crisis

is getting national attention.[5] During a visit in 2023, several Portland residents told me that "things have gotten bad" since the COVID-19 pandemic and the protests in 2020. If Portland's reputation as a "White utopia" has been disrupted, it is unclear how this might affect the daily experiences of longtime Black residents.

Finally, there are several new organizations focused on Black life in Northeast Portland. One is Albina Vision Trust (AVT), a nonprofit organization that is leading the redevelopment of Lower Albina, an area where many Black families were displaced by urban renewal. AVT is using public and private funds to acquire land and implement a plan that includes housing, a waterfront park, mixed commercial development, and an "interconnected series of accessible hubs geared towards meeting the existential needs of Lower Albina's residents."[6] AVT plans to develop ninety-four acres and build 1,000 housing units.

Albina Vision Trust was founded in 2017, but none of the interviewees mentioned the organization. However, as of 2024, AVT has a large social media following and is frequently discussed in the local news. The organization held workshops and community planning meetings throughout 2020 and 2021.[7] In 2023, AVT broke ground on Albina One, a $63.5 million complex with 94 housing units, including 16 units for people holding Section 8 vouchers and 76 units eligible for the North/Northeast Preference Policy. According to one *Oregonian* article, Albina One "aims to turn gentrification into Black-reentrification."[8] Additionally, in 2022 Phil Knight, the co-founder of Nike, contributed $400 million to establish the 1803 fund and invest in the "Rebuild Albina" project, which "aims to transform current and future generations of Black Portland through investments in education, place and culture and belonging in the Albina community."[9]

Albina Vision Trust and the Rebuild Albina project declare that their goal is to rebuild a Black community in Northeast neighborhoods. Their websites include futuristic digital collages and architectural renderings showing Black people happily occupying public space.[10] What will it take to create the future that is represented in these images? How can White space and White spacemaking be disrupted in a predominantly White city? Can large-scale or billionaire-funded projects enable these efforts? How can the goal of making

Black people feel at home and culturally, economically, socially, and politically secure be realized within a society structured by White supremacy? How do social class, gender, sexuality, and disability intersect with race to shape the meaning of being "at home" in place? It is my hope that scholars will pursue these questions in future research.

Acknowledgments

I could not have written this book if not for the generosity and kind- 179
ness of the people I interviewed in Portland. I am deeply appreciative
of the fifty-three individuals who shared their time and their thoughts
with me. I thank my editor, Elizabeth Branch Dyson, for believing in
this project and readily offering support and guidance. This book is
much improved because of the thoughtful suggestions made by four
reviewers. Thank you to Annette Lareau for her steadfast support
and for providing very detailed comments on multiple drafts of this
manuscript. I value the feedback I received from Michael Bader, Tony
Brown, Joseph Ewoodzie, and Karolyn Tyson. Angela Frederick, Rachel Fish, and Alex Friedus read preliminary analyses and posed useful questions about the project. Roseann Liu, Cary Beckwith, Elaine
Allard, Kate Cairns, Radhika Natarajan, Dara Shifrer, and Imani Hope
supported this project in a variety of ways. Thanks to Beth Slovic
for her generous friendship and Portland expertise. Thanks also to
Radhika, Paddy, and Asa for making me feel at home during my research trips to Portland. I feel exceedingly fortunate to be a member
of the Rice University sociology faculty. Thank you to my wonderful
colleagues who make it a joy to come to work each day, especially
department chair Jim Elliott. Thanks also to my former colleagues
at Reed College and Swarthmore College. I am grateful to Eduardo
Bonilla-Silva for spending a semester at the University of Pennsylva-

nia and teaching a course on American racism that had an enormous impact on my development as a scholar. Thank you to the kora players, especially Toumani Diabate, whose music facilitates my writing. I am blessed to be part of an incredibly loving and supportive family. To the Evans, Hope, King, Goodman, Goodwin, Gibbs, and Barnhardt families: I love you all and am so thankful to be one of you. I am particularly grateful for my father, Nate, and my brothers, Nathan and Jason, and their families. Thank you, Scott, for being a tremendously supportive partner and co-parent. I thank my two sons for filling my days with joy, purpose, love, and creativity.

Appendix   The Research Process

DATA COLLECTION

The primary sources of data for this project are in-depth qualitative interviews with forty-one Black adults who grew up in Northeast Portland. I conducted interviews between 2017 and 2019. I also convened a focus group with seven Black adults who grew up in Northeast Portland. I subsequently conducted one-on-one interviews with three of the focus group participants (included in the forty-one referenced above). Demographic information about the sample is summarized in table 2. In the early stages of the project, I interviewed eight other adults. Six of the eight were Black and spent time in Northeast Portland but did not grow up there. The remaining two were a White man and a Latina woman who grew up in Northeast Portland and worked for a local civic engagement organization. None of these eight interviewees are quoted in the manuscript; however, their knowledge helped me to understand the broader context and to interpret references made in subsequent interviews.

The sample is predominantly middle class, but it includes working-class and middle-class adults. My assessment of social class is based on education and occupation. The majority of the interviewees were college educated. Many worked for several years before enrolling in college and attended classes while working and raising children. The colleges most frequently attended were Portland State University (13), Portland Community College (8), and the University of Oregon (5).

TABLE 2. Interview sample

AGE (MEAN = 42)		
19–29	10	22%
30–39	11	25%
40–49	9	20%
50–59	9	20%
60+	6	13%
GENDER		
Man	20	45%
Woman	24	53%
Nonbinary	1	2%
EDUCATION		
High school/GED	12	27%
Some college	9	20%
Bachelor's degree	17	38%
Graduate degree	7	15%
HOUSING STATUS		
Renter	21	47%
Homeowner	24	53%
RESIDENTIAL LOCATION		
Lives in Northeast	16	36%
Lives outside of Northeast	29	64%

N = 45, including 41 Black interviewees who grew up in Northeast Portland, and 4 focus group participants who were not also interviewed.

Four interviewees attended historically Black colleges in the South. Two respondents graduated from elite institutions on the East Coast. Most of the middle-class interviewees worked for nonprofits, in local government, or as educators. Three held high-status positions: a non-profit executive director, a director of a city program, and an owner of a successful business. Working-class respondents did not have college degrees and held the following jobs: construction worker, office cleaner, building maintenance worker, grocery store cashier, building superintendent, and unemployed.

I used a variety of methods to recruit interview participants. I met some interviewees at events that were organized for Portland's Black residents. A former undergraduate student who is Black, grew up in Northeast Portland, and had a wide social network also helped me identify several people who were willing to be interviewed. I used snowball sampling to recruit additional participants. At the end of each interview, I asked respondents if they could recommend another person who might speak with me. Several people recommended that I interview individuals who are widely seen as community leaders and are often quoted by journalists and researchers. I avoided interviewing those who are seen as experts on Portland gentrification and instead sought to interview "regular" people. Nonetheless, I did interview four people who had a public-facing persona because of their job or volunteer work. Given that I recruited some participants from events that were organized for Black Portland residents, I expect that my sample is somewhat skewed toward people who had positive feelings about Northeast Portland as a historically Black place.

I conducted the interviews in places that were convenient for respondents, including in their homes, in my office, in interviewees' offices, in quiet restaurants, and in library study rooms at the Portland Community College campus on North Killingsworth Avenue. If we met in a restaurant or café, I would buy a drink or snack for the interviewee. Otherwise, interviewees did not receive compensation or gifts. All of the names of interviewees are pseudonyms. To maintain confidentiality, I also change some details about some interviewees' occupations. Many said that they would not mind if I used their real names in my publications. To some extent, I would prefer to use participants' real names so that they might have their experiences memorialized in print. However, providing confidentiality is an important way to ensure that participants can share their perspectives and experiences without fearing that what they say might be misinterpreted or used against them in some way.

In addition to in-depth interviews, I conducted participant observation at eleven events that were specifically organized for Black people or Northeast Portland residents. These included Good in the Hood and the Black community preview of the Historic Williams Art Project. I also conducted participant observation in Northeast Portland coffee shops. I spent time walking around the neighborhood and becoming acquainted with streets and intersections that were important to interviewees. I took detailed field notes from these observations. I primarily use field notes to provide context and depth to my interview data analysis. I also reviewed community documents, materials in Portland archives, and news articles. I use real names of people who made statements at public events where journalists were present (e.g., the Historic Black Williams Art Project event) or who were quoted in newspaper stories.

My status as both an insider and an outsider gave me an advantageous position from which to conduct this research. Interviewees expected that as a Black woman I understood and had firsthand experience with anti-Black racism. It is likely that they would not have been as forthcoming about their experiences with racism had they been interacting with White or other non-Black interviewers. As someone who grew up in a New Jersey suburb, I was an outsider among Black people who grew up in Portland. While observing events, I occasionally noticed some tension between longtime Black residents and Black newcomers. Some longtime residents expressed annoyance about newcomers who complained about Portland being a White city but did not make an effort to learn about its existing Black community or Northeast's history as a Black place. In interviews, I presented myself as someone who knew very little about Portland but was eager to learn. Generally, my subjects responded well to this approach. However, a few people who chose not to be interviewed seemed to mistrust my motivations as an outsider.

I transcribed all of the interviews and uploaded them to qualitative data analysis software. I then did multiple rounds of coding. I first used codes that separated sections of data by topic, which allowed me to see how all of the respondents discussed the topics I asked about during the interview. The subsequent rounds used more analytical codes that reflected emergent themes I identified while reading transcripts and reviewing coded data. Simultaneously, I read widely in order to identify theoretical and empirical work that could help interpret what I was learning from the data.

RESEARCH MOTIVATIONS

The questions that motivate this study emerge from my own experiences and observations as a Black woman and an urban dweller. I began doctoral studies at the University of Pennsylvania just a few weeks after my eldest child was born. During my first years at Penn, I spent many hours in the playgrounds of my West Philadelphia neighborhood. Simultaneously, I was conducting research about the social networks that developed among parents of young children through informal interactions on playgrounds.[1] I noticed that when I went to the park with my husband, who is White, other White parents would initiate conversation. When I was alone, most White parents did not acknowledge me unless we already knew each other.

Elijah Anderson's "The White Space" (2015) provided a useful framework for thinking about Black experiences in predominantly White social spaces. The article also raised new questions about how longtime Black residents think and feel about urban neighborhood change. Anderson describes angry Black people scowling as they walked past a new brewery that represented "a White invasion" in a gentrifying West Philadelphia neighborhood; however, he did not ask longtime residents how they thought or felt. My home happened to be just two blocks from that brewery and my family ate there often. As a Black gentrifier, I wanted to understand how longtime Black residents were thinking about the brewery and other racialized forms of neighborhood change. However, I could not find scholarship that systematically examined these perspectives. The White space framework focused on middle-class Black people. Was it also useful for explaining the experiences of poor and working-class Black people in White space?

Another impactful event occurred in Portland, Oregon, where I moved with my family in 2015. About four months after my arrival, I visited a Montessori school to which I was considering transferring my son. Almost everyone I observed in the school was White. At the end of the tour, the prospective parents and tour guide gathered in a waiting area near the front door. I was sitting in a chair with the main door of the school behind me when I observed a change in the facial expression of the White parent who faced me. She smiled nervously and her eyes opened wider, almost with pity. I immediately thought, "there is a Black person behind me." I slowly turned and saw a Black girl around seven years old and a woman who may have been her grandmother entering the school through the front door. In Portland, I was aware that I was often the only Black person in a grocery store or coffee shop. However, I had not realized that in just a few months I had developed the ability to recognize White reactions to the appearance of Black people in White space.

The combination of my experiences in Philadelphia and Portland led me to initiate this project. I wanted to understand what it was like to be Black and grow up in a city that largely functioned as a White space. Once I learned that the city I observed as a newcomer in 2015 was very different from the city Black adults who grew up in Portland remembered from their youth, I turned my attention to their experience with that transition.

Notes

CHAPTER ONE

1 Withers, "Whiteness and Culture"; Walton, "Habits of Whiteness."

2 Hern, *What a City Is For*; Woody, "Emotions and Ambient Racism in America's Whitest Big City."

3 Rizzari, "Re-Imaging a Neighborhood."

4 Gibson, "Bleeding Albina."

5 Anderson, "'The White Space.'"

6 Brunsma et al., "The Culture of White Space"; Combs, *Bodies Out of Place*.

7 Anderson, "'The White Space.'"

8 Combs, "Everyday Racism Is Still Racism."

9 Shaw and Sullivan, "'White Night'"; Freeman, *There Goes the 'Hood*; Hwang, "Gentrification Without Segregation?"; Lees, Slater, and Wyly, *Gentrification*.

10 Hwang, "While Some Things Change, Some Things Stay the Same."

11 Lees, Slater, and Wyly, eds., *The Gentrification Reader*.

12 For example, in "The Culture of White Space," Brunsma et al. assert that "Gentrification involves the displacement of lower income individuals— minorities in particular—and an influx of new, typically middle-class and affluent residents." See also Dantzler, "The Urban Process under Racial Capitalism"; Rucks-Ahidiana, "Theorizing Gentrification as a Process of Racial Capitalism."

13 For example, Deener (in *Venice: A Contested Bohemia in Los Angeles*) argues that Black residents felt economically marginalized by new stores that opened in gentrified Venice. And Brunsma et al. write in "The Culture of White Space" that "White business owners and consumers then create a new sense of place by injecting *middle-class values* into these spaces." Rather than highlighting the way race and class intersect, this account flattens race and class into a single axis of oppression. Gentrification is a useful heuristic device that has developed new knowledge about neighborhood change, but it has limitations as an analytical framework. See the discussion of "intersectionality as a heuristic" in Collins, *Intersectionality as Critical Social Theory.*

14 Williams, "Race and Class: Why All the Confusion?"

15 Dantzler, "The Urban Process under Racial Capitalism."

16 Du Bois and Eaton, *The Philadelphia Negro.*

17 Drake, Cayton, and Pattillo, *Black Metropolis*, 387.

18 Drake, Cayton, and Pattillo, 385.

19 Pattillo, *Black Picket Fences.* Other examples can be found in non-academic writing, for example: Baldwin, *Notes of a Native Son*; Wright, "The Ethics of Living Jim Crow."

20 Hunter and Robinson, *Chocolate Cities.* Also see Freeman, *A Haven and a Hell.*

21 Taylor, "The Great Migration."

22 Brooks and Rose, *Saving the Neighborhood*; Pearson, "'A Menace to the Neighborhood'"; Sugrue, *The Origins of the Urban Crisis.*

23 Freund, *Colored Property.*

24 Rothstein, *The Color of Law.*

25 Hirsch and Connolly, *Making the Second Ghetto*; Satter, *Family Properties*; Shabazz, *Spatializing Blackness.*

26 Pritchett, "The Public Menace of Blight."

27 Fullilove, *Root Shock.*

28 Massey and Denton, *American Apartheid*; Wilson, *The Truly Disadvantaged.*

29 Sharkey, *Stuck in Place*; Goffman, *On the Run*; Anderson, *Code of the Street*; Wilson, *The Truly Disadvantaged.*

30 Korver-Glenn, *Race Brokers*; Shedd, *Unequal City*; Rios, *Punished*; Pager and Shepherd, "The Sociology of Discrimination"; Sewell, "The Racism-Race Reification Process."

31 Duneier, *Ghetto*; Freeman, *A Haven and a Hell.*

32   Hunter et al., "Black Placemaking."

33   McKittrick, "On Plantations, Prisons, and a Black Sense of Place."

34   Feagin, *The White Racial Frame.*

35   hooks, *Yearning.*

36   hooks, 42, 47.

37   Lacy, *Blue-Chip Black.*

38   Massey and Denton, *American Apartheid.*

39   Cairns, "Youth, Temporality, and Territorial Stigma"; Lamont et al., *Getting Respect.*

40   Lewis, *In Their Own Interests*; Lipsitz, *How Racism Takes Place.*

41   Howell and Korver-Glenn, "The Increasing Effect of Neighborhood Racial Composition on Housing Values, 1980–2015"; Taylor, *Race for Profit.*

42   Lewis, *In Their Own Interests,* 90.

43   Lewis, *In Their Own Interests*; Logan and Molotch, *Urban Fortunes.*

44   Lipsitz, *How Racism Takes Place,* 64.

45   Lipsitz, 55.

46   Lipsitz, 53.

47   Lipsitz, 61.

48   Wacquant, "Territorial Stigmatization in the Age of Advanced Marginality"; Freeman, *A Haven and a Hell.*

49   Gibson, "Bleeding Albina."

50   Hern, *What a City Is For*; Betancur and Smith, *Claiming Neighborhood*; Duneier, *Slim's Table.*

51   Some scholars who dismiss the plausibility of intra-class congregation seem to misinterpret Robin D. G. Kelley's assertion that working-class social movements do not need middle-class leaders. Kelley critiques analyses that ignore class conflict and the potentiality for the interests of Black middle-class and Black working-class actors to be contradictory (Kelley, *Race Rebels*). Yet Kelley contends that Black neighborhoods were fruitful sites of resistance against racism, sexism, and material deprivation in the first half of the twentieth century. He writes: "Hidden in homes, dance halls, and churches, embedded in expressive cultures, is where much of what is choked back at work or in White-dominated space can find expression . . . 'congregation' enables Black communities to construct and enact a sense of solidarity" (51).

52   For example, in *Jim Crow Nostalgia*, Boyd argues that middle-class Black residents presented a nostalgic and inaccurate story of a middle-class Black past while lobbying for a Black gentrified future that they claimed was a continuation of the past.

53   See Fainstein and Nesbitt, "Did the Black Ghetto Have a Golden Age?"

54   Allen, "Black Geographies of Respite."

55   Boyd, *Jim Crow Nostalgia*; Hyra, *The New Urban Renewal*; Pattillo, *Black on the Block*; Taylor, *Harlem: Between Heaven and Hell*.

56   Feagin and Sikes, *Living with Racism*; Anderson, *Black in White Space*.

57   Brunsma et al., "The Culture of White Space."

58   White watching describes the way White people watch Black people, assess behavior, and enforce penalties in public space. White watching takes place in settings where Whites establish norms and enforce them. It is in a society where White people are able to use the law and the criminal justice system on behalf of their interests. There is no comparable practice among Black people that we might call "Black watching." Some Black people may be suspicious of, curious about, or resistant to White people entering majority Black spaces. However, Black people are not motivated and incentivized to reinforce the racial order through spatial domination. Moreover, because White supremacy structures American society, Black people rarely have the power to establish and enforce behavioral norms in public.

59   Combs, *Bodies Out of Place*; McNamarah, "White Caller Crime."

60   Bonilla-Silva, "Feeling Race."

61   Lowe, Stroud, and Nguyen, "Who Looks Suspicious?"; Lowe et al., "'I Live Here.'"

62   Moore, "The Mechanisms of White Space(s)."

63   Brunsma et al., "The Culture of White Space"; Dantzler, "The Urban Process under Racial Capitalism"; Deener, *Venice*; Martucci, "Shopping Streets and Neighborhood Identity."

64   Combs, *Bodies Out of Place*.

65   Small, "Four Reasons to Abandon the Idea of 'the Ghetto.'"

66   Anderson, "'The White Space,'" 13.

67   Anderson, *Streetwise*. Scholars who write about place-based racial exclusion, including Karyn Lacy, Mary Pattillo, and Elijah Anderson, have focused primarily on the experiences of the Black middle class. At the same time, gentrification researchers emphasize social class as the mode of change and capitalist exploitation as a mechanism of exclusion. Scholars have paid

far less attention to place-based racial exclusion that is experienced across social class.

68   Helmuth, "'Chocolate City, Rest in Peace'"; Brunsma et al., "The Culture of White Space"; Werth and Marienthal, "'Gentrification' as a Grid of Meaning."

69   Brunsma et al., "The Culture of White Space."

70   Elliott-Cooper, Hubbard, and Lees, "Moving beyond Marcuse."

71   Elliott-Cooper, Hubbard, and Lees.

72   Ramírez, "City as Borderland."

73   Martin, "Fighting for Control."

74   Fried, "Grieving for a Lost Home"; Fullilove, *Root Shock*.

75   Brown-Saracino, *A Neighborhood That Never Changes*.

76   Pattillo, *Black on the Block*; Taylor, *Harlem: Between Heaven and Hell*.

77   Boyd, *Jim Crow Nostalgia*; Pattillo, *Black on the Block*.

78   Taylor, *Harlem: Between Heaven and Hell*.

79   Prince, *African Americans and Gentrification in Washington, DC*.

80   Hwang and Ding, "Unequal Displacement"; Rucks-Ahidiana, "Theorizing Gentrification as a Process of Racial Capitalism."

81   Dantzler, "The Urban Process under Racial Capitalism."

82   Massey et al., "Riding the Stagecoach to Hell."

83   Rucks-Ahidiana, "Theorizing Gentrification as a Process of Racial Capitalism."

84   Korver-Glenn, *Race Brokers*.

85   Tuck and McKenzie, *Place in Research*.

86   Combs, *Bodies Out of Place*.

87   Quizar, "Land of Opportunity."

88   Quizar.

89   Quizar.

90   Bonilla-Silva, *Racism Without Racists*.

91   My analysis draws on critical race theory. Like critical race theorists, I understand racism to be embedded in social systems such as the law, the real estate market, banking, and education. I do not perceive racism to be an anomaly in an otherwise equitable society.

92   Combs, "Everyday Racism Is Still Racism"; McNamarah, "White Caller Crime."

93   Hunter et al., "Black Placemaking."

94   Abbott, *Greater Portland*; Hern, *What a City Is For*; Woody, "Emotions and Ambient Racism in America's Whitest Big City."

95   Portland Housing Bureau, "Displacement in North and Northeast Portland—An Historical Overview," Your Neighborhood, Your Voice, accessed March 21, 2024, https://www.portlandoregon.gov/phb/article/655460; Van Wing, "Knight Investment Follows History of Disinvestment in Portland's Albina Neighborhood"; Norcross, "A Freeway Once Tore a Black Portland Neighborhood Apart."

96   These perspectives are an example of counternarratives, or counter-storytelling, which is a methodology used by critical race theorists. Counternarratives are stories told from the perspective of marginalized groups that disrupt taken for granted, dominant explanations for racial inequality. The term refers to the ways legal scholars tell stories that make more compelling and engaging arguments about racism and the law (e.g., Harris, "Whiteness as Property").

97   Nearly all of the respondents were descendants of Black people who were enslaved in the American South. Interviewees' parents or grandparents migrated to Portland from the South in the mid-twentieth century. Two of the respondents had one African immigrant parent. To my knowledge, there were no other immigrants or descendants of immigrants in the sample. Three of the respondents had one White parent. All of the respondents identified as Black, except for one who identified as "mixed."

98   Omi and Winant, *Racial Formation in the United States.*

99   Ludema, Cooperrider, and Barrett, "Appreciative Inquiry."

100   McKittrick, "On Plantations, Prisons, and a Black Sense of Place."

101   Hunter and Robinson, *Chocolate Cities.*

102   Hunter and Robinson, "The Sociology of Urban Black America."

103   Neely and Samura, "Social Geographies of Race: Connecting Race and Space."

104   McKittrick, *Demonic Grounds.*

105   Fullilove, *Root Shock.*

106   Albina was named after the daughter and wife of William Winter Page. Page bought the land that would become Albina from the men who first acquired it via land grant from the federal government. Lundmark, "The City of Albina and the Eliot Neighborhood."

CHAPTER TWO

1   Lasky, "Four Square Blocks: Portland"; Taylor, *Harlem: Between Heaven and Hell.*

2   Gibson, "Bleeding Albina"; Ause, "Black and Green"; Shaw and Sullivan, "'White Night'"; Sullivan and Shaw, "Retail Gentrification and Race"; Savitch-Lew, "Gentrification Spotlight."

3   Rizzari, "Re-Imaging a Neighborhood."

4   Korver-Glenn, Dantzler, and Howell, "A Critical Intervention for Urban Sociology."

5   Beckett et al., "Drug Use, Drug Possession Arrests, and the Question of Race."

6   Anderson, *Black in White Space*; Korver-Glenn, *Race Brokers*; Lipsitz, *How Racism Takes Place.*

7   Anderson writes, "With gentrification, as white buyers begin to look to disenfranchised Black communities, they invest not only their financial capital. But their racial capital. Their White skin, increasing the value of the property by moving in. By investing themselves, they realize their own racial capital." (Anderson, *Black in White Space*, 217).

8   Imarisha, "Why Aren't There More Black People in Oregon?"

9   Harris, "Whiteness as Property."

10   Hunter and Robinson, *Chocolate Cities.*

11   Brooks, "Race, Politics, and Denial," 2.

12   Berrey, *The Enigma of Diversity*; Burke, *Racial Ambivalence in Diverse Communities*; Mayorga-Gallo, *Behind the White Picket Fence.*

13   Portland Indian Leaders Roundtable, "Leading with Tradition: Native American Community in the Portland Metropolitan Area," accessed June 1, 2020, https://nayapdx.org/wp-content/uploads/2017/12/Leading-with -Tradition.pdf.

14   Millner, Abbott, and Galbraith, "Cornerstones of Community," 2.

15   Comprehensive Planning Workshop, "History of the Albina Plan Area."

16   Coleman, "Dangerous Subjects," 6.

17   Millner, Abbott, and Galbraith, "Cornerstones of Community."

18   Coleman, "'We'll All Start Even,'" 423. This language that depicts dispossession as a humanitarian act relies on the assumption that indigenous people are the "depraved," which is similar to the language White planners use to

explain why the destruction of a "blighted" community is for the benefit of its inhabitants.

19   Coleman, "'We'll All Start Even.'"

20   Coleman, "Dangerous Subjects."

21   Coleman; "Theophilus Magruder v. Jacob Vanderpool Case Documents," accessed March 26, 2024, https://scua.uoregon.edu/repositories/2/resources /1215.

22   Robbins, "Oregon Donation Land Law."

23   Coleman, "'We'll All Start Even'"; Brooks, "Race, Politics, and Denial."

24   For example, the historian Carl Abbott writes that the city's early elites "propped open the door of opportunity for *anyone* [emphasis added] who could help the city grow, whether U.S. born or immigrant from Europe" (Abbott, *Portland in Three Centuries*, 31). The first reference to Black people in his book appears twelve pages later, when he writes that "African-American population numbers were too small to make a major contribution on the city" in the late 1800s (43). This explanation minimizes the role of racism in determining the size and political power of Portland's Black population.

25   Even notably liberal scholars took for granted that a "Portlander" is a White person. For example, the historian and liberal activist E. Kimbark McColl claimed that Portlanders had a "deep-seated Anglo-Saxon bias." According to McColl, "Portlanders viewed their city as a center of problems: crime, rising taxes, minorities and welfare recipients." McColl locates minorities outside the category of Portlander. Although he was critiquing the Anglo-Saxon bias, McColl nonetheless takes for granted that Black (and other non-White) Portlanders are excluded from full membership. See Wollner, Provo, and Schablisky, "Brief History of Urban Renewal in Portland, Oregon."

26   Taylor, "Slaves and Free Men."

27   Taylor, "The Emergence of Black Communities in the Pacific Northwest," 197.

28   Bureau of Planning, Portland, Oregon, "Portland: The History of Portland's African American Community (1805 to the Present)."

29   Portland African American Leadership Forum, "PAALF Letter."

30   Pearson, "'A Menace to the Neighborhood.'"

31   Millner, Abbott, and Galbraith, "Cornerstones of Community," 14.

32   Bureau of Planning, Portland, Oregon.

33   Taylor, "The Emergence of Black Communities in the Pacific Northwest."

34   Abbott, *Greater Portland*.

35 Taylor, "The Emergence of Black Communities in the Pacific Northwest."

36 Abbott, *Greater Portland.*

37 Restrictive covenants were legal and enforced by the state until the 1948 *Shelley v. Kraemer* decision. Brooks and Rose, *Saving the Neighborhood*; Gonda, *Unjust Deeds*; Smith, "'Congenial Neighbors.'"

38 Bureau of Planning, Portland, Oregon, "Portland: The History of Portland's African American Community (1805 to the Present)."

39 Millner, Abbott, and Galbraith, "Cornerstones of Community."

40 Bureau of Planning, Portland, Oregon, "Portland: The History of Portland's African American Community (1805 to the Present)."

41 Taylor, "The Great Migration"; McElderry, "The Problem of the Color Line."

42 Burke, "The Model City."

43 Lang, "'A Place under the Sun.'"

44 "Council Document #2381"; "Council Minutes #4472."

45 Pearson, "A Menace to the Neighborhood."

46 Pearson, 175.

47 Women were excluded from the City Club until 1973. Watson and Rose, "She Flies with Her Own Wings."

48 City Club of Portland, "The Negro in Portland."

49 McElderry, "Building a West Coast Ghetto."

50 Gibson, "Bleeding Albina."

51 Blockbusting is a process whereby realtors, preying on Whites' racist fears, convince White homeowners that Black people are moving into their neighborhood. Under these conditions, White homeowners would sell their homes to realtors at a discounted rate. The realtors would then sell or rent the homes to Black home seekers, who had few options, at an inflated price. Gotham, "Beyond Invasion and Succession."

52 Gibson, "Bleeding Albina."

53 Wollner, Provo, and Schablisky, "Brief History of Urban Renewal in Portland, Oregon."

54 City Club of Portland, "The Negro in Portland."

55 United States Department of the Interior.

56 Wollner, Provo, and Schablisky, "Brief History of Urban Renewal in Portland, Oregon."

57   Bureau of Planning, Portland, Oregon, "Portland: The History of Portland's African American Community (1805 to the Present)"; Gibson, "Bleeding Albina."

58   City Club of Portland, "Report on Urban Renewal in Portland."

59   Lipsitz, *How Racism Takes Place.*

60   Gibson, "Bleeding Albina"; Lipsitz, *How Racism Takes Place.*

61   Serbulo and Gibson, "Black and Blue."

62   Cortright, "How a Freeway Destroyed a Neighborhood, and May Again."

63   Burke and Jeffries, *The Portland Black Panthers.*

64   Burke, "The Model City."

65   Burke.

66   Burke.

67   Legacy Emanuel Medical Center.

68   Legacy Emanuel Medical Center, 6; Woolley, "Reconciliation Project."

69   City Club of Portland, "Report on Urban Renewal in Portland," 46.

70   City Club of Portland, 46.

71   Burke and Jeffries, *The Portland Black Panthers.*

72   Woolley, "Reconciliation Project."

73   Bates, Curry-Stevens, and Coalition of Communities of Color, *The African American Community in Multnomah County.*

74   Toll, "Commerce, Climate, and Community."

75   Wollner, Provo, and Schablisky, "Brief History of Urban Renewal in Portland, Oregon."

76   Burke and Jeffries, *The Portland Black Panthers.*

77   Burke and Jeffries.

78   Feagin and Hahn, *Ghetto Revolts.*

79   Burke and Jeffries, *The Portland Black Panthers*; Sugrue, *The Origins of the Urban Crisis.*

80   Serbulo and Gibson, "Black and Blue."

81   Burke and Jeffries, *The Portland Black Panthers.*

82   Burke and Jeffries.

83   Johnson and Williams, "Desegregation and Multiculturalism in the Portland Public Schools."

84   Johnson and Williams.

85   Johnson and Williams.

86   Johnson and Williams.

87   Serbulo and Gibson, "Black and Blue."

88   Serbulo and Gibson.

89   Serbulo and Gibson.

90   Gibson, "Bleeding Albina," 6, 18.

91   Lane and Mayes, "Bank Redlining Creates Blueprint for Slum in North, Inner NE Portland."

92   *The Oregonian*/OregonLive, "Major Lenders Discourage Homeownership."

93   Gibson, "Bleeding Albina," 17.

94   Gibson.

95   Cate, "Untangling Prison Expansion in Oregon."

96   Cate.

97   Cate, 41.

98   Rizzari, "Re-Imaging a Neighborhood."

99   Duneier, *Ghetto*; Freund, *Colored Property*.

100 Beckett et al., "Drug Use, Drug Possession Arrests, and the Question of Race"; "Highlights by Race/Ethnicity for the 2021 Survey on National Drug Use and Health."

101 Bates, Curry-Stevens, and Coalition of Communities of Color, *The African American Community in Multnomah County*.

102 Oliver and Shapiro, *Black Wealth/White Wealth*.

103 Abbott, *Greater Portland*.

104 Lee et al., "Racial Differences in Urban Neighboring."

105 *The Oregonian*/OregonLive, "Albina 1996: Jeff and Susan Hartnett, Portrait of NE Portland Urban Pioneers."

106 Shaw and Sullivan, "'White Night.'"

107 Deener, "Commerce as the Structure and Symbol of Neighborhood Life"; Sullivan and Shaw, "Retail Gentrification and Race."

108 Gibson, "Urban Redevelopment in Portland," 169.

109 Pucci, "Creative Energy Injects New Life into Portland's Alberta Street."

110 Swart and Wolf, *Northeast Passage*; Bureau of Planning, Portland, Oregon, "Albina Community Plan"; interview data collected by the author.

111 Bureau of Planning, Portland, Oregon, "Portland's Boise Neighborhood Plan."

112 Burke, *Racial Ambivalence in Diverse Communities*; Mayorga-Gallo, *Behind the White Picket Fence*.

113 Gibson, "Urban Redevelopment in Portland."

114 Korver-Glenn, *Race Brokers*; Johnson and Shapiro, "Good Neighborhoods, Good Schools"; Korver-Glenn, Dantzler, and Howell, "A Critical Intervention for Urban Sociology."

115 Baker, "Denser Growth Gives Eliot Neighborhood a Healthy Boost."

116 Gibson, "Bleeding Albina."

117 Gibbons, *City of Segregation*.

118 Roy, "Dis/Possessive Collectivism."

119 Contemporary debates about racial segregation are discussed in Ellen and Steil, eds., *The Dream Revisited*.

120 Hepler, "The Hidden Toll of California's Black Exodus."

121 For example, according to census data, my great-grandparents' community, West Winter Park, Florida (census tract 159.01) was 79 percent Black in 1990 and 29 percent Black in 2020. See Kahrl, *The Land Was Ours*; Slocum, *Black Towns, Black Futures*.

122 Seamster, "The White City."

CHAPTER THREE

1 Seamon, *A Geography of the Lifeworld*.

2 Brown-Saracino, *A Neighborhood That Never Changes*.

3 Bonds and Inwood, "Beyond White Privilege."

4 Gillborn, "Rethinking White Supremacy."

5 Shim, "Token Fatigue."

6 Hunter and Robinson, *Chocolate Cities*.

7 Wacquant, "Territorial Stigmatization in the Age of Advanced Marginality"; Wacquant, *Urban Outcasts*.

8 Gibson, "Bleeding Albina."

9 hooks, *Belonging*.

10   hooks, *Belonging.*

11   Hunter et al., "Black Placemaking."

12   Combs, *Bodies Out of Place.*

13   Wiltse, "The Black-White Swimming Disparity in America."

14   "SEI: This Is Our Story," The Center for Self-enhancement, accessed March 24, 2024, https://www.selfenhancement.org/history. SEI is supported by local, state, and federal funds, as well as money from foundations and corporate sponsors.

15   Most SEI participants have been Black. However, the organization serves a racially diverse group of young people.

16   "Mission," House of Umoja, accessed October 17, 2019, https://www .houseofumoja.net/mission.html.

17   Federal Comprehensive Employment and Training Act, Congress.gov, "H.R.17526—93rd Congress (1973–1974): Comprehensive Employment and Training Act Amendments," November 26, 1974, https://www.congress.gov /bill/93rd-congress/house-bill/17526.

18   Hunter and Robinson, *Chocolate Cities.*

19   Anderson, *Streetwise.*

20   Deener, *Venice: A Contested Bohemia in Los Angeles*; Pattillo, *Black Picket Fences.*

21   Lipsitz, *How Racism Takes Place.*

22   Columbia Villa is a planned community in the northwest corner of Northeast Portland that was built to house defense workers in 1942–43. It was converted to housing for low-income families after World War II. Initially lauded for its landscaping and amenities, by the 1980s Columbia Villa was a hotbed of the drug trade. Interviewees, some of whom grew up in Columbia Villa, described it as "the projects of Portland." To them, Columbia Villa represented a stereotypical majority Black, poor, urban public housing complex. Using funds from the federal HOPE VI program, the Housing Authority of Portland redeveloped Columbia Villa as a mixed-income community called "New Columbia" in 2003–2005. Some interviewees mentioned this redevelopment as a mechanism by which longtime residents were displaced. See Gibson, "The Relocation of the Columbia Villa Community."

23   White working-class residents of gentrifying neighborhoods have offered similar accounts of being known and welcomed in the homes of neighbors, pre-gentrification (Brown-Saracino, *A Neighborhood That Never Changes*). However, it would be a mistake to interpret such accounts as analogous to the experiences shared here. Black people who knock on the

wrong door are at heightened risk of racial violence. Rolnick, "Defending White Space."

24   Browne, *Dark Matters*; Healy et al., "In a Nation Armed to the Teeth, These Tiny Missteps Led to Tragedy"; Hollingsworth, "Judge Rules White Man Will Stand Trial for Shooting Black Teen Ralph Yarl, Who Went to Wrong House."

25   Young, *Justice and the Politics of Difference*.

26   Lipsitz, *How Racism Takes Place*.

27   Fred Myers is a hypermarket chain founded in 1922 and headquartered in Portland, Oregon. In addition to groceries, Fred Myers stores often include a drugstore, a restaurant, and a bank and sell clothing, jewelry, home decor, home improvement materials, garden supplies, electronics, shoes, sporting goods, and toys.

28   The change in socialization practices Veronica is describing may also be attributed to the introduction of smartphones and social media.

29   Lindberg, "Violent Youth Gangs in Portland Oregon."

30   Duck, *No Way Out*; Pattillo, *Black on the Block*.

31   Du Bois, *The Souls of Black Folk*.

32   "Do gimp" refers to the practice of making lanyards and bracelets by tying knots out of plastic lacing, also called scoubidou and craftlace.

33   Mills, *The Racial Contract*.

34   Contreras, "There's No Sunshine."

35   Anderson, *Streetwise*.

36   Small, "De-exoticizing Ghetto Poverty."

37   McKittrick, "On Plantations, Prisons, and a Black Sense of Place."

38   Hunter and Robinson, "The Sociology of Urban Black America."

39   Conway, "New Directions in the Sociology of Collective Memory and Commemoration"; Olick, "Collective Memory."

40   Harris, "Whiteness as Property."

41   In his interview, Bilal volunteered an example of intra-racial conflict that changed over time: "When you're dark skinned and you grow up in the black community in the eighties, it just wasn't the most ideal thing to be back then. We still had a lot of self-hatred in our community, still had a lot of ignorance in our community. Back then, we still made fun of our—of the things that made us who we are: the size of our lips, our hair, our nose, our skin color, and so forth. Going to school, we would make fun of each other about these things and we didn't realize, at the time, as kids, what we

were doing. Dark skinned kids weren't the most attractive. As my mom used to tell me. The closer you were to the European standard of beauty, the more better off you were in this particular society. And so that's how it was back then. I was dark skinned. I was a little dude. I had to learn how to protect myself. I had to learn how to crack jokes. If I walk into a room, I'd scan the room and I had a joke for everybody because I had to defend myself. . . . It's different now. It almost changed overnight. You started to see the black medallions. I don't know if you remember the African symbols and it was around the time where the hip hop culture started to be more Afrocentric and you started to see your Denzel Washingtons and your Wesley Snipes and people like that . . . in Portland, that happened in probably the early nineties."

CHAPTER FOUR

1   Stein, *Capital City*.

2   Brown-Saracino, *A Neighborhood That Never Changes*.

3   hooks, *Yearning*.

4   Freeman, "Displacement or Succession?"

5   SEI is based in Northeast but increasingly provides services in schools where many Black students have moved, including in "the numbers" and Troutdale. SEI services may now be available in Bethany's area.

6   Rizzari, "Re-Imaging a Neighborhood."

7   Fullilove, *Root Shock*.

8   Atkins-Conwell and McCollum, "Final Report—Arterial Traffic Calming Program."

9   Centner, "Places of Privileged Consumption Practices."

10   Hoffmann, *Bike Lanes Are White Lanes*.

11   Harris et al., "Contested Spaces."

12   Brown-Saracino, ed., *The Gentrification Debates*.

13   Stein, *Capital City*.

14   Lipsitz, *How Racism Takes Place*; Shiffer-Sebba, "Understanding the Divergent Logics of Landlords."

15   I did not ask whether Terrence rents his property to his family members at the market rate.

16   A rent control law was passed in Oregon in 2019. Lyon, "Overview of Oregon's New Rent Control Law."

17   Boyd, *Jim Crow Nostalgia*; Pattillo, *Black on the Block*; Taylor, *Harlem: Between Heaven and Hell*. Taking the work of Boyd, Pattillo, and Taylor into consideration, I expected that middle-class respondents would blame poor people for their own disadvantage, offer cultural explanations for racial inequality, and celebrate middle-class people as role models. However, I only heard a version of this perspective from one interviewee, when a woman in her sixties said "my favorite [rapper] to hate is Lil Wayne. He looks like a damn fool. He's got tattoos all over his body, his pants hanging down his ass, a grill and he's about making the money. I understand that. I understand that but we don't have a strong middle-class Black community to anchor young people here. So they're just floating on their own."

18   Fullilove, *Root Shock*.

19   Portland City Council deemed Inner Northeast Portland an "impact area" based on a recommendation by the chief of police. In impact areas, the chief of police can encourage the OLCC to reject liquor license applications or place specific restrictions on liquor licenses, "such as allowing liquor sales only during limited hours, restricting the sale of alcoholic beverages associated with street drinkers, or other restrictions consistent with the Oregon liquor laws." Impact Areas, 14B 100.060, Portland City Code, accessed March 25, 2024, https://www.portland.gov/code/14/b100/060.

20   Terrence's comments convey what Abrutyn calls *social trauma*, including both collective and cultural trauma. Like many others, Terrence is pained by the loss of community and the reality of racial oppression, saying "it hurts me so bad to see how this neighborhood has changed." See Abrutyn, "The Roots of Social Trauma."

21   Hunter, "Black Logics, Black Methods."

22   Werth and Marienthal, "'Gentrification' as a Grid of Meaning."

23   Gibson and Abbott, "Portland, Oregon."

24   Fullilove, *Root Shock*.

25   Rugh and Massey, "Racial Segregation and the American Foreclosure Crisis."

26   Gibson, "Urban Redevelopment in Portland."

27   Slocum heard similar comments from residents of Black rural towns (Slocum, *Black Towns, Black Futures*).

28   Collins, *Black Sexual Politics*; Hill, "Do the Marriageable Men Want to Protect and Provide?"

29   "Racial and Ethnic Disparities in Multnomah County"; Brosseau, "Who's on Portland's Gang List"; Serbulo and Gibson, "Black and Blue."

30   Hunter et al., "Black Placemaking"; Quizar, "Land of Opportunity."

31 Taylor, "Background Brief on . . . Measure 11."

32 "About the Prison Policy Initiative Oregon Profile," Prison Policy Initiative, accessed March 21, 2024, https://www.prisonpolicy.org/profiles/OR.html.

33 Morenoff and Harding, "Incarceration, Prisoner Reentry, and Communities."

34 "City Council Hearing Drug Free Zone Ordinance"; Jessica Wyse, "Drug Free Zones in Portland, Oregon."

35 Center for Court Innovation, "Drug-Free Zones in Portland."

36 Franzen and Learn, "Rights Getting Zoned Out?"

37 Mode, "Portland's Expanding Zones Exclusion by Race."

38 Beckett and Herbert, *Banished.*

39 Franzen and Learn, "Rights Getting Zoned Out?"; "Portland Exclusion Zones," Oregon ACLU, accessed October 30, 2020, https://www.aclu-or.org/en/legislation/portland-exclusion-zones. This is no longer available; it last appears on Wayback Machine on June 5, 2023.

40 State of Oregon, Appellant, v. Robert J. James, Respondent, 9703-32435 (Court of Appeals of Oregon 1999).

41 Howell and Korver-Glenn, "The Increasing Effect of Neighborhood Racial Composition on Housing Values, 1980–2015"; D'Auria and Slovic, "A $22 Million Federal Lawsuit Says Portland Discriminated Against a Black Nightclub Owner"; Thames v. City of Portland, 3:16-cv-01634-JR (D. Or. December 15, 2019).

42 Howell and Korver-Glenn, "The Increasing Effect of Neighborhood Racial Composition on Housing Values, 1980–2015."

43 Dunn, "Owner of Shuttered Hip-Hop Club, the Fontaine Bleau, Details Allegations of Racial Discrimination by Portland City Hall and OLCC"; Willson, "Hip-Hop Club Owner Files Discrimination Lawsuit Against City of Portland, OLCC"; Griffin-Valade et al., "Policy Review."

44 Willson, "Hip-Hop Club Owner Files Discrimination Lawsuit Against City of Portland, OLCC"; Bowlin, "Portland Club Discrimination Case Settled"; Esteve, "Race Discrimination Trial Shines Troubling Light on Oregon Liquor Agency"; Dunn, "Owner of Shuttered Hip-Hop Club, the Fontaine Bleau, Details Allegations of Racial Discrimination by Portland City Hall and OLCC"; Busse, "Racism in a Bottle."

45 Willson, "Hip-Hop Club Owner Files Discrimination Lawsuit Against City of Portland, OLCC."

46 Bernstein, "Judge Throws Out Fontaine Bleau's Discrimination Suit."

47 Thames v. City of Portland, 3:16-cv-01634-JR (D. Or. December 15, 2019).

NOTES TO PAGES 105–114

48 Dunn, "Making Money the Easy Way"; Sottile, "Racist Policing Plagues Portland's Nightclubs."

49 Rollins, "Liquor License Dispute."

50 While I cannot confirm Terrence's specific claim, the Oregon Liquor Licensing Commission does have the authority to restrict liquor licenses if it "determines that a restriction is in the public interest or convenience under specific criteria." "The City of Portland's Liquor License Recommendation Process: A Community Guide," City of Portland Office of Neighborhood Involvement, accessed December 31, 2023, https://www.portlandonline.com/shared/cfm/image.cfm?id=160669.

51 Van Fleet, "The Long Goodbye."

52 Monahan, "Portland Officials Try to Place a 10pm Music Curfew on One of the City's Last Jazz Clubs."

53 Dewalt Prods., Inc. v. City of Portland, 19-35806 (9th Cir. November 6, 2020).

54 Gallagher, "'Re-Whitening' Non-White Spaces through Colorblind Narratives."

55 Lefebvre, "Blacklisted."

56 McElroy and Werth, "Deracinated Dispossessions."

57 Gallagher, "'Re-Whitening' Non-White Spaces through Colorblind Narratives."

58 Gallagher.

CHAPTER FIVE

1 Lasky, "Four Square Blocks: Portland."

2 Combs, "Everyday Racism Is Still Racism."

3 Du Bois, *The Souls of Black Folk.*

4 Anderson, "'The White Space.'"

5 Feagin, Vera, and Imani, *The Agony of Education.*

6 Morrison, *Playing in the Dark.*

7 According to Zillow, the estimated value of the house was $1 million.

8 Omi and Winant, *Racial Formation in the United States*; Bonilla-Silva, *Racism Without Racists.*

9 Anderson, "'The White Space.'"

10 Anderson, *Black in White Space.*

11 Anderson; Neckerman, Carter, and Lee, "Segmented Assimilation and Minority Cultures of Mobility."

12 Anderson, "'The White Space.'"

13 Jenkins, *Black Bourgeois.*

14 Feagin and Sikes, *Living with Racism.*

15 A 2002 article in the *Portland Business Journal* predicted that North Mississippi would join this group of trendy shopping streets. Stout, "North Portland District Enjoys Business Surge."

16 McNamarah, "White Caller Crime."

17 Anderson, *Streetwise.*

18 Kurwa, "Policing, Property, and the Production of Racial Segregation."

19 McNamarah, "White Caller Crime."

20 Lipsitz, *How Racism Takes Place.*

21 Gabbidon and Higgins, *Shopping While Black: Consumer Racial Profiling in America.*

22 Freeman, *There Goes the 'Hood*; Anderson, "'The White Space.'"

23 Similar findings appear in Sullivan and Shaw, "Retail Gentrification and Race." Sullivan and Shaw suggest that Black people simply feel uncomfortable in culturally unfamiliar places. Systemic racism and White supremacy are absent in this analysis.

24 Deener, *Venice: A Contested Bohemia in Los Angeles*; Sullivan and Shaw, "Retail Gentrification and Race."

25 Hoffmann, *Bike Lanes Are White Lanes*; Deener, "Commerce as the Structure and Symbol of Neighborhood Life."

26 Martucci, "Shopping Streets and Neighborhood Identity."

27 Martucci.

28 Deener, "Commerce as the Structure and Symbol of Neighborhood Life."

29 Sullivan and Shaw, "Retail Gentrification and Race."

30 Watt, "'It's Not for Us'"; Danley and Weaver, "'They're Not Building It for Us'"; Doucet, "Living Through Gentrification."

31 Brunsma et al., "The Culture of White Space"; Martucci, "Shopping Streets and Neighborhood Identity."

32 Martucci, "Shopping Streets and Neighborhood Identity."

33   Lange, "All Knit Up in Sweater Instagram."

34   Deener, "Commerce as the Structure and Symbol of Neighborhood Life"; Sullivan and Shaw, "Retail Gentrification and Race."

35   Long, "Sense of Place and Place-Based Activism in the Neoliberal City."

36   Using words like resentment, cynicism, defensiveness, and anger (e.g., Anderson, "The White Space"; Freeman, *There Goes the 'Hood*) to describe Black responses to the emergence of White cultural dominance does not account for the sense of loss associated with displacement. See Fullilove, *Root Shock*.

37   Freeman, *There Goes the 'Hood*.

CHAPTER SIX

1   Berrey, *The Enigma of Diversity*; Hyra, *Race, Class, and Politics in the Cappuccino City*; Underhill, "'Diversity Is Important to Me.'"

2   Withers, "Whiteness and Culture."

3   Robinson, *This Ain't Chicago: Race, Class, and Regional Identity*.

4   Campuzano, "Police Investigate Racist Threat against Good in the Hood."

5   Brown-Saracino, "From the Lesbian Ghetto to Ambient Community."

6   Boyd, *Jim Crow Nostalgia*.

7   Hyra, *Race, Class, and Politics in the Cappuccino City*.

8   Both women were highly involved community members (DePass later joined the Portland Public School Board, and Maxey leads a well-attended public lecture series, "Race Talks"). On conflicts over cycling infrastructure on North Williams Avenue, see Lubitow, Miller, and Shelton, "Contesting the North Williams Traffic Operations and Safety Project."

9   Maus, "Meeting on Williams Project Turns into Discussion of Race, Gentrification."

10   Tissot, "Of Dogs and Men."

11   Historic Black Williams Art Project, accessed November 24, 2020, http://blackwilliamsproject.com.

12   Billy Elks Lodge was severely damaged by fire in 2021.

13   Sankofa is a pictorial image from the Akan tribe and a word in the Twi language that means "it is not taboo to go back and retrieve what you have forgotten or lost"—see Temple, "The Emergence of Sankofa Practice in the United States."

14   Boyd, *Jim Crow Nostalgia*.

15 In *Black Towns, Black Futures*, Karla Slocum finds that "Little Leaguers" (local boys) and "Low Riders" (urban young men) were welcomed in a Black-town parade, even if elders may have complained about the aesthetics of urban Black men outside of the parade. Similarly, it may be that diverse social statuses were represented in the art, even if some residents criticized people from lower-status groups in other settings. However, such critiques did not appear in my interviews.

16 Hyra, *Race, Class, and Politics in the Cappuccino City*; Zukin, *Naked City*.

17 Majestic Realty Co., "Celebrating the Past, Developing the Future," June 2023, https://www.majesticrealty.com/downloads/SOQ_LO.pdf.

18 Njus, "Trader Joe's Is Mystery Grocer in Subsidized Northeast Portland Development."

19 PDC argued that the $2.9 million appraisal was inaccurate because it was based on a multilevel mixed use development, which was not feasible because of a sewer main on the property. Njus, "Three Obstacles for the NE Portland Lot Where Trader Joe's Fell Through."

20 Njus, "Trader Joe's Is Mystery Grocer in Subsidized Northeast Portland Development"; Parks, "Trader Joe's Decision to Pull out of NE Portland Leaves Neighbors, Opposition Dissatisfied."

21 Portland African American Leadership Forum rebranded as "Imagine Black" in 2020. This change was intended to incorporate all Black people, not just African Americans, in their vision to create "a world where people of African descent enjoy the rights, resources, and recognition to be a thriving, resilient, and connected community." "About Us," Imagine Black, accessed January 8, 2024, https://www.imagineblack.org/our-vision.

22 Portland African American Leadership Forum, "PAALF Letter."

23 Jan Lin provides additional examples of neighborhood groups contesting top-down development projects. See Lin, *Taking Back the Boulevard*.

24 The joke also denigrates indigenous people and language.

25 I identified both women via a Google search.

26 Burke, "The Model City."

27 Theen, "Trader Joe's"; "Hales, Trader Joe's Officials Will Meet next Week in Calif.—The Columbian."

28 Portland African American Leadership Forum, "The People's Plan," https://www.portlandoregon.gov/oehr/article/713241.

29 Sorenson, "Gordly Family Home to Become Center for Black Leadership"; Jaquiss and Monahan, "City Deal to Finance the Purchase of Avel Gordly's Home Raises Questions"; Gordly Burch House, accessed December 21, 2023, https://gordlyburchhouse.org/.

30   Portland Housing Bureau, "N/NE Neighborhood Housing Strategy," accessed March 21, 2024, https://www.portland.gov/phb/nnehousing.

31   Portland Housing Bureau, "North/Northeast Neighborhood Housing Strategy Oversight Committee."

32   N/NE Neighborhood Housing Strategy Oversight Committee. 2022. *Annual Report 2022*. Portland Housing Bureau.

33   Approximately 30 percent of home buyers earn less than 60 percent of AMI.

34   N/NE Neighborhood Housing Strategy Oversight Committee. 2022. *Annual Report 2022*. Portland Housing Bureau.

35   Thurber, Bates, and Halverson, "Evaluating the N/NE Preference Policy."

36   Betancur and Smith, *Claiming Neighborhood*.

37   Moore, *Invisible Families*; Polletta and Jasper, "Collective Identity and Social Movements."

38   Prado, "New Murals Celebrate Portland's African American History and Future."

39   Quizar, "Land of Opportunity."

40   Anderson, "Support Portland's Black-Owned Businesses."

41   Murals may promote racial tourism and heritage tourism: Hyra, *Race, Class, and Politics in the Cappuccino City*; Boyd, *Jim Crow Nostalgia*.

42   Summers, *Black in Place*.

43   "Portland Development Commission Announces New Name Reflecting Strategic Shift in Direction," Prosper Portland, May 10, 2017, https://prosperportland.us/portland-development-commission-announces-new-direction/.

44   Reed, "Evolving Tax Incentives."

45   Brown, "Majestic's Alberta Commons Retail Project Connects Community"; Morrison, "With Alberta Commons, Portland Sees a Chance to Do Redevelopment Right."

46   https://www.alberta-commons.com/blog/2019/4/16/three-established-businesses-to-relocate-to-alberta-commons, accessed October 14, 2022. Much of the same material is available at https://www.theskanner.com/news/northwest/28474-alberta-commons-grows.

47   Ahmed, "The Nonperformativity of Antiracism."

48   "People of Majestic Realty," accessed March 21, 2024, https://www.majesticrealty.com/people.

CHAPTER SEVEN

1   Harris, "Whiteness as Property."

2   Combs, *Bodies Out of Place.*

3   Hunter et al., "Black Placemaking."

4   Hern, *What a City Is For*; Betancur and Smith, *Claiming Neighborhood.*

5   Combs, *Bodies Out of Place*; DeAngelis, "Moving On Up?"; Feagin and Sikes, *Living with Racism*; McNamarah, "White Caller Crime"; Voigt et al., "Language from Police Body Camera Footage Shows Racial Disparities in Officer Respect."

6   For example, see Betancur and Smith, *Claiming Neighborhood.*

7   Collins, *Black Feminist Thought.*

8   Howell and Korver-Glenn, "The Increasing Effect of Neighborhood Racial Composition on Housing Values, 1980–2015."

9   The Combahee River Collective, *Combahee River Collective Statement.*

10 Some interviewees participated in gendered rite-of-passage programs for Black youth (e.g., The Prospective Gents). However, they did not link their participation in these programs to their experiences with racial change in Northeast Portland.

11 Some relevant texts include: Brown-Saracino, "From the Lesbian Ghetto to Ambient Community"; Brown-Saracino, *How Places Make Us*; Ghaziani, *There Goes the Gayborhood?*; Hunter et al., "Black Placemaking"; Hunter, "The Nightly Round"; Wilson, "How We Find Ourselves."

12 Anderson, *The Cosmopolitan Canopy.*

13 Lacy, "How to Convince a White Realtor You're Middle Class."

14 The fact that respondents did not experience downtown as White space is further evidence that White space cannot be collapsed into White institutional space. White space specifically references racialized *spatial* exclusion. It describes spaces where Black people are looked upon with suspicion and made to feel out of place. In contrast, White institutional space refers to the "cultural and ideological mechanisms that entrench White norms, beliefs, values, and logics" (Embrick and Moore, *White Space(s) and the Reproduction of White Supremacy*). Institutions in downtown Portland were structured as White institutional space, but they were not experienced by respondents as White space. An analysis that prioritizes Black experience must recognize that some places function as White institutional space, but are not experienced as White space.

15   Collins, "On the Microfoundations of Macrosociology"; Essed, *Understanding Everyday Racism.*

16   Zukin, *The Cultures of Cities*; Martucci, "Shopping Streets and Neighborhood Identity"; Helmuth, "'Chocolate City, Rest in Peace.'"

17   Brunsma et al., "The Culture of White Space."

18   For example, see Chapman and Brunsma, *Beer and Racism: How Beer Became White.*

19   Bonilla-Silva, *Racism Without Racists*; Bonilla-Silva, "Rethinking Racism"; Ray, "A Theory of Racialized Organizations."

20   Monk, "Linked Fate and Mental Health among African Americans"; Sternthal, Slopen, and Williams, "Racial Disparities in Health"; Thoits, "Stress and Health"; Williams, "Stress and the Mental Health of Populations of Color."

21   Assari, Gibbons, and Simons, "Depression among Black Youth."

22   Gallagher, "'Re-Whitening' Non-White Spaces through Colorblind Narratives."

POSTSCRIPT

1   Levinson, "As Portland Braces for More Protest Violence, Progressive Activists Agree on Who Is to Blame"; Levinson and Olmos, "In America's Whitest City, Black Activists Struggle to Separate Themselves from Anarchists."

2   Fonsegrives, "Portland: America's Liberal Utopia Loses Its Shine."

3   "Downtown Portland Vibrancy Tracker," accessed April 5, 2024, https://downtownportland.org/research-reports/downtown-recovery-tracker/.

4   City of Portland, "Homelessness," accessed April 6, 2024, https://www.portland.gov/wheeler/homelessness.

5   Kekatos, "Oregon Officials Declare State of Emergency to Address Fentanyl Crisis in Portland."

6   Cook, "Portland Public Schools One Step Closer to Selling Its Headquarters to Albina Vision Trust," KGW8 News, February 22, 2024, https://www.kgw.com/article/news/local/portland-public-schools-selling-district-headquarters-albina-vision-trust/283-cb2046d6-6ff3-4e70-b673-98798acef030#.

7   Albina Vision Trust, accessed April 6, 2024, https://albinavision.org/.

8   Eastman, "Portland Housing Complex Aims to Turn Gentrification to Black 'Re-Entrification.'"

9   1803 Fund, "Phil Knight announces $400M investment in Portland's Albina neighborhood," accessed April 5, 2024, https://static1.squarespace.com/static/6440362cf28de07b1a3ffc31/t/644802e92dd1314bbc34149d/1682440937221/Rebuild_Albina_Press_Release.pdf.

10   Albina Vision Trust; Hennebery Eddy Architects, Inc., "Albina Vision | Portland District Plan | Hennebery Eddy Architects," accessed April 7, 2024, https://www.henneberyeddy.com/project/albina-vision/.

APPENDIX

1   Bader et al., "Talk on the Playground."

Bibliography

Abbott, Carl. *Greater Portland: Urban Life and Landscape in the Pacific Northwest.*   213
  Philadelphia: University of Pennsylvania Press, 2011.
Abbott, Carl. *Portland in Three Centuries: The Place and the People.* Corvallis: Oregon State University Press, 2011.
Abrutyn, Seth. "The Roots of Social Trauma: Collective, Cultural Pain
  and Its Consequences." *Society and Mental Health,* November 30, 2023,
  21568693231213088. https://doi.org/10.1177/21568693231213088.
Ahmed, Sara. "The Nonperformativity of Antiracism." *Meridians: Feminism, Race, Transnationalism* 7, no. 1 (2006): 104–26.
Allen, Douglas L. "Black Geographies of Respite: Relief, Recuperation, and
  Resonance at Florida A&M University." *Antipode* 52, no. 6 (November 2020):
  1563–82. https://doi.org/10.1111/anti.12658.
Anderson, Elijah. *Black in White Space: The Enduring Impact of Color in Everyday Life.* Chicago: University of Chicago Press, 2021.
Anderson, Elijah. *Code of the Street: Decency, Violence, and the Moral Life of the Inner City.* New York: W. W. Norton, 2000.
Anderson, Elijah. *The Cosmopolitan Canopy: Race and Civility in Everyday Life.*
  New York: W. W. Norton, 2011.
Anderson, Elijah. *Streetwise: Race, Class, and Change in an Urban Community.* Chicago: University of Chicago Press, 1990.
Anderson, Elijah. "'The White Space.'" *Sociology of Race and Ethnicity* 1, no. 1
  (January 2015): 10–21. https://doi.org/10.1177/2332649214561306.
Anderson, Jen. "Support Portland's Black-Owned Businesses." *Travel Oregon*
  (blog), June 17, 2020. https://traveloregon.com/things-to-do/trip-ideas
  /discover-portlands-black-owned-businesses/.
Assari, Shervin, Frederick Gibbons, and Ronald Simons. "Depression among

Black Youth: Interaction of Class and Place." *Brain Sciences* 8, no. 6 (June 12, 2018): 108. https://doi.org/10.3390/brainsci8060108.

Atkins-Conwell, Crysttal, and Doug McCollum. "Final Report—Arterial Traffic Calming Program." Bureau of Traffic Management, City of Portland, September 1993. https://www.portland.gov/sites/default/files/2020-06/ncp-trn-2-03-ex-59346.pdf.

Ause, Carter. "Black and Green: How Disinvestment, Displacement and Segregation Created the Conditions for Eco-Gentrification in Portland's Albina District, 1940–2015." University Honors Theses, paper 269, Portland State University, January 1, 2016. https://doi.org/10.15760/honors.294.

Bader, Michael D. M., Annette Lareau, and Shani A. Evans. "Talk on the Playground: The Neighborhood Context of School Choice." *City & Community* 18, no. 2 (June 1, 2019): 483–508. https://doi.org/10.1111/cico.12410.

Baker, Nena. "Denser Growth Gives Eliot Neighborhood a Healthy Boost." *The Oregonian*, October 23, 1995.

Baldwin, James. *Notes of a Native Son*. Boston: Beacon Press, 2012.

Bates, Lisa K., Ann Curry-Stevens, and Coalition of Communities of Color. *The African American Community in Multnomah County: An Unsettling Profile*. Portland, OR: Portland State University, January 2014.

Beckett, Katherine, and Steven Kelly Herbert. *Banished: The New Social Control in Urban America*. Studies in Crime and Public Policy. Oxford: Oxford University Press, 2010.

Beckett, Katherine, Kris Nyrop, Lori Pfingst, and Melissa Bowen. "Drug Use, Drug Possession Arrests, and the Question of Race: Lessons from Seattle." *Social Problems* 52, no. 3 (August 2005): 419–41. https://doi.org/10.1525/sp.2005.52.3.419.

Bernstein, Maxine. "Judge Throws Out Fontaine Bleau's Discrimination Suit against City of Portland, State Liquor Control Commission." *The Oregonian*, September 6, 2019, sec. Crime.

Berrey, Ellen. *The Enigma of Diversity: The Language of Race and the Limits of Racial Justice*. Chicago: University of Chicago Press, 2015.

Betancur, John Jairo, and Janet L. Smith. *Claiming Neighborhood: New Ways of Understanding Urban Change*. Urbana: University of Illinois Press, 2016.

Bonds, Anne, and Joshua Inwood. "Beyond White Privilege: Geographies of White Supremacy and Settler Colonialism." *Progress in Human Geography* 40, no. 6 (December 2016): 715–33. https://doi.org/10.1177/0309132515613166.

Bonilla-Silva, Eduardo. "Feeling Race: Theorizing the Racial Economy of Emotions." *American Sociological Review* 84, no. 1 (2019): 1–25. https://doi.org/10.1177/0003122418816958.

Bonilla-Silva, Eduardo. *Racism Without Racists: Color-Blind Racism and the Persistence of Racial Inequality in America*. Lanham, MD: Rowman & Littlefield, 2010.

Bonilla-Silva, Eduardo. "Rethinking Racism: Toward a Structural Interpretation." *American Sociological Review* 62, no. 3 (June 1, 1997): 465–80. https://doi.org/10.2307/2657316.

Bowlin, Nick. "Portland Club Discrimination Case Settled: As Part of the Settlement, the Dress Code Used to Discriminate against Black Patrons Must Be Stopped." *High Country News*, July 21, 2019. https://www.hcn.org/issues/51.12 /race-portland-club-discrimination-case-settled.

Boyd, Michelle. *Jim Crow Nostalgia: Reconstructing Race in Bronzeville*. Minneapolis: University of Minnesota Press, 2008.

Brooks, Cheryl. "Race, Politics, and Denial: Why Oregon Forgot to Ratify the Fourteenth Amendment." *Oregon Law Review* 83, no. 2 (2004): 731–62.

Brooks, Richard R. W., and Carol M. Rose. *Saving the Neighborhood: Racially Restrictive Covenants, Law, and Social Norms*. Cambridge, MA: Harvard University Press, 2013.

Brosseau, Carli. "Who's on Portland's Gang List?—Oregonlive.com." *The Oregonian*, November 4, 2016. https://www.oregonlive.com/portland/2016/11/at _least_i_was_on_some_kind_of.html.

Brown, Lisa. "Majestic's Alberta Commons Retail Project Connects Community." *GlobeSt.Com*, October 22, 2019. https://www.globest.com/2019/10/22 /majestics-alberta-commons-retail-project-connects-community/.

Browne, Simone. *Dark Matters: On the Surveillance of Blackness*. Durham, NC: Duke University Press, 2015.

Brown-Saracino, Japonica. *A Neighborhood That Never Changes: Gentrification, Social Preservation, and the Search for Authenticity*. Fieldwork Encounters and Discoveries. Chicago: University of Chicago Press, 2009.

Brown-Saracino, Japonica. "From the Lesbian Ghetto to Ambient Community: The Perceived Costs and Benefits of Integration for Community." *Social Problems* 58, no. 3 (August 2011): 361–88. https://doi.org/10.1525/sp.2011.58 .3.361.

Brown-Saracino, Japonica. *How Places Make Us: Novel LBQ Identities in Four Small Cities*. Fieldwork Encounters and Discoveries. Chicago and London: University of Chicago Press, 2017.

Brown-Saracino, Japonica, ed. *The Gentrification Debates*. Metropolis and Modern Life. New York: Routledge, 2010.

Brunsma, David L., Nathaniel G. Chapman, Joong Won Kim, J. Slade Lellock, Megan Underhill, Erik T. Withers, and Jennifer Padilla Wyse. "The Culture of White Space: On the Racialized Production of Meaning." *American Behavioral Scientist* 64, no. 14 (December 2020): 2001–15. https://doi.org/10.1177 /0002764220975081.

Bureau of Planning, Portland, Oregon. "Albina Community Plan," October 1993. https://www.portland.gov/bps/planning/area-planning/area-and -neighborhood-plans.

Bureau of Planning, Portland, Oregon. "Portland: The History of Portland's African American Community (1805 to the Present)," 1993. http://hdl.handle.net /1794/5816.

Bureau of Planning, Portland, Oregon. "Portland's Boise Neighborhood Plan," October 1993. https://www.portland.gov/sites/default/files/2020-01/boise -neighborhood-plan-1993.pdf.

Burke, Lucas N. N. "The Model City: Civil Rights, the Black Panther Party, and the Revolution of Urban Politics in Portland, Oregon." Master of Arts thesis, University of Oregon, 2012.

Burke, Lucas N. N., and Judson L. Jeffries. *The Portland Black Panthers: Empowering Albina and Remaking a City*. Seattle: University of Washington Press, 2016.

Burke, Meghan. *Racial Ambivalence in Diverse Communities: Whiteness and the Power of Color-Blind Ideologies*. Lanham, MD: Lexington Books, 2012.

Busse, Phil. "Racism in a Bottle." *Portland Mercury*, August 3, 2000. https://www .portlandmercury.com/news/2000/08/03/22567/racism-in-a-bottle.

Cairns, Kate. "Youth, Temporality, and Territorial Stigma: Finding Good in Camden, New Jersey." *Antipode* 50, no. 5 (2018): 1224–43. https://doi.org/10.1111 /anti.12407.

Campuzano, Eder. "Police Investigate Racist Threat against Good in the Hood." *The Oregonian*, June 9, 2017, sec. Portland. https://www.oregonlive.com /portland/2017/06/racist_death_threats_good_in_the_hood_portland.html.

Cate, Sarah Diane. "Untangling Prison Expansion in Oregon: Political Narratives and Policy Outcomes." Master's thesis, Department of Political Science, University of Oregon, 2010.

Center for Court Innovation. "Drug-Free Zones in Portland," 2005. https://www .innovatingjustice.org/articles/drug-free-zones-portland.

Centner, Ryan. "Places of Privileged Consumption Practices: Spatial Capital, the Dot–Com Habitus, and San Francisco's Internet Boom." *City & Community* 7, no. 3 (September 2008): 193–223. https://doi.org/10.1111/j.1540-6040.2008 .00258.x.

Chapman, Nathaniel G., and David L. Brunsma. *Beer and Racism: How Beer Became White, Why It Matters, and the Movements to Change It*. Sociology of Diversity Series. Bristol, UK: Bristol University Press, 2020.

City Club of Portland. "The Negro in Portland: A Progress Report 1945–1957." Portland, OR, April 19, 1957. https://pdxscholar.library.pdx.edu/cgi /viewcontent.cgi?article=1178&context=oscdl_cityclub.

City Club of Portland. "Report on Urban Renewal in Portland." Portland, OR: City Club of Portland, 1971.

"City Council Hearing Drug Free Zone Ordinance." City Auditor—City Recorder—Council minutes, Portland, Oregon, February 5, 1997. https:// efiles.portlandoregon.gov/Record/3662700/.

Coleman, Kenneth. "'Dangerous Subjects': James D. Saules and the Enforcement of the Color Line in Oregon." Master of Arts thesis, History Department, Portland State University, 2014. http://search.proquest.com/openview /a883db64192002534eb0b5c5d89717c4/1?pq-origsite=gscholar&cbl=18750 &diss=y.

Coleman, Kenneth. "'We'll All Start Even': White Egalitarianism and the Oregon Donation Land Claim Act." *Oregon Historical Quarterly* 120, no. 4 (2019): 414–37.

Collins, Patricia Hill. *Black Feminist Thought: Knowledge, Consciousness, and the Politics of Empowerment*, 2nd ed. Routledge Classics. New York: Routledge, 2009.

Collins, Patricia Hill. *Black Sexual Politics: African Americans, Gender, and the New Racism*. Sociology Race & Ethnicity. New York: Routledge, 2006.

Collins, Patricia Hill. *Intersectionality as Critical Social Theory*. Durham, NC: Duke University Press, 2019.

Collins, Randall. "On the Microfoundations of Macrosociology." *American Journal of Sociology* 86, no. 5 (1981): 984–1014.

Combahee River Collective. *The Combahee River Collective Statement: Black Feminist Organizing in the Seventies and Eighties*. Freedom Organizing Series 1. Albany, NY: Kitchen Table/Women of Color Press, 1986.

Combs, Barbara. *Bodies Out of Place: Theorizing Anti-Blackness in U.S. Society*. Athens: University of Georgia Press, 2022.

Combs, Barbara Harris. "Everyday Racism Is Still Racism." *Phylon* 55, nos. 1 & 2, Special Volume: Remembering the 150th Anniversary of the Birth of W. E. B. DuBois and the 50th Anniversary of the Death of Martin Luther King Jr. (Summer/Winter 2018): 38–59.

Comprehensive Planning Workshop. "History of the Albina Plan Area." Department of Urban Studies, Portland State University, 1990. https://www
.portland.gov/sites/default/files/2020-01/albina-community-plan-history-of
-the-albina-plan-area-1990.pdf.

Contreras, Randol. "There's No Sunshine: Spatial Anguish, Deflections, and Intersectionality in Compton and South Central." *Environment and Planning D: Society and Space* 35, no. 4 (August 2017): 656–73. https://doi.org/10.1177
/0263775816677552.

Conway, Brian. "New Directions in the Sociology of Collective Memory and Commemoration." *Sociology Compass* 4, no. 7 (2010): 442–53. https://doi.org
/10.1111/j.1751-9020.2010.00300.x.

Cook, Katherine. "Portland Public Schools One Step Closer to Selling District HQ." *KGW8 News*, Portland, Oregon, February 22, 2024. https://
www.kgw.com/article/news/local/portland-public-schools-selling
-district-headquarters-albina-vision-trust/283-cb2046d6-6ff3-4e70-b673
-98798acef030#.

Cortright, Joe. "How a Freeway Destroyed a Neighborhood, and May Again." *City Commentary* (blog), March 18, 2019. https://cityobservatory.org/how-a
-freeway-destroyed-a-neighborhood-and-may-again/.

"Council Document #2381 (Returning Protests against the Settlement of Negroes in the Albina District)." City Auditor—City Recorder—Council Documents, August 25, 1943. #2156–#3339 (July 31, 1943–November 10, 1943). https://efiles.portlandoregon.gov/Record/11679837/.

"Council Minutes (Regarding a Negro Colony in Albina) #4472." City Auditor—City Recorder—Council Minutes, October 7, 1942. Vol. 124, p. 630–Vol. 126 (September 2, 1942–April 27, 1944). https://efiles.portlandoregon.gov/Record
/11683620/.

Danley, Stephen, and Rasheda Weaver. "'They're Not Building It for Us': Displacement Pressure, Unwelcomeness, and Protesting Neighborhood Investment." *Societies* 8, no. 3 (September 4, 2018): 74. https://doi.org/10.3390
/soc8030074.

Dantzler, Prentiss A. "The Urban Process under Racial Capitalism: Race, Anti-Blackness, and Capital Accumulation." *Journal of Race, Ethnicity and the City* 2, no. 2 (June 25, 2021): 1–22. https://doi.org/10.1080/26884674.2021.1934201.

D'Auria, Peter, and Beth Slovic. "A \$22 Million Federal Lawsuit Says Portland Discriminated Against a Black Nightclub Owner." *Willamette Week*, August 16, 2016. https://www.wweek.com/news/2016/08/16/a-22-million-federal-lawsuit-says-portland-discriminated-against-a-black-nightclub-owner/.

DeAngelis, Reed. "Moving On Up? Neighborhood Status and Racism-Related Distress among Black Americans." *Social Forces* 100 (June 1, 2022): 1503–32. https://doi.org/10.1093/sf/soab075.

Deener, Andrew. "Commerce as the Structure and Symbol of Neighborhood Life: Reshaping the Meaning of Community in Venice, California." *City & Community* 6, no. 4 (December 2007): 291–314. https://doi.org/10.1111/j.1540-6040.2007.00229.x.

Deener, Andrew. *Venice: A Contested Bohemia in Los Angeles*. Chicago: University of Chicago Press, 2012.

Doucet, Brian. "Living Through Gentrification: Subjective Experiences of Local, Non-Gentrifying Residents in Leith, Edinburgh." *Journal of Housing and the Built Environment* 24, no. 3 (September 2009): 299–315. https://doi.org/10.1007/s10901-009-9151-3.

Drake, Saint C., Horace R. Cayton, and Mary Pattillo. *Black Metropolis: A Study of Negro Life in a Northern City*. Chicago and London: University of Chicago Press, 2015.

Du Bois, W. E. B. *The Souls of Black Folk*. Chicago: A. C. McClurg and Co., 1903.

Du Bois, William E. B., and Isabel Eaton. *The Philadelphia Negro: A Social Study*. Reprint edition. Philadelphia: University of Pennsylvania Press, 1996.

Duck, Waverly. *No Way Out: Precarious Living in the Shadow of Poverty and Drug Dealing*. Chicago: University of Chicago Press, 2015.

Duneier, Mitchell. *Ghetto: The Invention of a Place, the History of an Idea*. First paperback edition. New York: Farrar, Straus and Giroux, 2017.

Duneier, Mitchell. *Slim's Table: Race, Respectability and Masculinity*. Chicago: University of Chicago Press, 1994.

Dunn, Katia. "Making Money the Easy Way." *Portland Mercury*, December 7, 2000. https://www.portlandmercury.com/news/2000/12/07/23503/making-money-the-easy-way.

Dunn, Lisa. "Owner of Shuttered Hip-Hop Club, the Fontaine Bleau, Details Allegations of Racial Discrimination by Portland City Hall and OLCC." *Willamette Week*, November 4, 2015.

Eastman, Janet. "Portland Housing Complex Aims to Turn Gentrification to Black 'Re-Entrification.'" *The Oregonian*, August 22, 2023. https://www.oregonlive.com/living/2023/08/portland-housing-complex-aims-to-turn-gentrification-to-black-re-entrification.html.

Ellen, Ingrid Gould, and Justin Steil, eds. *The Dream Revisited: Contemporary Debates about Housing, Segregation, and Opportunity*. New York: Columbia University press, 2019.

Elliott-Cooper, Adam, Phil Hubbard, and Loretta Lees. "Moving beyond Marcuse: Gentrification, Displacement and the Violence of Un-Homing." *Progress in Human Geography* 44, no. 3 (June 2020): 492–509. https://doi.org/10.1177/0309132519830511.

Embrick, David G., and Wendy Leo Moore. "White Space(s) and the Reproduction of White Supremacy." *American Behavioral Scientist* 64, no. 14 (2020): 1935–45. https://doi.org/10.1177/0002764220975053.

Essed, Philomena. *Understanding Everyday Racism: An Interdisciplinary Theory.* Thousand Oaks, CA: SAGE Publications, 1991.

Esteve, Harry. "Race Discrimination Trial Shines Troubling Light on Oregon Liquor Agency—Oregonlive.Com." *The Oregonian*, 2013. https://www.oregonlive.com/politics/2013/12/race_discrimination_trial _shin.html.

Fainstein, Norman, and Susan Nesbitt. "Did the Black Ghetto Have a Golden Age? Class Structure and Class Segregation in New York City, 1949–1970, with Initial Evidence for 1990." *Journal of Urban History* 23, no. 1 (November 1996): 3–28. https://doi.org/10.1177/009614429602300101.

Feagin, Joe R. *The White Racial Frame: Centuries of Racial Framing and Counter-Framing.* New York: Routledge, 2013.

Feagin, Joe R., and Harlan Hahn. *Ghetto Revolts: The Politics of Violence in American Cities.* New York: Macmillan, 1973.

Feagin, Joe R., and Melvin P. Sikes. *Living with Racism: The Black Middle-Class Experience.* Boston: Beacon Press, 1995.

Feagin, Joe R., Hernan Vera, and Nikitah Imani. *The Agony of Education: Black Students at White Colleges and Universities.* New York: Routledge, 1996.

Fonsegrives, Romain. "Portland: America's Liberal Utopia Loses its Shine." *Barron's*, February 10, 2024. https://www.barrons.com/news/portland-america-s -liberal-utopia-loses-its-shine-1ad5e744.

Forman, James, Jr. *Locking Up Our Own: Crime and Punishment in Black America.* New York: Farrar, Straus, and Giroux, 2017.

Franzen, R., and S. Learn. "Rights Getting Zoned Out? Some Say Civil Rights Are Trampled in Portland's High Traffic Drug Areas." *The Oregonian*, July 30, 2000, sec. A.

Freeman, Lance. "Displacement or Succession? Residential Mobility in Gentrifying Neighborhoods." *Urban Affairs Review* 40, no. 4 (March 2005): 463–91. https://doi.org/10.1177/1078087404273341.

Freeman, Lance. *A Haven and a Hell: The Ghetto in Black America.* New York: Columbia University Press, 2019.

Freeman, Lance. *There Goes the 'Hood: Views of Gentrification from the Ground Up.* Philadelphia, PA: Temple University Press, 2006.

Freund, David M. *Colored Property: State Policy and White Racial Politics in Suburban America.* Chicago: University of Chicago Press, 2010.

Fried, Marc. "Grieving for a Lost Home: Psychological Costs of Relocation." In *Urban Renewal: The Record and the Controversy*, edited by James Wilson, 359–79. Cambridge, MA: MIT Press, 1966.

Fullilove, Mindy Thompson. *Root Shock: How Tearing Up City Neighborhoods*

Hurts America, and What We Can Do About It. New York: One World/Ballantine, 2005.

Gabbidon, Shaun L., and George E. Higgins. *Shopping While Black: Consumer Racial Profiling in America.* Criminology and Justice Studies. New York London: Routledge, Taylor & Francis Group, 2020.

Gallagher, Charles A. "'Re-Whitening' Non-White Spaces through Colorblind Narratives." In *Routledge International Handbook of Contemporary Racisms,* edited by John Solomos. London: Taylor & Francis, 2020.

Ghaziani, Amin. *There Goes the Gayborhood?* Princeton Studies in Cultural Sociology. Princeton, NJ: Princeton University Press, 2014.

Gibbons, Andrea. *City of Segregation: 100 Years of Struggle for Housing in Los Angeles.* London: Verso, 2018.

Gibson, Karen, and Carl Abbott. "Portland, Oregon." *Cities* 19, no. 6 (December 2002): 425–36. https://doi.org/10.1016/S0264-2751(02)00075-6.

Gibson, Karen. "Bleeding Albina: A History of Community Disinvestment, 1940–2000." *Transforming Anthropology* 15, no. 1 (2007).

Gibson, Karen J. "The Relocation of the Columbia Villa Community: Views from Residents." *Journal of Planning Education and Research* 27, no. 1 (September 2007): 5–19. https://doi.org/10.1177/0739456X07299845.

Gibson, Karen. "Urban Redevelopment in Portland: Making the City Livable for Everyone?" In *The Portland Edge: Challenges and Successes in Growing Communities.* Washington, DC: Island Press, 2004.

Gillborn, David. "Rethinking White Supremacy: Who Counts in 'WhiteWorld.'" *Ethnicities* 6, no. 3 (September 2006): 318–40. https://doi.org/10.1177/1468796806068323.

Goffman, Alice. *On the Run: Fugitive Life in an American City.* New York: Picador, 2014.

Gonda, Jeffrey D. *Unjust Deeds: The Restrictive Covenant Cases and the Making of the Civil Rights Movement.* Chapel Hill: University of North Carolina Press, 2015.

Gotham, Kevin Fox. "Beyond Invasion and Succession: School Segregation, Real Estate Blockbusting, and the Political Economy of Neighborhood Racial Transition." *City & Community* 1, no. 1 (March 2002): 83–111. https://doi.org/10.1111/1540-6040.00009.

Griffin-Valade, LaVonne, Anika Bent-Albert, Eric Berry, Rachel Mortimer, and Constantin Severe. "Policy Review: Portland Police Bureau Policies and Practices Related to Hip-Hop Events." Office of the City Auditor, Portland, OR, 2014. https://www.portland.gov/ipr/publications/policy-reviews.

"Hales, Trader Joe's Officials Will Meet Next Week in Calif." *The Columbian,* March 21, 2014. https://www.columbian.com/news/2014/mar/21/hales-trader-joes-officials-will-meet-next-week-in/.

Harris, Brandon, Dorothy Schmalz, Lincoln Larson, Mariela Fernandez, and Sarah Griffin. "Contested Spaces: Intimate Segregation and Environmental Gentrification on Chicago's 606 Trail." *City & Community* 19, no. 4 (December 2020): 933–62. https://doi.org/10.1111/cico.12422.

Harris, Cheryl I. "Whiteness as Property." *Harvard Law Review* 106, no. 8 (June 1993): 1707–91. https://doi.org/10.2307/1341787.

Healy, Jack, Glenn Thrush, Eliza Fawcett, and Susan C. Beachy. "In a Nation Armed to the Teeth, These Tiny Missteps Led to Tragedy." *New York Times*, April 20, 2023, sec. US. https://www.nytimes.com/2023/04/20/us/wrong -house-shootings-guns.html.

Helmuth, Allison Suppan. "'Chocolate City, Rest in Peace': White Space-Claiming and the Exclusion of Black People in Washington, DC." *City & Community* 18, no. 3 (September 2019): 746–69. https://doi.org/10.1111/cico .12428.

Hepler, Lauren. "The Hidden Toll of California's Black Exodus." *CalMatters*, July 15, 2020, sec. Economy. http://calmatters.org/projects/california-black -population-exodus/.

Hern, Matt. *What a City Is For: Remaking the Politics of Displacement.* Cambridge, MA: MIT Press, 2016.

"Highlights by Race/Ethnicity for the 2021 Survey on National Drug Use and Health." Substance Abuse and Mental Health Services Administration, 2022. https://www.samhsa.gov/data/sites/default/files/2022-12 /2021NSDUHFFRHighlightsRE123022.pdf.

Hill, Marbella Eboni. "Do the Marriageable Men Want to Protect and Provide? The Expectation of Black Professional Hybrid Masculinity." *Gender & Society* 36, no. 4 (August 2022): 498–524. https://doi.org/10.1177 /08912432221102145.

Hirsch, Arnold R., and N. D. B. Connolly. *Making the Second Ghetto: Race and Housing in Chicago, 1940–1960.* Historical Studies of Urban America. Chicago and London: University of Chicago Press, 2021.

Hoffmann, Melody L. *Bike Lanes Are White Lanes: Bicycle Advocacy and Urban Planning.* Lincoln: University of Nebraska Press, 2016.

Hollingsworth, Heather. "Judge Rules White Man Will Stand Trial for Shooting Black Teen Ralph Yarl, Who Went to Wrong House." Associated Press, August 31, 2023. https://apnews.com/article/ralph-yarl-shooting-court-hearing -d2d210695772de5435c70039f0b36504.

hooks, bell. *Belonging: A Culture of Place.* New York: Routledge, 2009.

hooks, bell. *Yearning: Race, Gender, and Cultural Politics.* New York: Routledge, Taylor & Francis Group, 2015.

Howell, Junia, and Elizabeth Korver-Glenn. "The Increasing Effect of Neighborhood Racial Composition on Housing Values, 1980–2015." *Social Problems* 68, no. 4 (October 19, 2021): 1051–71. https://doi.org/10.1093/socpro/spaa033.

Hunter, Marcus Anthony. "Black Logics, Black Methods: Indigenous Timelines, Race, and Ethnography." *Sociological Perspectives* 61, no. 2 (April 2018): 207–21. https://doi.org/10.1177/0731121418758646.

Hunter, Marcus Anthony. "The Nightly Round: Space, Social Capital, and Urban Black Nightlife." *City & Community* 9, no. 2 (June 1, 2010): 165–86. https://doi .org/10.1111/j.1540-6040.2010.01320.x.

Hunter, Marcus Anthony, Mary Pattillo, Zandria F. Robinson, and Keeanga-Yamahtta Taylor. "Black Placemaking: Celebration, Play, and Poetry." *Theory, Culture & Society* 33, nos. 7–8 (December 2016): 31–56. https://doi.org/10 .1177/0263276416635259.

Hunter, Marcus Anthony, and Zandria F. Robinson. *Chocolate Cities: The Black Map of American Life*. Oakland: University of California Press, 2018.

Hunter, Marcus Anthony, and Zandria F. Robinson. "The Sociology of Urban Black America." *Annual Review of Sociology* 42, no. 1 (July 30, 2016): 385–405. https://doi.org/10.1146/annurev-soc-081715-074356.

Hwang, Jackelyn. "Gentrification Without Segregation? Race, Immigration, and Renewal in a Diversifying City." *City & Community* 19, no. 3 (September 2020): 538–72. https://doi.org/10.1111/cico.12419.

Hwang, Jackelyn. "While Some Things Change, Some Things Stay the Same: Reflections on the Study of Gentrification." *City & Community* 15, no. 3 (September 2016): 226–30. https://doi.org/10.1111/cico.12188.

Hwang, Jackelyn, and Lei Ding. "Unequal Displacement: Gentrification, Racial Stratification, and Residential Destinations in Philadelphia." *American Journal of Sociology* 126, no. 2 (September 1, 2020): 354–406. https://doi.org/10.1086/711015.

Hyra, Derek S. *The New Urban Renewal: The Economic Transformation of Harlem and Bronzeville*. Chicago: University of Chicago Press, 2008.

Hyra, Derek S. *Race, Class, and Politics in the Cappuccino City*. Chicago: University of Chicago Press, 2017.

Imarisha, Walidah. "Why Aren't There More Black People in Oregon? A Hidden History." PDXTalks, 2015. https://archives.pdx.edu/ds/psu/34187.

Jaquiss, Nigel, and Rachel Monahan. "City Deal to Finance the Purchase of Avel Gordly's Home Raises Questions." *Willamette Weekly*, October 11, 2016. https://www.wweek.com/news/2016/10/11/city-deal-to-finance-the-purchase-of-avel-gordleys-home-raises-questions/.

Jenkins, Candice Marie. *Black Bourgeois: Class and Sex in the Flesh*. Minneapolis: University of Minnesota Press, 2019.

Johnson, Ethan, and Felicia Williams. "Desegregation and Multiculturalism in the Portland Public Schools." *Oregon Historical Quarterly* 111, no. 1 (2010): 6–37. https://doi.org/10.5403/oregonhistq.111.1.0006.

Johnson, Heather Beth, and Thomas M. Shapiro. "Good Neighborhoods, Good Schools: Race and the 'Good Choices' of White Families." In *White Out: The Continuing Significance of Racism*, edited by Ashley W. Doane and Eduardo Bonilla-Silva. London: Psychology Press, 2003.

Kahrl, Andrew W. *The Land Was Ours: How Black Beaches Became White Wealth in the Coastal South*. Chapel Hill: University of North Carolina Press, 2012.

Kekatos, Mary. "Oregon Officials Declare State of Emergency to Address Fentanyl Crisis in Portland." *ABC News*, January 31, 2024. https://abcnews.go.com/US/oregon-officials-declare-state-emergency-address-fentanyl-crisis/story?id=106826829.

Kelley, Robin D. G. *Race Rebels: Culture, Politics, and the Black Working Class*. 1st Free Press paperback ed. New York: Free Press, distributed by Simon & Schuster, 1996.

Korver-Glenn, Elizabeth. *Race Brokers: Housing Markets and Racial Segregation in 21st Century Urban America*. New York: Oxford University Press, 2022.

Korver-Glenn, Elizabeth, Prentiss A. Dantzler, and Junia Howell. "A Critical Intervention for Urban Sociology." Preprint. SocArXiv, January 12, 2021. https://doi.org/10.31235/osf.io/zrj7s.

Kurwa, Rahim. "Policing, Property, and the Production of Racial Segregation." Preprint. SocArXiv, June 21, 2022. https://doi.org/10.31235/osf.io/wur89.

Lacy, Karyn. *Blue-Chip Black: Race, Class, and Status in the New Black Middle Class.* Berkeley: University of California Press, 2007.

Lacy, Karyn. "How to Convince a White Realtor You're Middle Class." *New York Times*, January 21, 2020, sec. Opinion. https://www.nytimes.com/2020/01/21/opinion/black-discrimination-study.html.

Lamont, Michèle, Graziella Moraes Dias da Silva, Jessica S. Welburn, Joshua A. Guetzkow, Nissim Mizrachi, Ḥanah Herzog, and Elisa P. Reis. *Getting Respect: Responding to Stigma and Discrimination in the United States, Brazil, and Israel.* Princeton and Oxford: Princeton University Press, 2016.

Lane, Dee, and Steve Mayes. "Bank Redlining Creates Blueprint for Slum in North, Inner NE Portland: 1990 Coverage from *The Oregonian*." Oregonlive.com, August 24, 2014. https://www.oregonlive.com/portland/2014/08/bank_redlining_creates_bluepri.html.

Lang, Melissa. "'A Place under the Sun': African American Resistance to Housing Exclusion." *Oregon Historical Quarterly* 119, no. 3 (2018): 365–96.

Lange, Alexandra. "All Knit Up in Sweater Instagram." *The New Yorker*, February 4, 2019. https://www.newyorker.com/culture/culture-desk/all-knit-up-in-sweater-instagram.

Lasky, Julie. "Four Square Blocks: Portland." *New York Times*, December 10, 2014. https://www.nytimes.com/2014/12/11/garden/four-square-blocks-portland.html%20December%2010.

Lee, Barrett A., Karen E. Campbell, and Oscar Miller. "Racial Differences in Urban Neighboring." *Sociological Forum* 6, no. 3 (September 1991): 525–50. https://doi.org/10.1007/BF01114475.

Lees, Loretta, Tom Slater, and Elvin K. Wyly. *Gentrification.* New York: Routledge, 2008.

Lees, Loretta, Tom Slater, and Elvin K. Wyly, eds. *The Gentrification Reader.* London: Routledge, 2010.

Lefebvre, Sam. "Blacklisted: How the Oakland Police Department Discriminates Against Rappers and Music Venues." *East Bay Express | Oakland, Berkeley & Alameda* (blog), April 26, 2017. https://eastbayexpress.com/blacklisted-how-the-oakland-police-department-discriminates-against-rappers-and-music-venues-2-1/.

Legacy Emanuel Medical Center. "Acknowledging the Past, Embracing the Future." Educational display, pdf file, accessed April 16, 2024. https://www.volgagermansportland.info/uploads/3/7/7/9/37792067/acknowledgingthepastembracingthefuture.pdf.

Levinson, Jonathan. "As Portland Braces for More Protest Violence, Progressive Activists and Police on Who Is to Blame." Oregon Public Broadcasting, September 25, 2020. https://www.opb.org/article/2020/09/25/progressive-activists-police-agree-blame-protests-elected-leaders/.

Levinson, Jonathan, and Olmos, Sergio. "In America's Whitest City, Black Activists Struggle to Separate Themselves from Anarchists." Oregon Public Broadcasting, November 25, 2020. https://www.opb.org/article/2020/11/23/portland-protest-racial-justice-oregon-black-lives-matter/.

Lewis, Earl. *In Their Own Interests: Race, Class, and Power in Twentieth-Century Norfolk, Virginia*. Berkeley: University of California Press, 1993.

Lin, Jan. *Taking Back the Boulevard: Art, Activism and Gentrification in Los Angeles*. New York: New York University Press, 2019.

Lindberg, Debra. "Violent Youth Gangs in Portland Oregon: A Study of the City's Response." Ph.D. diss., Portland State University, 1996.

Lipsitz, George. *How Racism Takes Place*. Philadelphia, PA: Temple University Press, 2011.

Logan, John R., and Harvey Luskin Molotch. *Urban Fortunes: The Political Economy of Place*. 20th anniversary ed., with a new preface. Berkeley: University of California Press, 2007.

Long, Joshua. "Sense of Place and Place-Based Activism in the Neoliberal City." *City* 17, no. 1 (February 1, 2013): 52–67. https://doi.org/10.1080/13604813.2012.754186.

Lowe, Maria R., Madeline Carrola, Dakota Cortez, and Mary Jalufka. "'I Live Here': How Residents of Color Experience Racialized Surveillance and Diversity Ideology in a Liberal Predominantly White Neighborhood." *Social Currents* 9, no. 3 (June 1, 2022): 207–25. https://doi.org/10.1177/23294965211052545.

Lowe, Maria R., Angela Stroud, and Alice Nguyen. "Who Looks Suspicious? Racialized Surveillance in a Predominantly White Neighborhood." *Social Currents* 4, no. 1 (February 1, 2017): 34–50. https://doi.org/10.1177/2329496516651638.

Lubitow, Amy, Thaddeus Miller, and Jeff Shelton. "Contesting the North Williams Traffic Operations and Safety Project." *Urban Studies and Planning Faculty Publications and Presentations* 101 (2013).

Ludema, James, David Cooperrider, and Frank Barrett. "Appreciative Inquiry: The Power of the Unconditional Positive Question." In *Handbook of Action Research*, edited by Peter Reason and Hilary Bradbury. London: Sage Publications, 2001.

Lundmark, Clint. "The City of Albina and the Eliot Neighborhood." Eliot Neighborhood (blog), April 16, 2007. https://eliotneighborhood.org/2007/04/16/409/.

Lyon, Vivien. "Overview of Oregon's New Rent Control Law." Oregon State Bar, 2019. Video recording, 6 min. 18 sec. State Library of Oregon Digital Collections. https://digital.osl.state.or.us/islandora/object/osl:885543.

Martin, Leslie. "Fighting for Control: Political Displacement in Atlanta's Gentrifying Neighborhoods." *Urban Affairs Review* 42, no. 5 (May 2007): 603–28. https://doi.org/10.1177/1078087406296604.

Martucci, Sara. "Shopping Streets and Neighborhood Identity: Retail Theming as Symbolic Ownership in New York." *City & Community* 18, no. 4 (December 2019): 1123–41. https://doi.org/10.1111/cico.12465.

Massey, Douglas, and Nancy Denton. *American Apartheid: Segregation and the Making of the Underclass.* Cambridge, MA: Harvard University Press, 1993.

Massey, Douglas S., Jacob S. Rugh, Justin P. Steil, and Len Albright. "Riding the Stagecoach to Hell: A Qualitative Analysis of Racial Discrimination in Mortgage Lending." *City & Community* 15, no. 2 (June 2016): 118–36. https://doi.org /10.1111/cico.12179.

Mayorga-Gallo, Sarah. *Behind the White Picket Fence: Power and Privilege in a Multiethnic Neighborhood.* Chapel Hill: University of North Carolina Press, 2014.

Maus, Jonathan. "Meeting on Williams Project Turns into Discussion of Race, Gentrification." BikePortland, July 21, 2011. https://bikeportland.org/2011/07 /21/racism-rears-its-head-on-williams-project-56633.

McElderry, Stuart. "Building a West Coast Ghetto: African-American Housing in Portland, 1910–1960." *Pacific Northwest Quarterly*, 2001. https://www.jstor.org /stable/40492659.

McElderry, Stuart. "The Problem of the Color Line: Civil Rights and Racial Ideology in Portland, Oregon, 1944–1965." PhD diss., University of Oregon, 1998.

McElroy, Erin, and Alex Werth. "Deracinated Dispossessions: On the Foreclosures of 'Gentrification' in Oakland, CA." *Antipode* 51, no. 3 (June 2019): 878–98. https://doi.org/10.1111/anti.12528.

McKittrick, Katherine. "On Plantations, Prisons, and a Black Sense of Place." *Social & Cultural Geography* 12, no. 8 (December 2011): 947–63. https://doi.org /10.1080/14649365.2011.624280.

McKittrick, Katherine. *Demonic Grounds: Black Women and the Cartographies of Struggle.* Minneapolis: University of Minnesota Press, 2006.

McNamarah, Chan. "White Caller Crime: Racialized Police Communication and Existing While Black." *Michigan Journal of Race & Law* 24, no. 2 (2019): 335. https://doi.org/10.36643/mjrl.24.2.white.

Millner, Darrell, Carl Abbott, and Cathy Galbraith. "Cornerstones of Community: Buildings of Portland's African American History." Portland State University Black Studies Faculty Publications and Presentations, August 1995. https://pdxscholar.library.pdx.edu/black_studies_fac/60/.

Mills, Charles W. *The Racial Contract.* Ithaca, NY: Cornell University Press, 2011.

Mode, Michael. "Portland's Expanding Zones Exclusion by Race." *The Oregonian*, July 30, 2000, sec. Local.

Monahan, Rachel. "Portland Officials Try to Place a 10pm Music Curfew on One of the City's Last Jazz Clubs: Lawyers Say City's Actions against Solae's Lounge Appear to Fit Pattern of Racial Bias against Black-Owned Nightclubs." *Willamette Week*, December 21, 2016. https://www.wweek.com/news /city/2016/12/20/portland-officials-try-to-place-a-10-pm-music-curfew-on -one-of-the-citys-last-jazz-clubs/.

Monk, Ellis P. "Linked Fate and Mental Health among African Americans." *Social Science & Medicine* 266 (December 2020): 113340. https://doi.org/10.1016/j .socscimed.2020.113340.

Moore, Mignon R. *Invisible Families: Gay Identities, Relationships, and Motherhood among Black Women.* Berkeley: University of California Press, 2011.

Moore, Wendy Leo. "The Mechanisms of White Space(s)." *American Be-*

havioral Scientist 64, no. 14 (2020): 1946–60. https://doi.org/10.1177
/0002764220975080.

Morenoff, Jeffrey D., and David J. Harding. "Incarceration, Prisoner Reentry, and
Communities." *Annual Review of Sociology* 40, no. 1 (July 30, 2014): 411–29.
https://doi.org/10.1146/annurev-soc-071811-145511.

Morrison, Erica. "With Alberta Commons, Portland Sees a Chance to Do Redevelopment Right." *OPB*, June 19, 2019. https://www.opb.org/news/article
/portland-oregon-alberta-commons-development-gentrification/.

Morrison, Toni. *Playing in the Dark: Whiteness and the Literary Imagination.* 1st
Vintage Books ed. New York: Vintage Books, 1993.

Neckerman, Kathryn M., Prudence Carter, and Jennifer Lee. "Segmented Assimilation and Minority Cultures of Mobility." *Ethnic and Racial Studies* 22, no. 6
(January 1999): 945–65. https://doi.org/10.1080/014198799329198.

Neely, Brooke, and Michelle Samura. "Social Geographies of Race: Connecting
Race and Space." *Ethnic and Racial Studies* 34, no. 11 (November 2011): 1933–
52. https://doi.org/10.1080/01419870.2011.559262.

Njus, Elliot. "Three Obstacles for the NE Portland Lot Where Trader Joe's Fell
Through." *The Oregonian*, March 10, 2014. https://www.oregonlive.com/front
-porch/2014/02/three_obstacles_for_the_ne_por.html.

Njus, Elliot. "Trader Joe's Is Mystery Grocer in Subsidized Northeast Portland
Development—Oregonlive.Com." *The Oregonian*, November 13, 2013. https://
www.oregonlive.com/front-porch/2013/11/trader_joes_is_mystery_grocer
.html.

Norcross, Geoff. "A Freeway Once Tore a Black Portland Neighborhood Apart.
Can New Infrastructure Spending Begin to Repair the Damage?" Oregon
Public Broadcasting, April 29, 2021. https://www.opb.org/article/2021/04/29
/federal-infrastructure-portland-albina-neighborhood/.

Olick, Jeffrey K. "Collective Memory: The Two Cultures." *Sociological Theory* 17,
no. 3 (November 1999): 333–48. https://doi.org/10.1111/0735-2751.00083.

Oliver, Melvin L., and Thomas M. Shapiro, eds. *Black Wealth/White Wealth: A New
Perspective on Racial Inequality.* New York: Routledge, 1995.

Omi, Michael, and Howard Winant. *Racial Formation in the United States.* London: Routledge, 2014.

Oregonian/OregonLive. "Albina 1996: Jeff and Susan Hartnett, Portrait of
NE Portland Urban Pioneers." OregonLive, August 24, 2014. https://www
.oregonlive.com/portland/2014/08/albina_1996_portrait_of_an_urb.html.

Oregonian/OregonLive, The. "Major Lenders Discourage Homeownership, Aid
Decline of NE Portland: 1990 Blueprint for a Slum Series." Oregonlive, August 24, 2014. https://www.oregonlive.com/portland/2014/08/major_lenders
_discourage_homeo.html.

Pager, Devah, and Hana Shepherd. "The Sociology of Discrimination: Racial
Discrimination in Employment, Housing, Credit, and Consumer Markets."
Annual Review of Sociology 34 (January 1, 2008): 181–209.

Parks, Casey. "Trader Joe's Decision to Pull out of NE Portland Leaves Neighbors, Opposition Dissatisfied—Oregonlive.Com." *The Oregonian*, February 4,

2014. https://www.oregonlive.com/portland/2014/02/trader_joes_decision_to
_pull_o.html.

Pattillo, Mary. *Black on the Block: The Politics of Race and Class in the City*. Chicago:
University of Chicago Press, 2007.

Pattillo, Mary. *Black Picket Fences, Second Edition: Privilege and Peril among the
Black Middle Class*. Edited by Annette Lareau. Chicago: University of Chicago
Press, 2013.

Pearson, Rudy. "'A Menace to the Neighborhood': Housing and African Americans in Portland, 1941–1945." *Oregon Historical Quarterly* 102, no. 2 (2001):
158–79.

Polletta, Francesca, and James M. Jasper. "Collective Identity and Social Movements." *Annual Review of Sociology* 27 (2001): 283–305.

Portland African American Leadership Forum. "PAALF Letter." OregonLive,
2013. http://media.oregonlive.com/portland_impact/other/PAALF%20letter
.docx.

Portland Housing Bureau. "North/Northeast Neighborhood Housing Strategy
Oversight Committee." Your Neighborhood, Your Voice, December 15, 2015.
https://media.oregonlive.com/portland_impact/other/NNE%20Combined
%20Presentation%2012%2015%202015.pdf.

Prado, Emilly. "New Murals Celebrate Portland's African American History and
Future." *Regional Arts and Culture Council* (blog), April 2, 2018. https://racc
.org/2018/04/02/new-murals-celebrate-portlands-african-american-history
-and-future/.

Prince, Sabiyha. *African Americans and Gentrification in Washington, DC: Race,
Class and Social Justice in the Nation's Capital*. Urban Anthropology. Farnham,
Surrey and Burlington, VT: Ashgate, 2014.

Pritchett, Wendell E. "The Public Menace of Blight: Urban Renewal and the Private Uses of Eminent Domain." *Yale Law & Policy Review* 21 (2003): 1.

Pucci, Carol. "Creative Energy Injects New Life into Portland's Alberta Street."
Seattle Times, March 10, 2005. https://www.seattletimes.com/life/travel
/creative-energy-injects-new-life-into-portlands-alberta-street/.

Quizar, Jessi. "Land of Opportunity: Anti-Black and Settler Logics in the Gentrification of Detroit." *American Indian Culture and Research Journal* 43, no. 2
(2019): 113–33. https://doi.org/10.17953/aicrj.43.2.quizar.

"Racial and Ethnic Disparities in Multnomah County." W. Haywood Burns
Institute for Justice Fairness and Equity, November 2019. https://www
.documentcloud.org/documents/6559824-Multnomah-R-E-D-Analysis-2019
-Final-November-19.html.

Ramírez, Margaret M. "City as Borderland: Gentrification and the Policing of
Black and Latinx Geographies in Oakland." *Environment and Planning D:
Society and Space* 38, no. 1 (February 2020): 147–66. https://doi.org/10.1177
/0263775819843924.

Ray, Victor. "A Theory of Racialized Organizations." *American Sociological
Review* 84, no. 1 (February 1, 2019): 26–53. https://doi.org/10.1177
/0003122418822335.

Reed, Andy. "Evolving Tax Incentives: A Shared Value Approach to Economic Development in Portland." Brookings Institution, May 29, 2018. https://www.brookings.edu/articles/evolving-tax-incentives-a-shared-value-approach-to-economic-development-in-portland/.

Rios, Victor M. *Punished: Policing the Lives of Black and Latino Boys*. New Perspectives in Crime, Deviance, and Law Series. New York: New York University Press, 2011.

Rizzari, Meredith. "Re-Imaging a Neighborhood: The Creation of the Alberta Arts District, Portland, Oregon." Master's thesis, Department of Geography, Portland State University, 2005. https://pdxscholar.library.pdx.edu/open_access_etds/4052/.

Robbins, William G. "Oregon Donation Land Law." In *Oregon Encyclopedia*, May 25, 2022. https://www.oregonencyclopedia.org/articles/oregon_donation_land_act/#.YoO2RC-B30o.

Robinson, Zandria F. *This Ain't Chicago: Race, Class, and Regional Identity in the Post-Soul South*. New Directions in Southern Studies. Chapel Hill: University of North Carolina Press, 2014.

Rollins, Michael. "Liquor License Dispute: Is Racism Involved?" *The Oregonian*, June 28, 1992.

Rolnick, Addie C. "Defending White Space." *Cardozo Law Review* 40 (2019): 1639.

Rothstein, Richard. *The Color of Law: A Forgotten History of How Our Government Segregated America*. New York: Liveright, 2018.

Roy, Ananya. "Dis/Possessive Collectivism: Property and Personhood at City's End." *Geoforum* 80 (March 2017): A1–11. https://doi.org/10.1016/j.geoforum.2016.12.012.

Rucks-Ahidiana, Zawadi. "Theorizing Gentrification as a Process of Racial Capitalism." *City & Community*, November 15, 2021. https://doi.org/10.1177/15356841211054790.

Rugh, Jacob S., and Douglas S. Massey. "Racial Segregation and the American Foreclosure Crisis." *American Sociological Review* 75, no. 5 (October 2010): 629–51. https://doi.org/10.1177/0003122410380868.

Satter, Beryl. *Family Properties: How the Struggle Over Race and Real Estate Transformed Chicago and Urban America*. New York: Picador, 2010.

Savitch-Lew, Abigail. "GENTRIFICATION SPOTLIGHT: How Portland Is Pushing Out Its Black Residents." Colorlines, April 18, 2016. http://www.colorlines.com/articles/gentrification-spotlight-how-portland-pushing-out-its-black-residents.

Seamon, David. *A Geography of the Lifeworld: Movement, Rest and Encounter*. London: Croom Helm, 1979.

Seamster, Louise. "The White City: Race and Urban Politics." *Sociology Compass* 9, no. 12 (December 2015): 1049–65. https://doi.org/10.1111/soc4.12326.

Serbulo, Leanne C., and Karen J. Gibson. "Black and Blue: Police-Community Relations in Portland's Albina District 1964–1985." *Oregon Historical Quarterly* 114, no. 1 (2013): 6–37.

Sewell, Alyasah Ali. "The Racism-Race Reification Process: A Mesolevel Political Economic Framework for Understanding Racial Health Disparities." *Sociol-*

ogy of Race and Ethnicity 2 (February 8, 2016): 1–31. https://doi.org/10.1177
/2332649215626936.

Shabazz, Rashad. *Spatializing Blackness.* Urbana, Chicago, and Springfield: University of Illinois Press, 2015.

Sharkey, Patrick. *Stuck in Place: Urban Neighborhoods and the End of Progress toward Racial Equality.* Chicago: University of Chicago Press, 2013.

Shaw, Samuel, and Daniel Monroe Sullivan. "'White Night': Gentrification, Racial Exclusion, and Perceptions and Participation in the Arts." *City & Community* 10, no. 3 (September 1, 2011): 241–64. https://doi.org/10.1111/j.1540
-6040.2011.01373.x.

Shedd, Carla. *Unequal City: Race, Schools, and Perceptions of Injustice.* New York: Russell Sage Foundation, 2015.

Shiffer-Sebba, Doron. "Understanding the Divergent Logics of Landlords: Circumstantial versus Deliberate Pathways." *City & Community* 19, no. 4 (December 2020): 1011–37. https://doi.org/10.1111/cico.12490.

Shim, J. "Token Fatigue: Tolls of Marginalization in White Male Spaces." *Ethnic and Racial Studies* 44, no. 7 (May 28, 2021): 1115–34. https://doi.org/10.1080
/01419870.2020.1779947.

Slocum, Karla. *Black Towns, Black Futures: The Enduring Allure of a Black Place in the American West.* Chapel Hill: University of North Carolina Press, 2019.

Small, Mario L. "De-exoticizing Ghetto Poverty: On the Ethics of Representation in Urban Ethnography." *City & Community* 14, no. 4 (December 2015): 352–58. https://doi.org/10.1111/cico.12137.

Small, Mario Luis. "Four Reasons to Abandon the Idea of 'the Ghetto.'" *City & Community* 7, no. 4 (December 1, 2008): 389–98. https://doi.org/10.1111/j
.1540-6040.2008.00271_8.x.

Smith, Greta. "'Congenial Neighbors': Restrictive Covenants and Residential Segregation in Portland, Oregon." *Oregon Historical Quarterly* 119, no. 3 (2018): 358–94.

Sorenson, Saundra. "Gordly Family Home to Become Center for Black Leadership." *Skanner News*, November 3, 2021. https://www.theskanner.com
/news/northwest/32274-gordly-family-home-to-become-center-for-black
-leadership.

Sottile, Leah. "Racist Policing Plagues Portland's Nightclubs." *High Country News*, February 18, 2019. https://www.hcn.org/issues/51.3/race-and-racism
-racist-policing-plagues-portlands-nightclubs.

Stein, Samuel. *Capital City: Gentrification and the Real Estate State.* Jacobin Series. London and Brooklyn, NY: Verso, 2019.

Sternthal, Michelle J., Natalie Slopen, and David R. Williams. "Racial Disparities in Health: How Much Does Stress Really Matter?" *Du Bois Review: Social Science Research on Race* 8, no. 1 (April 2011): 95–113. https://doi.org/10.1017
/S1742058X11000087.

Stout, Heidi. "North Portland District Enjoys Business Surge." *Portland Business Journal*, March 17, 2002.

Sugrue, Thomas J. *The Origins of the Urban Crisis: Race and Inequality in Postwar Detroit.* Princeton, NJ: Princeton University Press, 2014.

Sullivan, Daniel Monroe, and Samuel C. Shaw. "Retail Gentrification and Race: The Case of Alberta Street in Portland, Oregon." *Urban Affairs Review* 47, no. 3 (May 1, 2011): 413–32. https://doi.org/10.1177/1078087410393472.

Summers, Brandi Thompson. *Black in Place: The Spatial Aesthetics of Race in a Post-Chocolate City.* Chapel Hill: University of North Carolina Press, 2019.

Swart, Cornelius, and Spencer Wolf. *Northeast Passage: The Inner City and the American Dream.* SydHonda Cinema Productions, 2001. Documentary video recording, 55:45. https://www.youtube.com/watch?v=U83_LFs_q60&t=41s.

Taylor, Bill. "Background Brief on . . . Measure 11." State of Oregon, *Legislative Committee Services* 2, no. 1 (May 2004). https://www.oregonlegislature.gov/citizen_engagement/Reports/2004IG_Measure_11.pdf.

Taylor, Keeanga-Yamahtta. *Race for Profit: How Banks and the Real Estate Industry Undermined Black Homeownership.* Chapel Hill: University of North Carolina Press, 2019.

Taylor, Monique. *Harlem: Between Heaven and Hell.* Minneapolis: University of Minnesota Press, 2002.

Taylor, Quintard. "The Emergence of Black Communities in the Pacific Northwest: 1865–1910." *Journal of Negro History* 64, no. 4 (October 1979): 342–54. https://doi.org/10.2307/2716942.

Taylor, Quintard. "The Great Migration: The Afro-American Communities of Seattle and Portland during the 1940s." *Arizona and the West* 23, no. 2 (1981): 109–26.

Taylor, Quintard. "Slaves and Free Men: Blacks in the Oregon Country, 1840–1860." *Oregon Historical Quarterly* 83, no. 2 (1982): 153–70.

Temple, Christel N. "The Emergence of Sankofa Practice in the United States: A Modern History." *Journal of Black Studies* 41, no. 1 (September 2010): 127–50. https://doi.org/10.1177/0021934709332464.

Theen, Andrew. "Trader Joe's: Portland Mayor Charlie Hales Makes Strong Push for Grocery Store, Announces $20 Million Affordable Housing Plan." *The Oregonian*, March 10, 2014. https://www.oregonlive.com/portland/2014/03/trader_joes_portland_mayor_cha_1.html.

Thoits, Peggy A. "Stress and Health: Major Findings and Policy Implications." *Journal of Health and Social Behavior* 51, no. 1 suppl. (March 1, 2010): S41–53. https://doi.org/10.1177/0022146510383499.

Thurber, Amie, Lisa Bates, and Susan Halverson. "Evaluating the N/NE Preference Policy." Prepared for the N/NE Oversight Committee. Portland Housing Bureau, 2021. https://pdxscholar.library.pdx.edu/socwork_fac/552/.

Tissot, Sylvie. "Of Dogs and Men: The Making of Spatial Boundaries in a Gentrifying Neighborhood." *City & Community* 10, no. 3 (September 2011): 265–84. https://doi.org/10.1111/j.1540-6040.2011.01377.x.

Toll, William. "Commerce, Climate, and Community: A History of Portland and Its People: Race and Progressive Resistance." Oregon History Project, 2003. https://www.oregonhistoryproject.org/narratives/commerce-climate-and-community-a-history-of-portland-and-its-people/portland-neighborhoods/race-and-progressive-resistance/#.YafNIy9h1rQ.

Tuck, Eve, and Marcia McKenzie. *Place in Research: Theory, Methodology, and Methods*. New York: Routledge, 2015.

Underhill, Megan R. "'Diversity Is Important to Me': White Parents and Exposure-to-Diversity Parenting Practices." *Sociology of Race and Ethnicity*, August 6, 2018,. https://doi.org/10.1177/2332649218790992.

United States Department of the Interior. "National Register of Historic Places Multiple Property Documentation Form: African American Resources in Portland Oregon, from 1851 to 1973." July 1, 2020. https://www.portland.gov/sites/default/files/2020-09/mpd_final.pdf.

Van Fleet, Toby. "The Long Goodbye." *Willamette Week*, January 3, 2006. https://www.wweek.com/portland/article-5200-the-long-goodbye.html.

Van Wing, Sage. "Knight Investment Follows History of Disinvestment in Portland's Albina Neighborhood." Oregon Public Broadcasting, May 2, 2023. https://www.opb.org/article/2023/05/02/albina-portland-history-phil-knight/.

Voigt, Rob, Nicholas P. Camp, Vinodkumar Prabhakaran, William L. Hamilton, Rebecca C. Hetey, Camilla M. Griffiths, David Jurgens, Dan Jurafsky, and Jennifer L. Eberhardt. "Language from Police Body Camera Footage Shows Racial Disparities in Officer Respect." *Proceedings of the National Academy of Sciences* 114, no. 25 (June 20, 2017): 6521–26. https://doi.org/10.1073/pnas.1702413114.

Wacquant, Loïc. "Territorial Stigmatization in the Age of Advanced Marginality." *Thesis Eleven* 91, no. 1 (November 2007): 66–77. https://doi.org/10.1177/0725513607082003.

Wacquant, Loïc. *Urban Outcasts: A Comparative Sociology of Advanced Marginality*. Reprinted. Cambridge: Polity Press, 2010.

Walton, Emily. "Habits of Whiteness: How Racial Domination Persists in Multiethnic Neighborhoods." *Sociology of Race and Ethnicity* 7, no. 1 (January 1, 2021): 71–85. https://doi.org/10.1177/2332649218815238.

Watson, Tara, and Melody Rose. "She Flies with Her Own Wings: Women in the 1973 Oregon Legislative Session." *Oregon Historical Quarterly* 111, no. 1 (2010): 38–63. https://doi.org/10.5403/oregonhistq.111.1.0038.

Watt, Paul. "'It's Not for Us': Regeneration, the 2012 Olympics and the Gentrification of East London." *City* 17, no. 1 (February 2013): 99–118. https://doi.org/10.1080/13604813.2012.754190.

Werth, Alex, and Eli Marienthal. "'Gentrification' as a Grid of Meaning: On Bounding the Deserving Public of Oakland First Fridays." *City* 20, no. 5 (August 24, 2016): 719–36. https://doi.org/10.1080/13604813.2016.1224484.

Williams, David R. "Stress and the Mental Health of Populations of Color: Advancing Our Understanding of Race-Related Stressors." *Journal of Health and Social Behavior* 59, no. 4 (December 2018): 466–85. https://doi.org/10.1177/0022146518814251.

Williams, Johnny E. "Race and Class: Why All the Confusion?" In *Race and Racism in Theory and Practice*, edited by Berel Lang. Lanham, MD: Rowman & Littlefield Publishers, 2000.

Willson, Kate. "Hip-Hop Club Owner Files Discrimination Lawsuit against City

of Portland, OLCC." *Willamette Week*, January 24, 2017. https://www.wweek
.com/portland/blog-31673-hip-hop-club-owner-files-discrimination-lawsuit
-against-city-of-portland-olcc.html.

Wilson, Alex. "How We Find Ourselves: Identity Development and Two-Sprit
People." *Harvard Educational Review* 66, no. 2 (1996): 303–18.

Wilson, William J. *The Truly Disadvantaged: The Inner City, the Underclass, and
Public Policy*. Second edition. Chicago and London: University of Chicago
Press, 2012.

Wiltse, Jeff. "The Black-White Swimming Disparity in America: A Deadly Legacy
of Swimming Pool Discrimination." *Journal of Sport and Social Issues* 38, no. 4
(August 2014): 366–89. https://doi.org/10.1177/0193723513520553.

Withers, Erik T. "Whiteness and Culture." *Sociology Compass* 11, no. 4 (April
2017): e12464. https://doi.org/10.1111/soc4.12464.

Wollner, Craig, John Provo, and Julie Schablisky. "Brief History of Urban Renewal in Portland, Oregon." ProsperPortland, 2019. https://prosperportland
.us/wp-content/uploads/2019/07/Brief-History-of-Urban-Renewal-in
-Portland-2005-Wollner-Provo-Schablisky.pdf.

Woody, Ashley. "Emotions and Ambient Racism in America's Whitest Big City."
Social Problems 70, no. 4 (December 3, 2021): 981–98. https://doi.org/10.1093
/socpro/spab074.

Woolley, Jeana. "Reconciliation Project: The Emanuel Hospital Urban Renewal
Project." City of Portland, January 2012. https://www.portland.gov/phb
/nnehousing/documents/emanuel-hospital-urban-renewal-project/download.

Wright, Richard. "The Ethics of Living Jim Crow." In *Uncle Tom's Children*. New
York: Harper & Brothers, 1938.

Wyse, Jessica. "Drug Free Zones in Portland, Oregon: Legitimate Social Policy
or Legal Moving Target?" *The Michigan Journal of Public Affairs* 1 (Summer
2004). https://www.researchgate.net/publication/237366744_DRUG_FREE
_ZONES_IN_PORTLAND_OREGON_LEGITIMATE_SOCIAL_POLICY_OR
_LEGAL_MOVING_TARGET, full text available from the article's author.

Young, Iris Marion. *Justice and the Politics of Difference*. Princeton Classics.
Princeton, NJ: Princeton University Press, 2022.

Zukin, Sharon. *The Cultures of Cities*. Oxford: Blackwell Publishers, 1996.

Zukin, Sharon. *Naked City: The Death and Life of Authentic Urban Places*. Reprint
edition. Oxford: Oxford University Press, 2011.

Index